The Bible On Trial

by Wayne Jackson

The Bible on Trial

By Wayne Jackson

ISBN: 1-932723-11-0   978-1-932723-11-3

Christian Courier Publications
P.O. Box 690308
Stockton, CA 95269-0308
(209) 472-2475
http://www.christiancourier.com

Table of Contents

Like Timothy (Acts 16:1), I was born to parents who did not share a common faith. My mother's family had a rich Christian background. Her grandfather was Dr. John B. Hardeman, a prominent Christian physician who lived in Henderson, Tennessee. Mother's uncle was the celebrated N.B. Hardeman, co-founder of Freed-Hardeman University and one of the renowned preachers of his day. Her parents both attended the school in Henderson.

On the other hand, my father professed no religious affiliation at all. He once told my mother that he did not know whether or not there even is a God. I saw him reading the Bible only one time in my life. I never heard a prayer escape his lips and the only time I ever heard him use the name "God" was in profanity.

I hope I'm not misunderstood. I loved my dad very much. He was good to me in ways physical and material. He taught me moral principles pertaining to hard work and honesty in dealing with others, though he could not explain why those qualities were better than laziness and thievery. Once as a child I heisted a small wooden hammer from a young family friend. Dad gave me a moderate fanny-warming, and made me return the "loot," and apologize to my friend in the presence of his whole family.

I provide you this background so that you may know that as I matured, I wanted to know the truth. Who is right? Dad or mom? Is there a God? Has his will been revealed in the Bible?

After becoming a Christian at the age of seventeen, I began an earnest investigation of the Scriptures. I wanted to know if the Bible, to which I'd committed myself on the basis of faith, could stand the most rigorous investigation. Would the many historical, geographical, and scientific issues touched upon within those pages pass the test of critical examination? I must find out!

I thus began to build a library of scholarly books in defense of the Bible's claims, and a sizable collection of books designed to undermine the integrity of the Scriptures. I determined I would know the truth about this matter, no matter where the "chips" fell.

With the passing of the years I have become convinced beyond any shadow of doubt that the Bible is absolutely the perfect word of God; that the original autographs were verbally inspired and that, as Jesus said, "scripture cannot be broken" (John 10:35), though many an infidel has broken himself into pieces attempting to prosecute a case against the Bible.

This book contains some of my research, as I have sought to function as a defense advocate, against the prosecutorial chicanery of the anti-God community. They have put the Bible on trial. I have ventured to defend it. You must be the jury. Some of the material has been published before. Some of it is new. All of it together, I truly pray, will bless many who honestly seek the truth in the years that lie ahead.

— Wayne Jackson

God Has Spoken

"No book contains more truths, or is more worthy of confidence than the Bible."
— David Josiah Brewer (1837–1910), U.S. Supreme Court Justice

If God exists, and if he created the human family, one would expect that he has communicated with those made in his very image (Gen. 1:26–27). The truth is, God has spoken (Heb. 1:1). He has spoken abstractly, and he has communicated concretely.

ABSTRACT REVELATION

Abstract revelation has to do with God's presence as made known through his handiwork. David, king of Israel, declared: "The heavens declare the glory of God; and the firmament shows his handiwork" (Psa. 19:1). The visible universe eloquently testifies of the power and wisdom of its Creator (Rom. 1:20).

The ancient Greeks called the universe the *kosmos* (cf. English "Cosmos"), a term suggesting that which is characterized by order. Balbus, a Greek writer, asked: "Can one behold heaven, and contemplate what passes there, without discerning with all possible evidence, that it is governed by a supreme intelligence?" Interestingly, when atheist Carl Sagan wrote a book about the spectacular nature of the universe, he titled it, *Cosmos*—not *Chaos!*

The universe (and it is a uni-verse; not a multi-verse) is like a gigantic machine that has been intricately engineered. The term "astronomy" derives from two original terms signifying "star law," which hints of the laws that govern the heavenly bodies. Where there is law there must be a lawgiver. It is only because of the mathematical orthodoxy of the universe that astronomers can predict lunar or solar eclipses years in advance, or launch a spacecraft to the moon and land it with pinpoint precision.

The earth is moving in a 600,000-mile long orbit around the sun at a speed of 1,000 miles per minute. Its track is elliptical in design. Thus, at times it is closer to the sun than at other times. When closer to the sun, it moves faster; when farther away, slower. As the earth moves in its gigantic race-track-like orbit, it digresses from a straight line one-ninth of an inch every eighteen miles. If the turn were only one-tenth of an inch, our planet would freeze; if the adjustment were one-eighth of an inch, the earth would burn to a cinder. There is balance; someone designed it just right. That One was God.

By means of abstract revelation one can know that the Creator is powerful. The universe is estimated to be some twenty billion light years across (the distance light can travel in twenty billion years at the rate of 186,000 miles per second). Of course its extremities have not been fathomed. But the size speaks to the power of its Creator. The precision design reveals his wisdom. To really know God, however, and his will for humanity, requires more than abstraction; it requires concrete data.

CONCRETE REVELATION

In ancient times God spoke to select persons directly—men like Noah, Abraham, and Moses—and, through them he communicated his will verbally. Language is the vehicle of precise communication. Through Moses a written law was given to the Hebrew nation (ca. 1500 B.C.), a people divinely selected and ideally situated to influence the nations of the antique world, which they admirably did.

At precisely the most opportune time, God sent his Son, Jesus Christ, into the world as a revelation of himself (Jn. 1:18; cf. Gal. 4:4). That Christ existed is almost universally conceded; history overflows with the evidence. Friend and foe (e.g., philosopher Ernest Renan) alike have applauded his character. To study the life and attributes of Jesus is to get a picture of the Father himself, as conveyed in human form (Jn. 1:14; 14:9).

Out of that Judaeo-Christian background comes the most amazing book the world has ever known. It is called the Bible. It was composed over a span of some sixteen centuries—from Moses at Sinai to John the apostle on the island Patmos—a library of sixty-six books with a united theme: the Messiah is coming; he has arrived; he will return. That Messiah was Christ, the Lord.

The biblical documents are characterized by an amazing variety of evidences that authenticate the Book's claim of divine origin. In this volume some of these proofs will be discussed. Too, theories and arguments of the Bible's hostile critics will be addressed. Let infidelity put the Scriptures on trial. Let the prosecution attempt to make the case that the Old Book is a mere fraud. The defense will respond. The reader will be the jury, and the verdict will be reflected in the lives of those who judge the case. Ultimately, all will stand before the Great Judge and give account for their verdict!

This volume has been designed to do two things. First, it introduces a wide variety of evidences for the integrity of the Bible's claim that it is the inspired Word of God. Second, it is intended to review the critical theories (both in their most radical and more modified forms) that undermine the biblical claim of verbal inspiration.

For the past few centuries, biblical enemies have sought "invent" themselves by attacking the Grand Old Book of books. Having no original contribution to make to civilization, they, like parasites, have thought to sustain their miserable existences by attacking that of which they are ignorant, but which, tragically, has generated a malevolence within their blighted minds. Unfortunately for these wretched souls, the more they have vented their wrath upon sacred Scripture, the brighter it has become, while the more sinister they have shown themselves to be. In some bizarre sense, therefore, the world is indebted to them.

This present volume is sent forth with the deepest gratitude to Him whose influence lies ultimately behind it. Glory be to God Almighty for his wonderful and invigorating Book!

The Nature of Credible History

"No one can estimate or describe the salutary influence of the Bible. What would the world be without it?"
— John McLean (1785–1861), U.S. Supreme Court Justice

Historian David McCullough said that "we need history as much as we need bread or water or love."

History is tremendously important. When consulting a physician, it is crucial to have one's medical history. Frequently, in transacting business matters, chronicling one's financial history is essential. History is vitally important in religion; the Christian's faith, indeed his hope of eternal life, depends upon history.

Some religions are born merely of ideas—esoteric concepts initiated in the minds of fallible, illusionary people. They have no roots in actual history, hence are but vapors of no substance, wafting in the winds of passing time.

Christianity is not of such character. It is grounded in historical reality; its validity is determined by whether or not the events connected with its commencement actually happened. The documented evidence, and the case for its genuineness, is overwhelming.

What is "history"? History is not what "shall be," or what "is." Rather, it is what "was." The construction of the pyramids is history. The founding of our nation is history. Your birth is history. History was yesterday—even earlier today. When this sentence is closed with a period, it will be history.

How does one separate genuine history from the mythical? If the historical event was recent, the testimony of eyewitnesses certainly will be relevant. Written documents can be helpful. In our modern world, video could contribute significantly (e.g., in documenting the tragedy in New York of 9/11/01). The evaluation of historical evidence is a science all its own, and historians frequently disagree on the evidence. The credibility of documents, the reliability of witnesses, and the interpretation even of visuals can be controversial. The significance of the Zapruder film at the time of John Kennedy's assassination was disputed intensely.

REVISIONISM

Since the early centuries of the present era, there have been "revisionists" who have sought to "tamper" with the historical facts. A flood of rewritten monstrosities clutters the modern literary landscape.

Historical revisionists are of that journalistic species that, for some reason, are infuriated because certain events of history do not measure up to their perceptions of what is reported to have happened at a given point in time.

Additionally, in the frantic hope that they may implement some personal agenda that will affect the future, revisionist authors reconstruct certain historical episodes. Such outrageous fantasies may be palmed off as "science," "just fiction," or rationalized as a playful exercise in what "might have been." But make no mistake about it, the motive behind the subterfuge is deadly serious.

SECULAR REVISIONISM

There are numerous examples that illustrate what is meant by "revisionism." A century and a half ago, there was the Charles Darwin–Alfred Russell Wallace effort to deny man his divine origin, hence personal responsibility. This was aimed at providing humanity with the freedom to craft a new code of ethics (rather, non-ethics). After all, if mankind's existence can be explained naturally, instead of supernaturally, God is dismissed and, as the atheist Jean Paul Sartre reasoned, "everything indeed is permitted" (Marsak 1961, 485).

Over the last half-century there has been a movement to revise the history of Jewish persecution by Adolf Hitler and his Nazi regime during World War II. A few writers have denied that the Third Reich government had a policy of targeting Jewish people for extermination. In spite of ample eyewitness and photographic documentation that the Nazi regime executed more than five million Jews in the extermination camps of Germany, revisionists contend such never happened, or that this "purging" has been exaggerated grossly.

RELIGIOUS REVISIONISM

Over the past twenty centuries the indisputable facts of Christian history have been subjected to the revisionists' cut-and-paste techniques, with theories constantly emerging that bear no resemblance to reality.

In the post-apostolic period, the idea evolved that Peter founded the church in Rome, and became "the bishop" of that metropolis. Later, he was touted as the first "pope," and the head of the church on earth. Of course there is not one shred of biblical evidence for these assertions, but revisionists distort history to buttress the theory.

"Rationalists" correctly observe that no miracles are in evidence in the modern era. Consequently, they assume that supernatural events never occurred. Thus the life of Christ is rewritten to portray the supernatural "signs" for which he was renowned as ordinary events that, upon closer inspection, have perfectly natural explanations. Rudolph Bultmann (1884–1976), a prominent German theologian, characterized the literary surgical procedure as "demythologizing" the New Testament.

In 1966, Jewish writer Hugh J. Schonfield authored his infamous volume, *The Passover Plot*, in which he argued that Christ was a Messianic manipulator who plotted and perpetrated his own "death" (which he never intended to happen) in order to realize his grandiose dream of being the Jews' king.

A few years ago (1985), the mislabeled "Jesus Seminar" completely reconstructed the deeds and teaching of Christ with their color-coded massacre of the Gospel Narratives.

More recently there was Dan Brown's best-seller (along with the subsequent movie), *The Da Vinci Code*. This ludicrous volume fabricated history by making Jesus of Nazareth the husband of Mary Magdalene, and the father of an unidentified child. The so-called "Gospel of Judas," similarly has received significant publicity. With a literary makeover, it rehabilitates Judas Iscariot and transforms him into a hero grander than all the other apostles.

THE NATURE OF HISTORY

Some thirty years ago, noted scholar Stephen Neill, one-time professor of philosophy and religious studies at the University of Nairobi, prepared an essay that defined certain traits of genuine history (Green 1977, 71–78). Some of the observations made in that presentation annihilate the rotten foundations of revisionist "history." With my own applications accompanying Neill's canons of history, I submit the following.

History Is Unique

History is rather like a movie film—a long series of individual frames, frozen in time. Once an event transpires, no other event ever again will precisely replicate it. Many of us vividly remember the assassination of John F. Kennedy; the visual details via television are forever etched in our memories. Other assassinations have occurred, and doubtless will continue to as time progresses, but none will ever be a Xerox copy of that horrible day.

The events in Christian history were unique. For instance, there have been a number of historical situations that vaguely shared a few similarities to some of the circumstances in the life of Christ. Lincoln was assassinated as he attempted to emancipate the slaves. Gandhi was murdered as he opposed the harsh imperialism of England. Martin Luther King was killed as he led the civil rights movement.

Absolutely no one, however, has precisely replicated the unique life of the Son of God. Christ claimed a relationship with God rivaled by no one else. His teaching and works were supernatural. Even his enemies inadvertently conceded such (Jn. 11:47–48), and his deeds impacted world history. The mystical notion that history is cyclical, and that it may repeat itself eventually, e.g., in the recycling of one's former life into another form (reincarnation) is a fantasy with no basis in reality.

History Is Unpredictable

One might reasonably speculate that eventually there will be military conflict between the United States and Iran, or possibly with North Korea, but no ordinary human being can predict the future with precision (see Isa. 41:21–24).

This fact is one of the things that makes the Bible so remarkable. There are hundreds of detailed prophecies recorded in the

Scriptures. J. Barton Payne's *Encyclopedia of Biblical Prophecy* lists 1,239 prophecies in the Old Testament, and 578 in the New Testament, for a total of 1,817. These encompass 8,352 verses. It must be noted, however, that the total depends upon how one has calculated the prophetic information. Actually, there are many more prophetic points than those figures reflect.

For example, while some would consider Isaiah 53 a "prophecy" pertaining to the coming Messiah, there are more than two dozen individual "prophecies" within that narrative of twelve verses. Most of the Old Testament prophecies have been fulfilled already; and the "non-conditional" prophecies that have been fulfilled demonstrate amazing and infallible accuracy.

History Is Not Repeatable

No matter how much the movies and television may fantasize about entering a "time-machine" and returning into the past, it cannot, and will not, be done.

How I have wished on occasion that I could return to the times of my childhood for just one day, visiting the old home place and seeing my mother at the stove, preparing supper for her family. I would throw my arms about her neck and thank her with many tears for having blessed my life so abundantly. But the historical terrain cannot be reclaimed. We cannot return to the "good old days."

In religious matters, certainly we will never witness those miracles that adorned the era of the apostolic church. They had a temporary design and were divinely terminated with the close of the first century (1 Cor. 13:8–13).

It is almost certain the modern church will never experience the rapid growth of Christianity, as was the case at the commencement of the movement, for Heaven's great plan of redemption was accommodated by centuries of planning, setting in place the most ideal circumstances that facilitated the initial success of the movement. Paul calls that day "the fullness of time," i.e., the ripest era possible for the gospel harvest (cf. Gal. 4:4).

History Is Unalterable

No matter how men may wish it were otherwise, history is what it was. It cannot be changed. Alexander the Great's conquest of Tyre cannot be altered to suggest that the Greek general led the victorious Union Army at the battle of Gettysburg. Hitler's death cannot be recast as the peaceful demise of an aged, benevolent gentleman in Argentina.

Christ cannot be joined to a first-century woman in marriage by modern literary hocus pocus (e.g., *The Da Vinci Code*; and even earlier, a similar fabrication by Brigham Young of Mormon fame). The traitor who sold out Jesus cannot be subjected to moral cosmetic surgery that creates loyalty (The Gospel of Judas), and the Savior cannot be un-crucified or left in a tomb.

Thomas Arnold of Rugby described Christ's resurrection as the "best-attested fact in human history" (Thomas 1939, 2569), and this historical reality cannot be repudiated simply because someone has determined in his own mind that the reanimation of a dead body cannot occur. The case for Jesus' resurrection will stand or fall on the historical documentation available—and that is considerable.

As Professor Neill sharply observed: "There is no heresy so dead that someone will not attempt to resuscitate it; there is no error so frequently denounced that someone will not try once more to deck it in the garments of truth" (Green 1977, 72). Practically speaking, that is why it is so important to do today what you will be unable to do tomorrow. Those religions that advocate a "time-warp" are characterized by a mind-warp. Those sects that have invented postmortem "plans" for the salvation of those now deceased (e.g., purgatory, baptism for the dead, etc.) have ignored this reality regarding history.

History Is Irreversible

Paul the apostle was haunted by the bitter memories of his pre-Christian days when he so viciously persecuted the cause of Jesus of Nazareth, putting to death both men and women (cf. Acts 26:10–11; Eph. 3:8; 1 Tim. 1:13). But the past could not be reversed. The only remedy for relief was pardon.

From a personal vantage point, none of us can reverse the countless blunders that marred our earlier days. Horrible acts cannot be undone; the bullet cannot retrace its path back into the pistol. Razor-sharp, wounding words cannot be unwritten or unspoken.

But one can be penitent, and profusely thankful to God for the forgiveness that is available through the atoning death of Jesus Christ.

Those who are motivated by faith in Christ, who confess that faith, repent of their wrongs, and become united with the Lord in the likeness of his burial and resurrection through baptism (Rom. 6:3–4; Col. 2:12), can be refreshed with the confidence that he is pardoned. And what a burden that lifts from the soul.

One's history cannot be changed by an impossible reversal of action. But the spiritual consequences of such may be removed, even though temporal penalties linger on. This is as amazing as it is exhilarating! "Thanks be to God for his unspeakable gift" (2 Cor. 9:15).

GUIDELINES FOR DETERMINING GENUINE HISTORY

George Rawlinson (1812–1902) was Camden Professor of History at Oxford University for twenty-eight years. In 1859, Rawlinson delivered a series of eight lectures in the famous Bampton Series at Oxford. The general theme explored was: "The Historical Evidences of the Truth of the Scripture Records."

My copy, an 1877 edition, contains 225 pages of text, with 211 pages of notes that reference 306 sources, both ancient and contemporary. To say that Rawlinson was a competent judge of what constitutes genuine history would be a gross understatement.

In his initial lecture, Professor Rawlinson introduced four canons (rules, principles) for the determination of true history, as opposed to mythological narratives. Here we introduce these in an abbreviated, though accurate, fashion (1877, 39ff). The four degrees proceed from the strongest to the weakest.

Eye-witness Testimony

When an event is described by a "credible witness" who had the means of observing that which he depicts, such testimony possesses the "highest degree of credibility."

Second-hand Testimony

When an event is recorded by a writer who obtained his information directly from eyewitnesses of the event, the testimony must be considered as probably true. This is the "second degree" of historical credibility.

Oral Tradition

The third level of evidence has to do with oral tradition. When an event is considerably distant from the one who records it, and the writer obtained the information through oral tradition; if the data represents events of public notoriety that were important enough to have affected national life, or have been commemorated by established ritualism, the events probably are substantially true. Oral history is regarded as fairly reliable for about one hundred fifty years.

Corroborating Societies

When the traditions of one people are supported by those of another, especially by those of a remotely distanced and antagonistic people, the probability of the events is greatly increased. This is even more the case if it can be shown that there has been no collusion between the two groups.

THE NEW TESTAMENT RECORDS

How does this relate to the New Testament records? Marvelously! The New Testament passes the credibility test with flying colors.

There were eight New Testament writers: Matthew, Mark, Luke, John, Peter, Paul, James, and Jude. Let us look carefully at these men.

- ◆ Peter, John, and Matthew were in the original apostolic company; they were with Jesus during his ministry, hence wrote as eyewitnesses of the things they saw and heard.

- ◆ James (not the brother of John; cf. Acts 12:2) was a leader in the Jerusalem church (Acts 15:13; cf. Gal. 2:9), and a half-brother of Jesus (Gal. 1:19; cf. Acts 1:14). At first he did not believe on Christ (Jn. 7:5), but later happily acknowledged himself as "a servant of God and the Lord Jesus Christ" (Jas. 1:1). James' credibility is extremely high. Too, Jude was a brother of James (Jude 1), and thus also a half-brother of Jesus.

- ◆ Mark was the son of Mary of Jerusalem. Mary was the aunt of Barnabas (Col. 4:10). She must have had a close relationship with the apostles since

Peter went to her house when released from prison (Acts 12:12ff). The familiarity of this family with the apostles is confirmed by Peter's reference to Mark as his "son" (1 Pet. 5:13), suggesting a spiritual relationship (cf. 1 Tim. 1:2). Thus, Mark himself would have been a witness of many of Jesus' deeds. Several ancient writers (e.g., Papias, Irenaeus, and Tertullian) testify that Mark's Gospel reflects Peter's influence.

◆ Luke was a Greek whose Gospel narrative was grounded in the eyewitness testimony of those familiar with Christ "from the beginning" (1:1–4). After studying these writings carefully, Sir William Ramsay, who once was a skeptic, declared that "Luke's history is unsurpassed in respect of its trustworthiness" (1979, 81).

◆ Paul, of course, was a scholar of no meager ability. He was contemporary with Christ and became acquainted with some of the apostles (cf. Gal. 1:18). His defenses of Christianity are classic (see Acts 22; 26).

All of these men were inspired of God, but in this brief piece, we have examined their credibility only in the light of recognized historical principles. Their writings pass the test superbly.

When one is grounded in truth, he is not "tossed to and fro and carried about with every wind of doctrine, by the sleight of men, in craftiness, after the wiles of error" (Eph. 4:14). Christianity is a religion grounded in history; one must not attempt to tamper with it!

Chapter 2

Were the New Testament Writers Credible "Witnesses"?

Of the Divine character of the Bible, I think no man who deals honestly with his own mind and heart can entertain a reasonable doubt. For myself, I must say, that having for many years made the evidences of Christianity the subject of close study, the result has been a firm and increasing conviction of the authenticity and plenary inspiration of the Bible. It is indeed the Word of God.
— Simon Greenleaf (1783–1853), professor of law, Harvard University

The New Testament abounds with words that carry a legal significance. The Greek verb *martureo* is used seventy-six times in the New Testament, and the nouns *marturia* (thirty-seven times), *martus* (thirty-five times), and *marturion* (nineteen times) compose a family of literary kinsmen that have an important emphasis in New Testament literature.

Such terms as "witness," "bear witness," "testify," "testimony," etc., arise within the word group. Our English word "martyr" derives from this stem—a martyr being one who provides "witness" to the genuineness of his testimony by the willingness to forfeit his own life, if necessary, in the affirmation of truth (see Rev. 17:6; cf. 20:4).

A sampling of how the various expressions are employed is a profitable study. In one of his post-resurrection appearances, Jesus spoke to a group of disciples (which included the eleven apostles). Regarding his death and resurrection, the Savior said: "You are witnesses of these things" (Lk. 24:48). To the apostles he later charged, "[Y]ou shall be my witnesses both in Jerusalem, and in all Judaea and Samaria, unto the utter most part of the earth" (Acts 1:8). They would "witness" personally in many places throughout the antique world, and their oral and written testimony would reach even farther.

In his sermon at the house of Cornelius, Peter affirmed the authenticity of the "witness" of the apostles who heard Jesus' words and saw his amazing deeds, and even the Savior himself following his resurrection (Acts 10:39–41; cf. 3:15; 4:33; 5:30–32; 13:29–31; 1 Pet. 5:1). Similarly Paul, who saw the resurrected Lord en route to Damascus, was commissioned as a witness for Jesus (Acts 22:15; 23:11; 26:16; 2 Thes. 1:10).

THE CHALLENGING DILEMMA

In view of the multiple New Testament passages that stress the importance of the witnesses and their testimony regarding Christ, the crucial nature of this theme cannot be exaggerated.

One could scarcely do better in introducing the subject than to quote the celebrated Simon Greenleaf (1783–1853). Greenleaf was Dane Professor of Law at Harvard University, and one of the founders of the law school at that university. His multi-volume work, *A Treatise on the Law of Evidence*, is considered one of the classics of judicial literature. I have owned and benefited from this scholarly, three-volume production for many years.

Originally a Jewish agnostic, Greenleaf became convinced of the truth of Christianity by his study of the Gospel accounts from the standpoint of their legal credibility. He wrote:

> The things related by the [Gospel] Evangelists are certainly of the most momentous character, affecting the principles of our conduct here, and our happiness for ever. The religion of Jesus Christ aims at nothing less than the utter overthrow of all other systems of religion in the world; denouncing them as inadequate to the wants of man, false in their foundations, and dangerous in their tendency. It not only solicits the grave attention of all, to whom its doctrines are presented, but it demands their cordial belief, as a matter of vital concernment. These are no ordinary claims; and it seems hardly possible for a rational being to regard them with even a subdued interest; much less to treat them with mere indifference and contempt. If not true, they are little else than the pretensions of a bold imposture, which, not satisfied with having already enslaved millions of the human race, seeks to continue the encroachments upon human liberty, until all nations shall be subjugated under its iron rule. But if they are well founded and just, they can be no less than the high requirements of Heaven, addressed by the voice of God to the reason and understanding of man, concerning things deeply affecting his relations to his sovereign, and essential to the formation of his character and of course to his destiny, for both this life and for the life to come (1903, vii–viii).

In considering this issue, it is only appropriate that one reflect upon the qualifications necessary to establish a *bona fide* witness, and thus determine the character of his testimony. Consider the following criteria essential for a credible witness, and how the testimony of the New Testament writers meets the standard required.

Competent

It is first required of a witness that he be competent. No small child, incapable of distinguishing fact from fiction, is qualified. Equally disabling are conditions such as insanity, impairment of the mind by frequent intoxication, drug use, or mental incapacitation by virtue of disease or old age. Were the writers of the New Testament competent? Let us consider but a few illustrations.

Matthew was a tax collector employed by the Roman government for the collecting of revenues in Palestine (Mt. 9:9). He would have garnered import–export dues, as well as road, bridge, and harbor fees. Such a complicated position of recordkeeping and accountability to the Roman government would have required considerable mental skill.

Luke was a Greek of high sophistication; he was a medical doctor (Col. 4:14). "He was quite clearly an educated man, and he writes very good Greek (note his reference to 'their language' in Acts 1:19; Aramaic was not Luke's language). He starts with a paragraph in classical style (1:1–4). His writing is a combination of a Hebraic strain and good Hellenistic Greek. This versatility points to a writer of no mean competence" (Carson, Moo, and Morris 1992, 115). Blaiklock, himself a recognized classical scholar, wrote concerning the first four verses of Luke's Gospel, that they "are a remarkable piece of Greek written in the manner of the best Greek historians" (1972, 3). William Barclay characterized verses 1–4 as "the best bit of Greek in the New Testament" (1956b, 1). The Gospel of Luke, together with the book of Acts, constitutes about one-fourth of the bulk of the New Testament.

Paul's competence scarcely can be questioned. His reputation was well established among the Jews (Acts 26:4; Gal. 1:14). He had been educated under the celebrated rabbi, Gamaliel (Acts 22:3). His "much learning" was recognized even by his antagonists (Acts 26:24). His thirteen epistles are an abiding testimony to his knowledge, brilliant logic, and skill—as marvelous literary tools under the guiding influence of the Spirit of God.

Informed

A credible witness "must have had the means of obtaining knowledge—in other words, must have observed, or had the opportunity to observe, the matters to which he testifies" (Greenleaf 1899, 527).

As we briefly noted in the previous chapter, the New Testament writers are most impressive in this regard. Matthew, John, and Peter were a part of the original twelve disciples, hence had firsthand knowledge of Jesus from the beginning of his ministry until his ascension—a period of some three and one-half years.

Luke's information, while secondhand, was derived from eyewitnesses (Acts 1:2), and, as Sir William Ramsay (once skeptical of Luke's accuracy) declared, "Luke's history is unsurpassed in respect of its trustworthiness" (1979, 81), because it can be checked for accuracy in so many particulars.

Mark lived in Jerusalem with his mother Mary (Acts 12:12), and he was an associate of Peter (1 Pet. 5:13), thus in a position to be quite familiar with the facts pertaining to Jesus.

Jude was a brother to James (Jude 1), who was a half-brother to Jesus (Gal. 1:19), hence these siblings had occasion to know precisely the nature of the evidence for the origin of Christianity. The New Testament writers were eminently qualified for their roles in conveying the truth about Christ.

Integrity

The character of a witness is of paramount importance. Under the law the veracity of a witnesses' character is assumed to be good "until it has been affected by some of the opponent's discrediting evidence" (Greenleaf 1899, 603–604). This means that the New Testament writers must be regarded as faithful witnesses, unless their testimony can be impeached—and that has not been done with reference to the New Testament documents.

In connection with the matter of integrity, "potential motive" should be taken into consideration. By this we mean, does the witness have any vested interest that might tend to distort or enhance his testimony (e.g., financial, social, or personal safety considerations).

I recently sat in a courtroom where a man was on trial for first-degree murder. His wife, with whom he had an on-and-off relationship, was called by the defense to testify on behalf of the man's character. He had been arrested after a high-speed chase; in his car were four guns and some fifty rounds of ammunition. The lady was asked whether or not she had ever seen her husband in possession of guns, and she firmly replied, "No!" Upon cross-examination, the prosecutor destroyed her credibility by citing a police report she once had filed, charging her husband with pointing a loaded shotgun at her face! Credibility matters.

The question then must be, first of all, **what did the authors of the New Testament documents have to gain** for their testimony in support of Christ and his system of religious teaching? The answer is, absolutely nothing—pertaining to this world. While the deaths of some of the New Testament writers are shrouded in the shadows of antiquity, regarding others there **is** information.

Tertullian (A.D. 200) refers to Peter's martyrdom in Rome (*De Praescriptione* XXXVI), and Eusebius, a fourth century historian, echoed that sentiment, adding that the apostle was crucified head-downward (*Ecclesiastical History* III.1.2.).

John was exiled to the island of Patmos (Rev. 1:9), Paul was persecuted tremendously for his testimony regarding Jesus (see 2 Cor. 11:23–27), and finally met his death in Rome.

According to the historical records available, God's apostle to the Gentiles was beheaded at Aquae Salviae, about three miles outside the city of Rome on the Ostian Way (see Bruce 1977, 450–451).

At this point I cannot but recall the case of Lord George Lyttleton (1709–1773). In the early 1700s, the Oxford-educated member of the British Parliament, who had succumbed to the skeptical influences of his day, determined to do an expose of the alleged "conversion" of Paul. He aimed to show that the apostle's radical change could be explained on the bases of dishonest motives, e.g., personal gain, etc. After a scholarly investigation of the available data, he was forced to completely reverse his views. Accordingly, in 1747 he published his book, *Observations on the Conversion of St. Paul*, in which he argued that there is no reasonable way to explain the abrupt turn-around of Saul of Tarsus, the vicious persecutor, to Paul, the tireless missionary—except by the post-resurrection appearances of Christ to the apostle.

James, the Lord's half-brother, was stoned at the behest of a Jewish priest in conjunction with the Sanhedrin (Josephus, *Antiquities of the Jews* 20.9.1).

An interesting consideration of the fates of the twelve is to be found in William Barclay's volume, *The Master's Men*, and also in Dr. William S. McBirnie's book, *The Search for the Twelve Apostles*.

Before we conclude this section of our discussion, we should note that the early English judicial system placed great emphasis upon the religious convictions of witnesses. It was contended that a person was deemed competent as a witness "if he believes in the being of God, and a future state of rewards and punishments; that is, that Divine punishment will be the certain consequence of perjury" (Greenleaf 1899, 507). That is why the phrase, "so help me God," is a vestige still in the court system, though the basic proposition is scarcely found in the progressively corrupt system of today's judiciary. It hardly needs to be pointed out that the biblical writers labored under the inflexible conviction that they were accountable before God for the truthfulness of their testimony.

INCIDENTAL SIGNS OF WITNESS INTEGRITY

While it certainly is the case that a witness is required to testify truthfully—with reference to friend or foe—it is not expected that one who witnesses for a friend will reveal **uncomplimentary** or **embarrassing** details that are not pertinent to the testimony. It also is anticipated that when one is witnessing with reference to an adversary, some tendency toward **negativity** would not be unexpected.

When testimony actually runs **contrary** to these expectations, however, it significantly underscores the credibility of the witness all the more dramatically. There are numerous New Testament examples that illustrate this principle. We will mention but a brief sampling involving the four writers of the Gospels.

The Testimony of Matthew

The testimony of Matthew relative to the apostolic company (of which he was a member) is stunning. First of all, as noted above, Matthew was a publican, i.e., a tax collector. Normally, "a tax-gatherer was debarred from being either a witness or a judge" (Barclay 1959, 59). The fact that Jesus chose one of that profession to be one of his "witnesses" is profound evidence that the integrity of the man was of such pristine quality that it eclipsed the suspicion normally associated with the job. This is powerful evidence of Matthew's credibility and an example of Jesus' brilliance. Consider, then, the following factors that reveal the objectivity of this apostle.

Matthew records the harshness of the disciples (he being among the number) in sending away a poor woman who sought mercy from Christ on behalf of her daughter (15:23). He recalls the Lord's rebuke of the group because of their "little faith" (16:8). He bluntly reviews Peter's chastisement of the Lord, and Christ's piercing response, "Get behind me, Satan, you are a stumbling-block to me" (16:22–23). Matthew tells of the disciples' lack of faith as demonstrated by their inability to heal a demon-possessed, epileptic man (17:14–17). There are many more such examples of Matthew's honest testimony, even though casting his friends (and himself) in an uncomplimentary light.

The Testimony of Mark

We have mentioned already the closeness of Mark to the apostle Peter (1 Peter 5:13). Several ancient writers (e.g., Papias, Irenaeus, and Tertullian) testify that Mark's Gospel reflects Peter's influence.

Mark is frank about the disciples' unwarranted criticism of Jesus (4:38; 5:31), and their frequent periods of spiritual dullness (4:13; 6:52; 8:17). He does not hesitate to mention the concern of Christ's family regarding the Savior's mental stability (3:21, 31–35).

Though likely a convert of Peter's, Mark describes the apostle's thrice denial of his Lord, and the strong oaths accompanying the horrible deed (14:66ff). He even reveals the disciples' initial disbelief and hardness of heart following Jesus' resurrection (16:14). The integrity of the narrative is incredible.

The Testimony of Luke

Though Luke, a Gentile biographer, was not an eyewitness of Jesus and his deeds, he did interview eyewitnesses and he "traced the course of all things accurately from the first," thus detailing the "certainty" of the matters under investigation (1:1–4). He related secondhand matters, which doubtless included both oral and written data. As noted earlier, his combined books of the Gospel and Acts constitute about one-fourth of the New Testament.

The historian tells of Mary's aggravation with twelve-year old Jesus as he remained in Jerusalem following a Passover feast (2:48). He reports the rejection of Jesus in his old hometown, Nazareth (4:28–29). Luke speaks of the confusion of John the Baptizer (while in prison) concerning the identity of Christ (7:19). The writer discusses the disciples' lack of confidence in the Lord during a storm on the Sea of Galilee (8:24–25). He mentions the disciples' egotism when they encountered a man casting out demons, but who was not a part of their immediate company (9:49).

Luke uncompromisingly tells of James and John's impulsive, hostile offer to call fire from heaven to consume some Samaritans (9:54), and he records the parable in which a despised Samaritan was the hero, and the Jews the villains (10:30ff). Furthermore, when a group of ten lepers was miraculously healed by Christ, the beloved physician noted that only a Samaritan was thankful enough to return and express praise to the Lord (17:11ff).

Luke also reveals the ugly quarrel among the disciples as to which would be the greatest, and of Jesus' rebuke of the less-than-humble group (22:24–27). The historian describes the despondency of those disciples traveling toward Emmaus, who appeared to labor under the conviction that the redemption of Israel had been frustrated by Christ's death (24:18–21). He recounts that even the eleven apostles, after seeing the wounds on Jesus' resurrected body, "still disbelieved for joy and wondered" (24:41). No forger would have included such circumstances that critics might twist into negative arguments.

The Testimony of John

A curious fact that lends itself to John's inspired restraint as a witness for Christ is the selective brevity of his Gospel narrative. Though he was the disciple closest to Jesus, he nonetheless reduces the events of Jesus' earthly ministry to slightly over one month of the Savior's 1,260 days of public activity—an incredible reflection of divine design. But the brevity is entirely understandable when one understands that the purpose of John's Gospel is to provide pinpoint focus to the unique identity of Jesus as the Christ, the Son of God, by means of the signs he performed (20:30–31).

John notes that Nathanael at first questioned that Jesus could be the Messiah since he was from Nazareth, a city with a sordid reputation (1:46). He records Mary's presumptiveness at the wedding in Cana (2:3–4). John tells of the incident of Jesus conversing with a Samaritan woman in public—a disgraceful act by the standards of that culture (4:9, 27). That the Samaritans were attracted to Christ would have ignited racial animosity even on the part of the disciples and, as a consequence, they might have been inclined to pass her by in silence (4:39).

The apostle hesitates not to reveal that many of the disciples were provoked at Jesus' teaching, and "went back, and walked with him no more" (6:66). He acknowledges that even his brothers [half-brothers] "did not believe on him" (7:5). John records the Jewish charge that Christ was the issue of "fornication" (8:41), a subtle slur that he was born out of wedlock—but incidentally confirming the virgin birth report.

The apostle tells of the Jewish disbelief, even though many Hebrews had witnessed Christ's miracles (12:37). He identifies Peter as the man who impetuously cut off the ear of Malchus, servant of the high priest (18:10). John unhesitatingly reports that Thomas refused to believe in Christ's resurrection unless he personally felt of the wounds in Jesus' hands and side (20:25). These are compelling facts that a biased witness might well have omitted.

Testimony Regarding Judas

Finally, there is this matter. Judas, one of the twelve, betrayed his Master for a paltry thirty pieces of silver. One might think that each of the Gospel writers, in his own unique way, would have taken the opportunity to ventilate his feelings of bitter disappointment and disgust regarding the rogue. But such was not the case. All four chronicle the treachery of the traitor, but in the calmest, most objective fashion imaginable.

When one reads the accounts in Matthew (26:47–56), Mark (14:43–52), Luke (22:47–53), and John (18:1–11), there is a total absence of volatile language with reference to Judas (much more so than is characteristic of this article). His horrible deed is related with a matter-of-factness that is inexplicable in terms of human emotional reaction. No string of adjectives reviles the knave, no rage is indicated, and no hatred is expressed. One might suggest these men had every right to express their outrage, but they did not. Why? Their role was to "witness," not to editorialize!

Thus, they were testifying as witnesses—not grandstanding! Witnesses indeed. Incomparable witnesses! Entirely credible witnesses! They pass the legal test with unparalleled excellence. Believe them!

Chapter 3

A General Survey of Evidences for Bible Inspiration

"Why may not the Bible, especially the New Testament, without note or comment, be read and taught as a Divine Revelation in the college, its general principles expounded, its evidences explained, and its glorious principles of morality inculcated?"
— Joseph Story (1779–1845), U.S. Supreme Court Justice

That the Bible claims to be inspired is seen easily by anyone who takes the time to examine its text. The fact that such a claim is made would not of itself, of course, guarantee that the claim is genuine. Many documents, which are clearly impious frauds, assert inspiration (e.g., The Book of Mormon). The question, therefore, is this: is there sufficient evidence to warrant the conclusion that the Bible is, in fact, a volume of divine origin? There is indeed, and it is to such matters that the reader's attention is now directed.

THE UNITY OF THE SCRIPTURES

Is it reasonably possible that forty men, from varying backgrounds, and scattered across more than 1,500 years in time, could have designed some sixty-six metal components, which accidentally came together to form a precision machine that revolutionized the world? Impossible! Exactly—from the human vantage point. But that is precisely the kind of thing that happened in the case of the Bible.

The sacred Scriptures were written by some forty different persons, over a span of some 1,600 years. These authors, from a variety of cultural and educational backgrounds, writing in three different languages (Hebrew, Aramaic, and Greek), produced a volume of sixty-six books that is characterized by such an amazing unity and beautiful continuity as to be inexplicable on the basis of mere human origin.

For example, from Genesis to Revelation there is a marvelous unfolding of the general theme of man's fall from his holy estate, God's plan for his redemption (as carefully worked out across the centuries), the atoning death of Jesus Christ, and the ultimate victory of the Christian system. No serious student of this matter can fail to be awed by this vast body of consistent evidence that can only argue for an inspired document.

Moreover, there are thousands of instances of minute agreement between the biblical writers in matters of history, culture, geography, biography, etc., for which there is absolutely no explanation, save that there was a divine oversight involved in the production. Those who would explore this point further are encouraged to study J. J. Blunt's *Undesigned Coincidences in the Writings Both of the Old and New Testament* and William Paley's "Horae Paulinae" in *The Works of William Paley*. See the more detailed discussion on "The Unity of the Bible" elsewhere in this volume.

THE FLAWLESS ACCURACY OF THE BIBLE

If the Bible is the verbally inspired Word of God, one ought to be able to expect it to be absolutely accurate in the various areas of subject matter upon which it touches. Works that are strictly human—no matter how scholarly or painstaking the authors—always are characterized by unintentional mistakes that betray fallibility. For example, when the famous Tacitus penned his renowned *History and Description of Germany*, it was flawed with so many errors that modern scholars are shocked. When *Encyclopaedia Britannica* was first published, it contained so many mistakes regarding places in America that the publishers of the *New American Cyclopedia* issued a special pamphlet exposing the blunders of its rival!

The Bible, however, is always amazingly accurate in its historical and geographical details. For example, biblical evidence indicates that Moses authored the Pentateuch (cf. Exodus 17:14; Joshua 1:7; Mark 12:26). This is confirmed by Josephus (*Against Apion* I.8), and numerous pagan writers. Hecataeus, Manetho, Lysimachus, Eupolemus, Tacitus, Juvenal, and Longinus all credit Moses with the laws that distinguished the Jews from other nations (see Rawlinson 1877, 254ff). Critics once scoffed at the mention of the Hittites in the biblical narratives (Genesis 23:10; 26:34) because supposedly they never existed. Yet, the archaeological discoveries at ancient Boghazkoy (in Turkey) have exploded that criticism, and confirmed the "authenticity of the 'background material' of the Old Testament" (see: *Bulletin of the American School of Oriental Research* 1953, 18).

In the late 1800s, Sir William Ramsay, a scholar who was skeptical of the authenticity of the book of Acts, led an archaeological expedition to Asia Minor with the intention of disproving the historicity and accuracy of Luke's narrative. After years of research—literally digging up the evidence—Ramsay was forced to conclude that Acts was historically accurate.

In Acts, Luke mentions thirty-two countries, fifty-four cities, and nine Mediterranean islands. He also mentions ninety-five persons, sixty-two of which are not named elsewhere in the New Testament. And his references, where checkable, are always correct. This is truly remarkable in view of the fact that the political–territorial situation of his day was in a state of almost constant flux. How does one account for Luke's precision? Inspiration!

In his monumental work, *Lands of the Bible*, J. W. McGarvey included a chapter titled, "An Argument from the Agreement of the Land and the Book." Therein he stated:

> A fictitious narrative, located in a country with which the writer is not personally familiar, must either avoid local allusions or be found frequently in conflict with the peculiarities of place and of manners and customs. By this conflict the fictitious character of the narrative is exposed (375).

McGarvey observed that there are hundreds of instances in which the Bible can be checked for accuracy. For example, are the Scriptures always correct topographically, or are compass references accurate? Is the way from Jerusalem to Gaza "south" of Samaria (Acts 8:26)? Is Bethel really "west" of Ai (Genesis 12:8)? McGarvey pointed out that "in not a single instance of this kind has any of the Bible writers been found at fault" (378). In concluding his argument, the author asked: "How could they [the Bible writers] have done what learned and careful men of their own age and of subsequent ages have failed to do, unless they were guided, as they claim to have been, by wisdom from on high?" (386).

For a more detailed presentation of this argument, see the chapter, "The Amazing Accuracy of the Bible."

PROPHECY

The prophet Isaiah based the credibility of his message on the validity of predictive prophecy. To the promoters of idolatry in his day, he issued a challenge:

> Let them bring them forth, and declare unto us what
> shall happen: declare ye the former things, what
> they are, that we may consider them, and know the
> latter end of them; or show us the things to come
> (Isaiah 41:22).

He is asking this: "You, who claim to speak revelations in the name of your gods, does subsequent history corroborate your predictions?" Well, what of the Bible? Does it pass the prophecy test?

Exactly what is predictive prophecy? Thomas H. Horne declared that it is "a miracle of knowledge, a declaration or representation of something future, beyond the power of human sagacity to discern or to calculate" (1841, 1.119). In order for prophecy to be valid, the following criteria must obtain. It must involve: (a) proper timing (i.e., significantly preceding the fulfillment); (b) specific details—not vague generalities or remote possibilities; and (c) exact fulfillment—not merely a high degree of probability. Consistent with these standards, the prophecies of the Bible come through with flying colors.

Prophecies of Nations

As God's plan of redemption was unfolding, numerous prophecies were given regarding the rise, decline, and fall of various nations. For example: (a) Israel's history is portrayed vividly in Deuteronomy 28:47–68. Study this narrative carefully and compare it with history. (b) When Israel became involved in idolatry, Isaiah foretold that the Lord would raise up the Assyrians, as the "rod of [His] anger" to punish them (10:5–6); but, after that was accomplished, Jehovah announced, the Assyrians themselves would be destroyed (10:12, 24–25). History reveals that this is exactly what happened (2 Kings 17:24; 18:13). (c) When the kingdom of Judah lapsed into a state of spiritual decay, the prophets announced that Babylon would punish them (Jeremiah 25:9–11; Habakkuk 1:5) and indeed, captivate them for seventy years (Jeremiah 25:11–12). The history of those events is available (2 Kings 24–25; 2 Chronicles 36:21). (d) But even mighty Babylon, "the glory of Kingdoms," was to be destroyed by the Medes and Persians (Isaiah 13), and, as every school boy knows, that is just what happened (Daniel 5:28). Numerous other Old Testament examples complement the foregoing.

Prophecies of People

In 2 Kings 18:13, the text indicates that Sennacherib, king of Assyria, came up against the fortified cities of Judah and took them. Assyrian records indicate that forty-six cities were captured. It was prophesied, however, that he would not be able to take the city of Jerusalem (2 Kings 19:32–34). Sennacherib's forces came to Jerusalem—his annals boast that he shut up Judah's king, Hezekiah, "like a bird in a cage" (see Pritchard 1955, 288)—but for some unexplained reason the city was never taken. [In a visit to the Oriental Institute at the University of Chicago, where a prism recording Sennacherib's exploits is housed, this writer was amused at the guide's puzzlement as to why the king never took Jerusalem. The Bible tells us. God destroyed 185,000 Assyrian soldiers in one night (2 Kings 19:35ff).] It was foretold further that the Assyrian king would return to his own land and there fall by the sword (2 Kings 19:7). Some twenty years later he was assassinated by his own sons, who smote him with the sword, while he was worshipping in his pagan temple (Isaiah 37:37–38).

Or what of the good king Josiah? His work was foretold (and he was called by name) more than three hundred years before it was fulfilled (1 Kings 13:2; 2 Kings 23:15–16). The ministry of King Cyrus of Persia (he, too, being called by name) was prophesied more than a century-and-a-half before the monarch was born (Isaiah 44:28; 45:1). It is on account of such remarkable prophecies as these that liberal critics want to re-date the books of the Bible at a very late period.

Messianic Prophecies

Sidney Collett has declared that of the approximately eight hundred prophecies in the Old Testament, no less than 333 center in the person of Jesus Christ (n.d., 192). The panorama of prophecy regarding the Son of God is nothing short of miraculous and is a demanding evidence for Bible inspiration. For example, there are prophecies about:

- His Lineage—He would be born of woman (Genesis 3:15; Galatians 4:4); of the seed of Abraham (Genesis 22:18; Luke 3:34); of the tribe of Judah (Genesis 49:10; Hebrews 7:14); of the royal lineage of David (2 Samuel 7:12; Luke 1:32); and, to the virgin Mary (Isaiah 7:14; Matthew 1:22–23).

- The Time of His Coming—Christ was to appear during the days of the Roman reign (Daniel 2:44; Luke 2:1), while Judah still possessed her own king (Genesis 49:10; Matthew 2:22). He would be killed some four hundred and ninety years after the command to restore Jerusalem at the end of the Babylonian captivity (457 B.C.), i.e., in A.D. 30 (Daniel 9:24ff). [NOTE: For additional documentation and discussion of this material, see Jackson, *Daniel's Seventy Weeks.*]

- His Nature—Jesus was to be both human and divine; though born, he was eternal (Micah 5:2; John 1:1, 14); though a man, he was Jehovah's "fellow" (Zechariah 13:7;

John 10:30; Philippians 2:6). He was to be gentle and compassionate in his dealing with people (Isaiah 42:1–4; Matthew 12:15–21). He would be perfectly submissive to his heavenly Father (Psalm 40:8; Isaiah 53:11; John 8:29; 2 Corinthians 5:21; 1 Peter 2:22).

- His Betrayal, Death, Resurrection—It was foretold that the Lord would be betrayed by a friend (Psalm 41:9) for thirty pieces of silver (Zechariah 11:12). He was (John 13:18; Matthew 26:15). He would be spit upon and beaten (Isaiah 50:6) and in death his hands and feet would be pierced (Psalm 22:16). This is precisely what happened (Matthew 27:30; Luke 24:39). Though he would be killed, amazingly, his flesh would not experience corruption, but he would be raised from the grave (Psalm 16:10; Acts 2:22ff).

These are but a sampling of the more than three hundred prophecies relating to the Lord. In his interesting book, *Science Speaks*, mathematician Peter W. Stoner selected just eight of the Old Testament prophecies concerning Christ, and estimated that the odds of these being fulfilled accidentally would be approximately 1 in 10^{17} (that is one followed by seventeen zeros)! He then illustrated in the following fashion:

Suppose we take 10^{17} silver dollars and lay them on the face of Texas. They will cover all of the state 2 feet deep. Now mark one of these silver dollars and stir the whole mass thoroughly, all over the state. Blindfold a man and tell him that he can travel as far as he wishes, but he must pick up one silver dollar and say that this is the right one. What chance would he have of getting the right one? (1963, 106–107).

Horne was quite correct when he wrote:

> The book which contains these predictions is
> stamped with the seal of heaven: a rich vein of evi-
> dence runs through the volume of the O.T.; the Bible
> is true; infidelity is confounded forever; and we may
> address its patrons in the language of Saint Paul,
> "Behold, ye despisers, and wonder and perish!"
> (1841, 1.126).

Chapter 4

A Profile of Bible Prophecy

"The authenticity of the writings of the prophets, though the men themselves are human, is established by such things as the prediction of highly significant events far in the future that could be accomplished only through a knowledge obtained from a realm which is not subject to the laws of time as we know them.

One of the great evidences is the long series of prophecies concerning Jesus the Messiah. These prophecies extend hundreds of years prior to the birth of Christ. They include a vast amount of detail concerning Christ himself, His nature and the things He would do when He came—things which to the natural world, or the scientific world, remain to this day completely inexplicable."
— Robert Morris Page (1903–1970), physicist

An examination of the lexical literature reveals that scholars are undecided as to the etymology of the term "prophet." Some think the noun is from an Arabic term meaning "spokesman" (Smith 1928, 10), whereas others have contended that the root is a Hebrew form which signifies a "bubbling up," as when water issues from a hidden fountain (Girdlestone n.d., 239). This would suggest the idea of the inspiration behind the prophet. It is now more commonly believed, however, that the word may be of Akkadian origin and that it may denote "to be called" (Unger and White 1980, 310).

Perhaps the best way to determine the meaning of the term is to examine the manner in which the Bible employs it. The classic passage which sets forth the role of the prophet is Exodus 7:1–2:

> And Jehovah said unto Moses, see, I have made you as God to Pharaoh; and Aaron your brother shall be your prophet. Thou shall speak all that I command thee; and Aaron thy brother shall speak unto Pharaoh.

A prophet was simply a spokesman for God. The prophet was also called a "seer." Note how the terms "prophet" and "seer" are interchanged in 1 Samuel 9:9:

> Beforetime in Israel, when a man went to inquire of God, thus he said, Come, and let us go to the seer; for he that is now called a Prophet was beforetime called a Seer.

Some scholars suggest that the term "prophet" stressed the objective or active work of God's spokesman, whereas "seer" underscored the subjective method of receiving divine revelation, i.e., by "seeing" (Freeman 1968, 40). A prophet was also designated as a "man of God" (2 Kgs. 4:9), a "servant of the Lord" (Ezek. 38:17), and a "messenger of Jehovah" (Mal. 3:1).

There are a number of truths that need to be appreciated if one is to understand the function of prophecy in biblical literature. Let us consider the following points.

THE PANORAMA OF PROPHECY

In discussing prophecy, one needs to make a clear distinction between "foretelling" and "forthtelling." Many assume, and erroneously so, that all prophecy is foretelling, i.e., predictive in its nature. However, prophecy also concerns the revelation of events that occurred in the past; it may deal with present circumstances (i.e., contemporary with the prophet), or it can look forward to the future.

For example, Moses was a prophet (Dt. 18:15), yet when he recorded the creation activity of Genesis 1, he was giving a divinely inspired account of what transpired during the first week of earth's history. Certainly he was not present to witness those events. His prophetic testimony looked into the past. On the other hand, when the prophet addressed certain situations during Israel's forty-year sojourn in the wilderness, he was dealing with current conditions in the lives of his fellow Hebrews. Amos was a prophet who wrote many things "he saw concerning Israel" (Am. 1:1).

Finally, the prophet's vision sometimes was directed into the future where he foretold details regarding certain people and events. In passing, we might simply mention several categories relating to predictive prophecy. For instance, there are prophecies that relate to individuals. The mission of Josiah was foretold more than three centuries before his birth (cf. 1 Kgs. 13; 2 Kgs. 23). The role of the Persian king, Cyrus, in releasing the Hebrews from Babylonian captivity, was described more than a century and a half before his reign (cf. Isa. 44:28; 45:1ff; see below). The fate of cities and nations is prophetically announced in various scriptures. Daniel's descriptions of the Babylonian, Medo-Persian, Greek, and Roman empires are nothing short of miraculous (cf. Daniel, chapters 2, 7, 8). Too, there is the matter of Messianic prophecy. Of the hundreds of prophecies in the Old Testament, at least three hundred (plus) center on the coming Christ. (See: http://www.vojo.com/rev/messianic_prophecies.htm.)

The design of predictive prophecy was to establish the credibility of God and, ultimately, the authenticity of his sacred

Scriptures. In this article, we will be dealing principally with the predictive nature of biblical prophecy.

GENUINE PREDICTIVE PROPHECY—THE TEST

Predictive prophecy may be defined as:

> a miracle of knowledge, a declaration, or description, or representation of something future, beyond the power of human sagacity to discern or to calculate, and it is the highest evidence that can be given of supernatural communion with Deity, and of the truth of a revelation from God (Horne 1841, 1.119).

There are a number of criteria for determining the genuineness of prophecy—as opposed to speculative prediction. Prophecy must involve the following:

- Proper timing—the oracle must significantly precede the person or event described. It must be beyond the realm of reasonable calculation so as to preclude the possibility of an "educated guess." When one "prophesies" that it will rain tomorrow—with a weather front moving in—it hardly evinces divine intervention.

- The prophecy must deal in specific details, not vague generalities that are capable of being manipulated to fit various circumstances. To predict that "someone" will do "something" at "sometime" is not terribly impressive.

- Exact fulfillment, not merely a high degree of probability, must characterize the prediction. A prophet who is eight percent accurate is no prophet at all!

In this connection we may observe that the prophets of the Bible, when uttering their declarations, spoke with absolute confidence. They frequently employed a verbal form known as the perfect state, which suggests completed action. One scholar calls it the "perfect of confidence" (Watts 1951, 17). It speaks of the event as if it had already occurred (though still in the future), thus stressing the certainty of its fulfillment. Isaiah could therefore say, "For unto us a child is born" (9:6), even though the incarnation of Christ was still several centuries away. Prophecy was never couched with an uncertain "maybe," or an ambiguous "perhaps."

The divine standard for a true prophet is stated by Moses. "When a prophet speaks in the name of Jehovah, if the thing follow not, nor come to pass, that is the thing which Jehovah has not spoken" (Dt. 18:22). In Isaiah 41:23, a challenge is issued to the false gods of paganism: "Declare the things that are to come hereafter, that we may know that you are gods"

Jeane Dixon (1904–97) was hailed as one of America's most famous psychic prophetesses. Just how good at prophecy was she?

> In the decade of the fifties were three presidential elections—one in '52, one in '56, and one in '60. During that time Jeane prophesied who would be the candidate for each of the major parties in all three of those elections, and who would win the elections. How did she do? She missed all of the candidates, all of the parties, and all of the winners of all the elections (Kennedy 1980, 16).

Clearly, predictive prophecy is a very important element of the sacred Scriptures, and stands in bold relief to the counterfeit prophecies of today's world.

PROPHECY—CONDITIONAL OR ABSOLUTE?

While we have noted that the prophets spoke with confidence, it is also important to observe that some prophecies obviously were conditional. This is especially true with reference to predictions that contained warnings of impending judgment upon wicked peoples. The doom prophetically announced was dependent upon whether or not that nation would turn from its evil.

For example, when Jonah went to the city of Nineveh, he announced: "Yet forty days, and Nineveh shall be overthrown" (3:4). However, that warning obviously was conditional as evidenced by the fact that when the people of Nineveh repented, and "God saw their works that they turned from their evil way," he withdrew the judgment and did not destroy them (cf. 3:10). Similarly, when God promised the Israelites that the land of Canaan would be their inheritance, that pledge was contingent upon their fidelity to Jehovah. Note the testimony of Joshua 23:16:

> When ye transgress the covenant of Jehovah your God, which he commanded you, and go and serve other gods, and bow down yourselves to them; then will the anger of Jehovah be kindled against you, and ye shall perish quickly from off the good land which he hath given unto you.

The Hebrew nation did apostatize and lost its special privileges with God (cf. Mt. 21:43). Those religionists and politicians today who argue for Israel's intrinsic right to Palestinian territory overlook this very critical element of Bible prophecy (see Jackson 1997, 168–174).

On the other hand, some prophecies were absolute. Predictions concerning the coming Messiah were not predicated upon human response; they were fulfilled with amazing accuracy. The Messiah was to be: the seed of woman (Gen. 3:15), the offspring of Abraham (Gen. 22:18), from the tribe of Judah (Gen. 49:10), born to a virgin (Isa. 7:14), in the town of Bethlehem (Mic. 5:2), etc. There was nothing conditional about these statements.

THE LANGUAGE OF PROPHECY

If one is to accurately interpret Bible prophecy, he must surely recognize that language of predictive literature can be either literal or figurative. But how does one determine the nature of prophetic terminology? In some instances common sense will dictate the character of the prophecy. If a literal view implies impossibility, or an absurdity, it obviously is figurative. The context will frequently shed light on the situation. In many instances, the issue will be settled by how the New Testament writers (who quote or cite the prophecies) viewed the matter. When Old Testament writers declared that Christ would be the offspring of Abraham (Gen. 22:18), or that he would be raised from the dead (Psa. 16:10), they made straightforward predictions that were fulfilled literally.

However, when Isaiah announced that John the Baptizer would "make level in the desert a highway for our God" (40:3), he was not suggesting that John would engineer a freeway project in the Palestinian wilderness; rather, the language was a symbolic description of John's preparatory work preliminary to the ministry of Jesus (cf. Mt. 3:1ff). When the prophet foretold that "the lion shall eat straw like an ox" (Isa. 11:7), he was not suggesting that Jehovah intended to redesign the dental–digestive processes of the animal kingdom in the alleged "millennial" age. He was figuratively suggesting the peaceful atmosphere that would be characteristic of the church of Christ as the various nations flowed into it (cf. Isa. 11:10;

Rom. 15:12). Thus, it is vital that the nature of the language in biblical prophecy be correctly identified.

THE PROPHET AND HIS GENERATION

Liberal critics of the Bible deny the reality of predictive prophecy (as well as other miraculous elements in the Scriptures). Frequently they ask: "What relevance would the prophecy have had to an antique generation which would never see it fulfilled?" It is for this reason that they desperately seek some application that would be contemporary with the prophet himself (as, for example, postulating a young maiden of Isaiah's day who would conform to his virgin-birth prophecy—7:14). The fact is some prophecies had no immediate relevance to their contemporary generation. Those ancients would not fully understand the predictions—except dimly through the eye of faith. Abraham, through prophecy, was promised that his seed would receive Canaan for an inheritance, though he himself never saw the fulfillment (cf. Gen. 15:12ff; Heb. 11:8–16).

Not even the prophets understood the meaning of many of their inspired utterances. Peter discusses this very matter in 1 Peter 1:10–12. God's redemptive plan, as previewed by the Old Testament messengers, was a "mystery," which can now be perceived only by means of New Testament revelation (Eph. 3:1–13).

PARTIAL AND COMPLETE FULFILLMENT

Those with loose theological leanings are sometimes prone to say that certain prophecies of the Old Testament had a rather immediate fulfillment, but that the New Testament writers sometimes lifted these passages from their original contexts and gave them meanings foreign to their original design. One writer, for example, has asserted "Paul paraphrased passages without regard to their original context, or meaning . . . It is as though the words of scripture convey a convincing power within themselves apart from their original context" (Batey 1969, 134). In this writer's judgment, this is a most careless statement that does not reflect well upon the apostle.

In the first place, whenever possible, one should attempt to ascertain precisely how the New Testament writer is appealing to the Old Testament passage. But that is not always easy. Is the New Testament writer merely borrowing language from an Old Testament text? Is he employing an ancient scripture illustratively? Or does he mean to affirm that a New Testament incident is actually a "fulfillment" of prophecy? We must remember that ancient writers did not use the same literary devices employed today. Quotation marks, colons, ellipsis marks, brackets, etc., were unknown to them. In view of this, we may not always know just how they were utilizing the language of the former Scriptures. Since we are largely ignorant of their procedures, criticism of them is hardly appropriate (Pache 1969, chapter 10). See our chapter on how the New Testament writers used texts from the Old Testament.

Is it not possible that the omniscient Holy Spirit, who guided both the Old Testament prophets and the New Testament inspired writers, could have directed certain prophecies to ancient Israel, but also could have known that a future event would ultimately fulfill the meaning of his words? What is wrong with such a view? Absolutely nothing. It surely is possible, and it preserves the integrity of the New Testament writers. Let me suggest an example to illustrate this point.

In a psalm that obviously had a primary application to David (Psa. 69; cf. Rom. 11:9), the psalmist prayed that his enemies might be divested of their power (v. 25). Yet centuries later Peter declared, with an application to the traitor Judas, "It was needful that the scripture should be fulfilled, which the Holy Spirit spoke through the mouth of David concerning Judas, 'Let his habitation be made desolate, and let no man dwell therein'" (Acts 1:20). We thus note that, consistent with his own purposes, the Holy Spirit may give a prophecy multiple applications.

Consider the case of Psalm 2:7, where Jehovah said: "Thou art my son; this day have I begotten thee." In the New Testament, this statement is applied to Christ in several different senses. First, it is employed to demonstrate that Christ is superior to the angels, for the Father never addressed any angelic being, saying, "You are my son, this day have I begotten thee" (cf. Heb. 1:5). (This is a truth which the "Jehovah's Witnesses"—who claim that Christ was a created angel—would do well to learn.)

Secondly, Psalm 2:7 is applied by Paul to Christ's resurrection from the dead. The apostle argues that "God hath fulfilled the same unto our children, in that he raised up Jesus; as also it is written in the second psalm, 'Thou art my son'" (Acts 13:33). It was, of course, by his resurrection that Jesus was declared to be the Son of God with power (Rom. 1:4). It was entirely appropriate that the psalm be applied to the Lord's resurrection.

Finally, the writer of Hebrews uses the psalm to prove that Christ glorified not himself to be made our high priest; rather, such a role was due to his relationship as the Son of God (5:5). Again, we absolutely must stress that the Holy Spirit, who inspired the original psalm, surely had all of these various thoughts in mind as is evidenced by his guidance of the New Testament writers as they employed his language.

TYPOLOGICAL PROPHECY

The Old Testament contains numerous examples of a device called a "type." A type may be defined as a "figure or ensample of something future and more or less prophetic, called the 'Antitype'" (Bullinger 1968, 768). A simpler description of a type might be a pictorial prophecy. For example, Melchizedek, who was both king of Salem and a priest of God, prophetically symbolized the Son of God who rules as our King and serves as our High Priest (cf. Psa. 110:4; Heb. 5:5–10; 6:20; 7:1–17). Jonah's three-day confinement in the belly of the great fish was a pictorial prediction of Christ's three-day entombment (cf. Mt. 12:40), and his resurrection from the dead. Typology is an important form of prophecy.

The foregoing principles by no means exhaust the topic of Bible prophecy. They are, however, illustrative of the kinds of factors that need to be considered in pursuing this sort of study. Again, let us remind ourselves that prophecy is one of the crucial proofs for establishing the credibility of the Holy Scriptures. Let us therefore study this area of biblical information carefully and employ it properly in our defense of the faith.

AN AMAZING CASE OF PROPHECY

One of the truly astounding prophecies of the Bible is found in the last verse of Isaiah 44, together with chapter 45:1ff (an unfortunate chapter break). It has to do with Cyrus, king of Persia. According to the historian Herodotus (*The Histories* i.46), Cyrus was the son of Cambyses I. He came to the Persian throne in 559 B.C. Nine years later he conquered the Medes, thus unifying the kingdoms of the Medes and the Persians.

Cyrus is mentioned some twenty-three times in the literature of the Old Testament. Isaiah refers to Cyrus as Jehovah's "shepherd," the Lord's "anointed," who was providentially appointed to facilitate the divine plan. God would lead this monarch to "subdue nations" and "open doors" (an allusion to the Jews' release from Babylonian captivity). He would make "rough places smooth," i.e., accommodate the Hebrews' return to their Palestinian homeland. He would ultimately be responsible for the rebuilding of Jerusalem and the reconstruction of the temple.

Amazingly, the king would accomplish these noble tasks even though he did not "know" Jehovah (45:4–5). In other words, though he was a pagan in sentiment and practice, yet, as an unconscious tool in the hands of the Lord, he would contribute mightily to the Jewish cause, and so, indirectly, to the coming of God's greater Anointed, Jesus of Nazareth.

The fulfillment of these plain and specific predictions is set forth in 2 Chronicles 36:22, 23 and Ezra 1:1–4, 7, 8; 3:7; 4:3. The *Encyclopedia Britannica*, an unlikely source, acknowledged that "in 538 [B.C.] Cyrus granted to the Jews, whom Nebuchadressar had transported to Babylonia, the return to Palestine and the rebuilding of Jerusalem and its temple" (1958, 940).

What many people do not realize in reading Isaiah 44:28ff is that the heathen ruler was named by the prophet long before the monarch was even born. Isaiah prophesied in the reigns of Uzziah, Jotham, Ahaz, and Hezekiah (1:1). His ministry thus occurred in the latter portion of the eighth century B.C. (ca. 740–701 B.C.). This was some one hundred fifty years before Cyrus came to the throne!

Incredible declarations of this nature have led critics (who reject the possibility of predictive prophecy) to suggest that these portions of the book of Isaiah were added much later— after the fact, as it were. A popular reference work states:

> Because the book of Isaiah includes prophecies concerning events during and after the Exile, critical scholars generally attribute portions of the book to one, two, or more prophets in addition to Isaiah (esp. Deutero-Isaiah, chs. 40–55; Trito-Isaiah, chs. 56–66) (Myers 1987, 531).

Here is an example of how the liberal viewpoint is reflected even by a professor in a Christian university. In discussing the promises set forth in Isaiah 44:26–28, John T. Willis of Abilene Christian University says:

> All of these promises assume that Jerusalem and the cities of Judah have been razed, that the temple is no longer standing, that Cyrus is on the scene and swiftly growing in power, and that the return of the exiles is imminent (1980, 380).

If such is the case, then the material could not possibly have been written by the prophet Isaiah since he died long before these events transpired. The author, in spite of his claim of a conservative approach to the book (31), clearly reflects his opinion that this portion of the book of Isaiah was authored by a writer of the sixth century B.C. (cf. 381). These assertions plainly contradict the New Testament (cf. Jn. 12:37–41).

Against such a viewpoint we have the assurance of Scripture itself. Earlier, in 41:25ff, Isaiah had spoken of the coming of "one . . . from the rising of the sun." Though not called by name, the allusion is clearly to Cyrus, who would bring good tidings regarding Jerusalem.

In 41:26, Isaiah makes it plain that the mission of Cyrus was a matter of prophecy, not educated speculation. It is a reflection of compromised faith to postulate a late date for these prophecies.

Finally, as an interesting sidelight, we note that Josephus, the Jewish historian, states that the Jews in Babylonian captivity showed Cyrus the prophecies of the Old Testament Scriptures that contained his name and described his role in the scheme of God. The historian says that it was this circumstance that motivated the ruler "to fulfill what was written" (*Antiquities of the Jews* 11.1.2), and thus to issue his edict permitting Israel's return to her homeland.

Excavations at Babylon (1879–82) led to the discovery of a clay barrel, known as the Cyrus Cylinder, which contained a marvelous historical confirmation of the biblical narrative. It portrays the benevolent policies of Cyrus in the following fashion: "All of their peoples I gathered together and restored to their dwelling-places" (Price 1920, 234).

Predictive prophecy is a compelling evidence for the divine origin of the Holy Scriptures.

Chapter 5

The Unity of the Bible

"The Books of Scripture illustrate and expound each other; as in the mariner's compass, the needle's extremity, though it seems to point purposely to the north, doth yet at the same time discover both east and west, as distant as they are from it and each other, so do some texts of Scripture guide us to the intelligence of others, for which they are widely distant in the Bible."
— Robert Boyle (1626–1691), father of modern chemistry

The Bible claims to be the divinely inspired Word of God. Is there any support for this affirmation? Evidences for the inspiration of the Bible fall into two general categories. Some evidences are classified as external in nature, while others are viewed as internal. For instance, artifacts from the field of archaeology, which corroborate the historical statements of the Scriptures, are external evidences. An example would be the discovery of the Nabonidus Cylinder, which demonstrated that Belshazzar (Dan. 5) was a real Babylonian king, and not a mythical character, as some early critics contended (Wiseman 1980, 183).

On the other hand, certain proofs of biblical inspiration are internal in character. That is, they are a part of the fabric of the Book itself. They are self-authenticating phenomena from within the Sacred Volume that bear testimony to the fact that the production of the Holy Scriptures must have been orchestrated by a superintending Mind. One such evidence of inspiration is the incredible unity that is characteristic of the Bible.

In order to appreciate the marvelous unity that pervades the Sacred Volume, one must first understand that the Bible was written by approximately forty different men, in three languages (Hebrew, Aramaic, and Greek), over a vast span of time. From the composition of the Pentateuch (possibly the book of Job was penned even earlier), to the final completion of Revelation, some sixteen hundred years of history were involved.

The holy writings came out of a variety of cultural backgrounds, and the documents were penned by a diverse group of authors (shepherds, fishermen, professional men, scholars, etc.). In view of this fact, one might well expect the final form of the Scriptures to be a tangled mishmash of divergent subjects that are quite often marred by conflict and lack of continuity. Such a circumstance, however, is far from the case. The fact is, the Bible evinces such an astounding harmony, such a consistent flow, that it utterly defies any naturalistic explanation. Unquestionably, there was a unifying Source behind the composition. It is as though the Bible were a magnificent symphony that clearly has been orchestrated by a single Master. Let us consider several lines of evidence that support the concept that the Scriptures could only have come ultimately from God.

UNITY OF THEME

There is a unity of theme that saturates the whole of the divine oracles. The Bible is the story of one problem, sin; with one solution, Jesus Christ (Geisler and Nix 1986, 194). In Genesis, Christ is the promised seed (3:15); in Exodus, he is the Passover lamb (chapter 12); in Leviticus, he is the holy sacrifices (chapters 1–5); in Numbers, he is the brazen serpent (chapter 21), etc. Christ is found, either directly or indirectly, in every book of the Bible.

The redemptive thread that runs through the Scriptures is wonderfully illustrated by a comparison between Genesis and Revelation, the first and last books of the holy canon.

In Genesis the origin of the heavens and Earth is revealed (1:1), while in Revelation the consummation of earthly affairs is effected, and the old order is replaced by a "new heaven and earth" (i.e., heaven itself), spiritual in nature. Further, the deceptive Satan, who seduced our original parents (Gen. 3:1ff), is to be cast into hell where he deceives no more (Rev. 20:10). Man, who was originally perfect, but who fell into sin (Genesis 3:6), is, by virtue of his obedience, granted the opportunity to become perfect again (Rev. 7:14; 22:14). All of this is made possible, of course, by the seed of woman (Gen. 3:15), who was the offspring of David (Rev. 22:16); who, as a consequence of his sacrifice (Gen. 4:4), became an enthroned Lamb (Rev. 5:12). Thus, the sorrow of Eden (Gen. 3:16) will be transformed into the joy of heaven (Rev. 21:4), and that tree of life, from which our early parents were separated (Gen. 3:22–24), will be our glad possession once more (Rev. 22:14). Appropriately, there is a remarkable concurrence between Genesis and Revelation.

UNITY OF PLAN

The Bible also has a unified plan of development. Consider the following. In Genesis there is the record of humanity's pristine origin, and then mankind's tragic fall into a sinful state. Moreover, there is also the initial suggestion that a benevolent God was beginning to unfold a plan for the remedy of this disaster (Gen. 3:15). A specific family line (i.e., the Hebrew nation) was selected for the accomplishment of this task (Gen. 12:1ff; 22:18).

But man needed to learn precisely what "sin" is. How was this concept to be defined? In response to that need, a written law was given. The books of Exodus through Deuteronomy record the giving of the law to Moses. This set of ordinances was designed to define sin, and to illuminate human rebellion in all of its horrible ugliness (Rom. 7:7, 13; Gal. 3:19). The historical books of the Old Testament reveal humanity's inability to perfectly keep a law system (Gal. 3:10), hence, they underscore the need for a Justifier—someone to do for man what he is incapable of doing for himself. The prophets of the Old Testament herald the coming of that Savior (Lk. 24:44). More than three hundred prophecies focus upon the promised Messiah.

After four silent centuries (the inter-biblical era), the Gospel writers inform us that the Justifier has come—Jesus of Nazareth. The books of Matthew, Mark, Luke, and John are carefully documented accounts of the life, death, and resurrection of the Son of God (Jn. 20:30–31). The evidence for the divine mission of Christ is overwhelming.

The book of Acts demonstrates how first-century men and women appropriated Jehovah's justifying grace unto themselves. It is an inspired manual on how to become a Christian. It is a historical record of how the church of Christ was established in Jerusalem, and flourished throughout the Roman Empire. The various epistles to churches and to individuals instructed saints how to grow toward spiritual maturity. Finally, the book of Revelation pictures (in vivid symbols) the ultimate and complete triumph of the cause of God over all hostile forces. Without question, the Bible contains a detailed continuity of plan.

UNITY OF DOCTRINE

The Bible is likewise characterized by doctrinal unity, by which we mean that the fundamental elements of its teaching system are harmonious. There is, of course, the development of certain theological themes within the Sacred Volume (e.g., the concept of immortality—cf. Job 14:14; 2 Tim. 1:10), yet there is no discord.

It is truly an astounding phenomenon that whereas biblical writers did not hesitate to criticize one another for personal flaws of conduct (see Gal. 2:11ff), and while one author might concede that another writer's production was difficult to understand (2 Pet. 3:16), never did the inspired writers critique, or attempt to refute, the doctrinal argumentation of their inspired companions. Contrast this with the conduct of theologians in this age—indeed, of any age! Note these brief examples of doctrinal harmony:

- The Scriptures affirm that there is but one God (Dt. 6:4; Jas. 2:19). By "one God" the biblical writers mean there is but a solitary divine nature. Yet, that divine essence is possessed by three distinct personalities—revealed in the New Testament as the Father, the Son, and the Holy Spirit (Gen. 1:1–2, 26; Mt. 28:19; Jn. 1:1; 2 Cor. 13:14).

- The universe is neither eternal, nor self-created; rather, it was brought into existence by Deity (Gen. 1:1; Psa. 33:6–9; Jn. 1:1–3; Heb. 11:3).

- Man is more than mere matter. In addition to flesh, he has a higher nature created in the image of God (Gen. 1:26; Eccl. 12:7; Dan. 7:15; Mt. 10:28; 1 Thes. 5:23).

- Blood is needed for the atonement of sin (Lev. 17:11; Mt. 26:28; Heb. 9:22; Rev. 7:14).

Contrast the doctrinal harmony of the Bible with modern works which allege inspiration, but which lack supporting evidence for the claim. For instance, the literature of Mormonism argues that polygamy is whoredom, sinful, etc. (Book of Mormon, Jacob 2:27; 3:5; 1:15; 2:23–24; Mosiah 11:2), yet plural marriages are elsewhere described as part of a new and everlasting covenant which may only be rejected upon the penalty of damnation (Doctrine and Covenants, 132:3–4).

FACTUAL HARMONY

Though the erudite works of men may be ever so skillfully produced, occasionally they are bound to incorporate factual mistakes that flaw the unity of the documents. Genuine disharmony, of course, would reveal the fact that a work was strictly human in origin. If, therefore, the Bible is the verbally inspired Word of God, we have the right to expect that it not be marred by contradictions, for Deity is not the author of confusion (or contradiction), but only of truth (1 Cor. 14:33; Jn. 17:17).

In the third century A.D., there lived a Syrian philosopher named Malchus Porphyry. Jerome once characterized him as "a rabid dog against Christ." Porphyry wrote fifteen books against Christianity. One of these was entirely devoted to an assemblage of "contradictions" which the infidel claimed he had detected in the Scriptures. The arguments of Porphyry, and his spiritual descendants, have been answered scores of times by devoted apologists across the centuries (see "Does the Bible Contradict Itself?" elsewhere in this volume). The fact of the matter is, the Bible reveals remarkable harmony in countless details; indeed, it has a consistency so precise that it could not have been contrived.

It might well be expected that the documents of the Scriptures would show a general unity. Broad and obvious agreements would prove little, for even forgers would be able to effect such concurrence. The Bible, however, is characterized by an infinite variety of minute details that are so obviously uncontrived that they evidence a guiding Force that was absolutely consistent. Such is a subtle, though convincing, evidence of divine inspiration.

In 1790, William Paley, the celebrated Anglican scholar, authored his famous volume *Horae Paulinae* (*Hours With Paul*). In this remarkable book, Paley demonstrated an amazing array of "undesigned coincidences" between the book of Acts and the epistles of Paul, which argue for the credibility of the Christian revelation. Paley stated:

> These coincidences, which are often incorporated or intertwined in references and allusions, in which no art can be discovered, and no contrivance traced, furnish numerous proofs of the truth of both these works, and consequently that of Christianity (1839, xvi).

In 1847, J. J. Blunt of Cambridge University released a companion volume titled, *Undesigned Coincidences in the Writings Both of the Old Testament and New Testament*. Professor Blunt argued that both Testaments contain numerous examples of "consistency without contrivance" which support the Scriptures' claim of a unified origin from a supernatural Source, namely God (1884, vii). The following examples illustrate the type of incidental, harmonious material of which we speak.

As a lad of seventeen years, Joseph was sold by his brothers into Egyptian slavery. Due to a false accusation lodged against him by a rejected woman, that godly young man was cast into prison. Joseph was confined in the place where the king's captives were "bound" (Gen. 39:20). Note that term "bound," for centuries later the Psalmist declared of Joseph, "His feet they hurt with fetters: He was laid in chains of iron" (Psa. 105:18).

When Pharaoh refused to release the Hebrew captives, Jehovah sent a series of plagues upon the Egyptians. One of the plagues was a devastating hail storm which destroyed the blooming flax in the fields (Ex. 9:31). Presently, the Israelites were delivered from Egypt. They journeyed into the wilderness of Sinai, where, on account of their lack of faith, they were forced to wander for four difficult decades. Finally, though, the younger generation entered Canaan. Their arrival in the Promised Land was exactly forty years from the time they left Egypt (Josh. 4:19), and thus shortly after the anniversary of that eighth plague which destroyed the blooming flax. The book of Joshua mentions that their entrance into Canaan was near harvest time (3:15). When agents were sent to spy out Jericho, they were concealed by Rahab under drying stalks of flax upon the rooftop of her house (Josh. 2:6). All of these seemingly insignificant details fit together like a hand in a glove. They are marvelous examples of "undesigned harmony."

The New Testament is no less remarkable for its uncanny unity. For example, when Jesus miraculously fed the five thousand, the inspired Mark records that the Lord seated his auditors upon the "green grass" (6:39), which is entirely in agreement with John's reference to the fact that this event occurred near the time of the Passover (6:4), which is, of course, in the spring—exactly when the grass is green in Palestine.

In the last chapter of Acts, Luke, describing Paul's two year Roman imprisonment, quotes the apostle as proclaiming: "[B]ecause of the hope of Israel I am bound with this chain" (28:20). During this period of incarceration, Paul penned four epistles—Ephesians, Philippians, Colossians, and Philemon. In his letter to the Ephesians, Paul alluded to his "chains" (6:20), in Philippians he refers to his "bonds" (1:7, 13–14, 17); similarly, see the references to his "bonds" in Colossians 4:3 and Philemon 10 and 13.

In his final letter to Timothy, Paul reminds his young companion that "from a babe you have known the sacred writings which are able to make you wise unto salvation through faith which is in Christ Jesus" (2 Tim. 3:15). The reference to the "sacred writings" is, of course, an allusion to the Old Testament Scriptures. Since Timothy had known the Old Testament writings from his earliest days, we would assume that his background was Jewish. Not surprisingly, then, we learn from the book of Acts that Timothy was "the son of a Jewess that believed but his father was a Greek" (16:1). It is worthy of further notice that when Paul commended Timothy for his faith, he alluded to the spirituality of both the lad's mother and grandmother, but no mention was made of the piety of Timothy's father (2 Tim. 1:5).

While it is true that there is an extraordinary unity within the writings of the Old Testament, and within the documents of the New Testament, the same sort of harmony exists between the Old and New Testaments. For instance, when Jesus died, his disciples prepared his body for burial by embalming it. John declares that the Jewish ruler Nicodemus brought spices—about a hundred pounds of myrrh and aloes—for this task (19:39). We thus conclude that it required large quantities of these spices for the embalming process. It is a recognized historical fact that the Egyptians were renowned for their skill in embalming. When Jacob died, the physicians of Egypt embalmed him (Gen. 50:2); likewise Joseph was embalmed when he expired (50:26). One would expect, therefore, that the Egyptians would require vast quantities of spices—like myrrh—for their embalming enterprise. Significantly, we learn from the Old Testament that myrrh was imported by camel caravans into Egypt! (Gen. 37:25).

Again we must stress this point. The Bible critic is likely to trivialize these examples as they are isolated from one another. When, however, literally hundreds and hundreds of these incidental details are observed to perfectly mesh, one begins to suspect that what has been called "undesigned coincidences" (from the human vantage point) become very obvious cases of divinely designed harmony—tiny footprints that lead only to the conclusion that God was the guiding Force behind the composition of the Sacred Scriptures.

The argument that emphasizes the unity of the Bible as an evidence for its inspiration is powerful indeed. Let us employ this form of reasoning as a tool for leading our contemporaries to a confidence in the Scriptures as the Word of God, the source of information pertaining to life everlasting.

Chapter 6

Does the Bible Contradict Itself?

"The belief of a future state of rewards and punishments, the entertaining just ideas of the main attributes of the Supreme Being, and a firm persuasion that He superintends and will finally compensate every action in human life (all which are revealed in the doctrines of our Savior, Christ) these are the grand foundations of all judicial oaths, which call God to witness the truth of those facts which perhaps may be only known to Him and the party attesting."
— Sir William Blackstone (1723–1780)

"I cannot have confidence in the Bible, for it is a book filled with contradictions."

I could not estimate how many times I have heard this charge against the Holy Scriptures over the past several decades. One thing, however, has been consistent about the allegation—the critic rarely can name even one alleged contradiction that the Bible is supposed to contain. He just "knows" that they are "in there" somewhere.

Those who allege that the Bible contains contradictions basically fall into two classes. First, there is the person who honestly believes this to be the case because he has heard the hackneyed charge repeated frequently; thus, he sincerely is misinformed about the facts. Second, there is that type of person who, from base motives, hates the Bible and so does not scruple to pervert its testimony in order to discredit the Sacred Volume. In either case, the Word of God is not at fault!

Preliminary to a consideration of this important theme, it should be noted that the principle of "innocent until proven guilty" applies to the Bible as much as to any other book. Books, like people, ought to be considered truthful and consistent unless it can be demonstrated that they are not. Great attempts have been made to absolve the Greek and Latin classics of contradictions, under the presumption that the authors did not contradict themselves. Surely the Bible deserves at least an equally charitable approach.

WHAT IS A CONTRADICTION?

It is fairly safe to say that most people have only a superficial concept of what constitutes a genuine contradiction. An important truth that must be hammered home repeatedly is this: a mere difference does not a contradiction make!

What, then, constitutes a contradiction? In logic, the Law of Contradiction is stated succinctly as follows: "Nothing can both be and not be" (Jevons 1928, 117). That is a very abbreviated form of the rule. Aristotle, in a more amplified format, expressed it this way: "That the same thing should at the same time both be and not be for the same person and in the same respect is impossible."

An analysis of the Law of Contradiction, therefore, would suggest the following. When one is confronted with an alleged contradiction, he must ask himself these questions: (1) Is the same thing or person under consideration? (2) Is the same time period in view? (3) Is the language that seems to be self-contradictory employed in the same sense? It is quite important that these questions be answered correctly.

For instance, let us analyze the following two statements: Robert is rich. Robert is poor. Do these statements contradict one another? The answer is—not necessarily! First, two different people named Robert could be under consideration. Second, two different time frames might be in view; Robert could have been rich but, due to financial disaster, he became poor. Third, the terms "rich" and "poor" might have been used in different senses; Robert could be spiritually rich but economically poor. The point is this: it never is proper to assume a contradiction exists until every possible means of harmonization has been fully exhausted. Now, let this principle be applied to the Bible.

Same Person or Thing

An infidel once announced that he had discovered a contradiction in the Bible. When challenged to produce it, he suggested that whereas Noah's ark, with all of its inmates, must have weighed many tons (Gen. 6), the Hebrew priests were said to have carried the ark across the Jordan River (Josh. 3). The poor fellow, in his profound simplicity, did not even know the difference between Noah's ark and the Ark of the Covenant! Slightly different "arks"—to say the least!

Again, the Scriptures affirm that faith saves apart from works; on the other hand, the New Testament declares that faith apart form works cannot save. "Surely," some contend, "this is a contradiction." The fact is, it is not, for different types of works are addressed in the Scriptures. Salvation involves works of obedience to the commands of Jesus Christ (Jas. 2:14ff; Phil. 2:12), but pardon cannot be obtained by works of the Mosaic Law (Romans 3:28; 4:2ff) or by boastful works of human merit (Eph. 2:9). There is no contradiction in the Bible on this point.

Same Time Reference

The Bible records: "God saw everything that he had made, and, behold, it was very good" (Gen. 1:31). And then: "And it repented Jehovah that he had made man on earth, and it grieved him at his heart" (6:6). The infidel cites both verses and claims that God simultaneously was satisfied and dissatisfied with his creation—neglecting to mention, of course, that the fall of man and hundreds of years of history separated the two statements!

Judas, one of the Lord's disciples, was empowered to perform miracles (cf. Mt. 10:1–18), yet he is called "the son of perdition" (Jn. 17:12). Is there a contradiction? No, for it was a couple of years after the time of the limited commission (Mt. 10) before Judas commenced to apostatize from the Lord (Jn. 12:6; 13:2, 27). The time element is important in understanding some passages.

Critics have charged the Bible with a mistake in connection with the time of Jesus' trial and death. Mark writes that the Lord was crucified at the third hour (Mk. 15:25), while John's account has the Savior being tried at the sixth hour (Jn. 19:14)—seemingly, therefore, three hours after his death. John's time reference, however, was based upon Roman civil days, while Mark computed according to Jewish time (cf. Westcott 1981, 282). Again, the "contradiction" dissolves.

Same Sense

If the Bible is to be understood, it is imperative that recognition be given to the different senses in which words may be employed. Normally, words are used literally, but they can be used figuratively as well.

In Matthew 11:14, John the Baptizer is identified as "Elijah." Yet, the forerunner of Christ, in John 1:21, plainly denied that he was Elijah. These verses are reconciled quite easily. Though John was not literally Elijah, physically reincarnated, nevertheless he was the spiritual antitype of the great prophet; he prepared the way for the Lord "in the spirit and power of Elijah" (Lk. 1:17).

Did the apostle Paul contradict himself when he affirmed on one occasion that he was "as touching the righteousness which is in the law, found blameless" (Phil. 3:6), and yet, at another time, he acknowledged that he was "chief" of sinners? (1 Tim. 1:15). Again, the answer must be "No." In the former passage, Paul was describing the reputation he enjoyed among his Hebrew contemporaries as a Pharisee, while in the latter verse he expressed the anguish he felt at having been a persecutor of the Christian Way. How sad it is that some are almost totally ignorant of the principles that resolve Bible difficulties.

LOGICAL IMPLICATIONS

One of the implications of the Law of Contradiction is the concept that "nothing can have at the same time and at the same place contradictory and inconsistent qualities" (Jevons 1928, 118). A door may be open or shut, but the same door may not be both open and shut at the same time. Open and shut are opposites, yet they are not contradictory unless they are affirmed of the same object at the same time. Here is the principle: opposites are not necessarily contradictory. Let this principle be applied to certain biblical matters.

Does the Bible contradict itself, as is often suggested, when it asserts that God both loves and hates? No, for though these terms are opposites, when used of God they do not express his disposition toward the same objects. God loves every sinner in the world (Jn. 3:16), but he hates every false way (Psa. 119:104). He loves righteousness, but hates iniquity (Psa. 45:7), and hence responds toward such with either goodness or severity (Rom. 11:22). No contradiction exists here.

Was Paul both "perfect" and "imperfect" at the same time? Some have charged that he so claimed. In Philippians 3:12, the apostle declared that he had not been "already made perfect," while in the fifteenth verse he wrote: "Let us, therefore, as many as are perfect, be thus minded." How is this problem resolved? A careful analysis of the language employed will solve this alleged discrepancy. When Paul claimed that he had not been "made perfect," he used a perfect tense form of the Greek term that literally suggested that the apostle had not arrived at a permanent state of perfection. On the other hand, in the latter verse Paul used an adjective that actually means full-grown or mature (note how the same term is used in contrast to infantilism in 1 Corinthians 14:20 and Ephesians 4:13). And so, while Paul denied that he was already in possession of permanent perfection, he did claim to possess spiritual maturity. There is no conflict between these passages.

Another important point to be emphasized is this: one must not confuse supplementation with contradiction. In a contradiction, two facts are mutually exclusive; in supplementation, two facts merely complement one another. If one says, for example, that John Doe is a husband, and then, of the same John Doe, that he is not a husband—this is contradiction. On the other hand, if one says that John Doe is a father—that is not a contradiction. It merely provides supplementation to statement number one. Many alleged Bible discrepancies can be answered by recognition of this principle.

The case of the healing of the blind men of Jericho presents an interesting study in supplementation (Mt. 20:29–34; Mk. 10:46–52; Lk. 18:35–43). Two prominent problems have been set forth. First, while both Mark and Luke mention the healing of one blind man, Matthew records the healing of two blind men. Second, Matthew and Mark indicate that the blind men were healed as Jesus was leaving Jericho, whereas Luke seems to suggest that a blind man was healed as the Lord "drew nigh" to the city. As a discussion of these passages is begun, let this vital consideration be remembered: if there is any reasonable way of harmonizing these records, no legitimate contradiction can be charged to the accounts!

How, then, shall these narratives be reconciled? Several reasonable possibilities have been posed by scholarly writers.

In the first place, the fact that two of the accounts mention only one man, while the other mentions two, need not concern us. Had Mark and Luke stated that Christ healed only one man, with Matthew affirming that more than one were healed, an error would be apparent. But such is not the case. If one says, "I have a son," he does not contradict himself by stating further, "I have a son and a daughter." The latter statement merely supplements the former. There is no discrepancy, therefore, with reference to the number of men involved.

But how may the second problem be resolved? Several reasonable possibilities have been advanced.

It is possible that three blind men were healed in the vicinity of Jericho on this occasion, and that the incident mentioned by Luke, as occurring when Jesus approached the city, might have represented a different miracle than that recorded by Matthew and Mark. This may not be the most likely explanation, but it cannot be disproved.

Edward Robinson argued that the verb *engizo*, rendered "drew near" (Lk. 18:35) also can mean "to be near." He cited evidence from the Septuagint (1 Kgs. 21:2—"it is near unto my house" [cf. Dt. 21:3; Jer. 23:23; Ruth 2:20; 2 Sam. 19:42]) and from the New Testament (Lk. 19:29; cf. Mt. 21:1; Phil. 2:30). He thus translated Luke 18:35 as "while he was yet nigh unto Jericho" (1855, 200). This view implies that Luke simply locates the miracle near Jericho; hence such can be harmonized with the other records.

Perhaps the most popular viewpoint among reputable writers is the fact that at the time of Christ there actually were two Jerichos. First, there was the Jericho of Old Testament history (Josh. 6:1ff; 1 Kgs. 16:34) that was located at the sight of Elijah's spring. In the first century, however, that city lay almost in ruins. About two miles south of that site was the new Jericho, built by Herod the Great. The Lord—traveling from the north toward Jerusalem—first would pass through the old Jericho, then some two miles to the southwest, would go through Herodian Jericho. The miracles under consideration, therefore, may have been performed between two towns. Accordingly, the references in Matthew and Mark to leaving Jericho would allude to the old city; whereas Luke's observation to drawing near to Jericho would refer to the newer community (see Robertson 1930–33, I.163).

In dealing with so-called contradictions in the Bible, let these principles carefully be remembered:

- No contradiction exists between verses that refer to different persons or things.

- No contradiction exists between passages that involve different time elements.

- No contradiction exists between verses that employ phraseology in different senses.

- Supplementation is not the same as contradiction.

One need show only the possibility of harmonization between two passage that appear to conflict in order to negate the force of an alleged discrepancy.

Finally, this point needs to be made: the differences in various Bible accounts of the same events actually demonstrate the independence of the divine writers and prove that they were not in collusion!

God, although using human writers in the composition of the Bible, is nevertheless its ultimate Author. And since the perfect God cannot be the source of confusion (1 Cor. 14:33) or contradiction (Heb. 6:18), it must be acknowledged that the Bible is perfectly harmonious. This does not mean that men will not struggle with difficult passages. If seeming discrepancies are discovered, let us apply ourselves to a diligent study in an effort to resolve them; but let us never foolishly charge God with allowing his sacred writers to contradict one another.

Chapter 7

When Silence Is Eloquent— An Argument for Inspiration

---

*"A thorough knowledge of the Bible
is worth more than a college education."*
— Theodore Roosevelt (1858–1919)

J. W. McGarvey (1829–1911) was once characterized by *The London Times* as the greatest Bible scholar on either side of the Atlantic. There is no question but that the professor of sacred history in the College of the Bible at Lexington, Kentucky—where he taught for forty-six years—was one of the most skillful defenders of the Scriptures of his day. His books on Christian evidences and other topics are still classics and should be circulated widely.

In the summer of 1893, McGarvey delivered a lecture on the "Inspiration of the Scriptures" before the YMCA at the University of Missouri. His arguments mainly appealed to certain evidences, internal to the New Testament itself, which argue for the Bible's supernatural origin. One of McGarvey's points was this: the very brevity of the New Testament narratives is astounding. For example, in connection with some of the most dramatic episodes of the New Testament, where we would expect the writers to satisfy our longing for loads of details, the sacred narrative contains only abbreviated descriptions.

Consider the episode of Christ's baptism. How many pages might have been consumed in describing this epochal event, had such been left to the literary skill of strictly human authors? God broke a verbal silence of fifteen centuries and audibly acknowledged his beloved Son. And yet, Matthew records the circumstance with but a dozen lines, Mark and Luke utilize about half that space, and John has only a sentence of about twelve words covering the occasion. McGarvey asked: "What man with a writer's instinct could have stopped short of many pages in describing the scene so as to do it justice?" (n.d., 6).

The scholarly professor cited other equally impressive examples of the startling restraint employed by the New Testament writers. It is quite reasonable, he argued, to conclude that God himself was supervising the composition of the documents. The Bible was not designed to satisfy our inquisitiveness. Only such materials as were consistent with the Lord's higher purpose were incorporated into the text.

McGarvey's argument is very compelling. Moreover, we are convinced that it may be pursued even further. A strong case can be made in favor of the Bible's inspiration on the basis of things that it omits altogether. In other words, the silence of the Scriptures—in areas where human curiosity clamors for information—is another internal evidence that reflects the heavenly origin of the biblical documents. Let us consider this matter.

NO ORIGIN FOR GOD

The Bible begins with the simple declarative, "In the beginning God created the heavens and the earth." Neither in Genesis 1, nor elsewhere in Holy Writ, are attempts made to explain the origin of the Creator of the universe. His self-existence is assumed as a primary truth. The prophets speak of his eternal presence without any adorning explanation. From everlasting to everlasting, he is the eternal God (cf. Psa. 90:2; Dt. 33:27).

The religions of ancient paganism postulate bizarre origins for their deities. Egyptian theology

> dwelt on the birth of the gods from Osiris, and told how he, the sun, brought forth the seven great planetary gods, and then the twelve humbler gods of the signs of the zodiac; they, in their turn, producing the twenty-eight gods presiding over the stations of the moon, the seventy-two companions of the sun, and other deities (Geikie n.d., 27).

How significant it is that Moses, who grew up in Egypt, incorporated no such foolishness into the Genesis record. A Babylonian creation epic, *Enuma Elish*, tells how pagan deities, Apsu and Tiamat, "procreated the other gods" (Mitchell 1988, 69). The mythology of India spoke of Brahma, "the father of all creatures," being hatched from a great egg of golden splendor. The Greeks constructed genealogical tables chronicling the history of their gods, etc.; but the Scriptures stand aloof from such absurdities.

NO DESCRIPTION OF GOD

The literature of heathenism is filled with representations of its gods. For instance, Baal, a Canaanite deity, frequently became a factor in the apostasy of the Hebrew people. Baal was a god of fertility. He is depicted on ancient monuments holding a lightning bolt in his hand (suggestive of his control of the weather); at other times his genital organ is prominently displayed because he was the "god of sex." His mother, Asherah, the patron goddess of sex, is depicted in a vulgar fashion in the artwork of ancient Ras Shamra (Boyd 1969, 117–122). El, the husband of Asherah, is portrayed as an old man with white hair and a beard (Smick 1988, 411). Many other pagan gods likewise are graphically and grossly represented.

The God of the Bible, however, is never given any sort of a physical description. While it is true that anthropomorphic (meaning "man form") language is employed frequently in Scripture to denote certain attributes of the Lord (e.g., the "eyes," "hands," etc., of the Lord)—because such figures are necessary to accommodate a human level of comprehension—nevertheless, the divine writers clearly stress that God is a spirit being and, as such, has no physical composition (Jn. 4:24; Lk. 24:39). He is invisible to human sight (1 Tim. 1:17; 6:16). If the Bible is a work of fiction, why is there no description of God?

NO DESCRIPTION OF JESUS CHRIST

When William Manchester wrote his acclaimed biography, *American Caesar—Douglas McArthur,* he referenced descriptions of the illustrious military commander on more than seventy pages (1978, 781). By way of contrast (though Jesus Christ is the central character of the Scripture, and is found either directly or indirectly in every book of the Bible), there is not one line in the New Testament giving a depiction of his physical attributes. In fact, the only remote reference to Jesus' appearance is a vague allusion in the book of Isaiah, where the Savior is represented as having "no comeliness" that his fellows would consider desirable (Isa. 53:2). Imagine that. No description is given of the most prominent person of the Bible, the founder of the Christian religion—only a passing prophetic remark that suggests he was less-than-handsome! What group of writers, desiring to ensure the success of Christianity, would have adopted such an approach?

THE SILENT YEARS

With the exception of the miraculous events connected with the birth of Jesus, we know little of the first thirty years of his life upon this earth. When he was eight days old, he was circumcised according to Jewish law (Lk. 2:21). Thirty-three days later he was presented in the temple (Lk. 2:22–39). There is the account of the visit of those wise-men from the east (Mt. 2:1–12), and then the flight into Egypt to escape the wrath of Herod (Mt. 2:13–23). There is a general reference to his settlement finally at Nazareth (Mt. 2:23; Luke 2:39–40), and then the record of a visit to Jerusalem when Jesus was twelve years old (Lk. 2:41–50). Following this, there is a blank space in the narrative that covers eighteen years in the life of Christ. Other than the generic notation that he was advancing in wisdom, stature, and in favor with God and men (Lk. 2:51–52), we know absolutely nothing of this time-span. Are we not curious? Would not an average human biographer have given some interesting data? That is a normal expectation.

It was this very circumstance that called forth a number of ancient spurious writings, known collectively as the Apocryphal Gospels. These extra-canonical documents arose because of the desire to have a fuller knowledge of certain periods of the life of Christ that the genuine Gospels omitted. Consider, for instance, the childhood Gospel of Thomas. It depicts the boy Jesus making little birds out of clay and causing them to fly away. Again, when another boy accidentally bumped into him, Jesus supposedly caused him to die immediately (see Findlay 1906, 671–685). No such absurdities deface the New Testament.

MISCELLANEOUS OMISSIONS

In addition to the foregoing cases, there are scores of biblical contexts within which there are strange absences of information (i.e., strange from a purely human viewpoint).

Moses

Moses is the most prominent character of the Old Testament. He is mentioned more than seven hundred fifty times in the Hebrew Scriptures, and approximately eighty times in the New Testament. At a very early age he was adopted by Pharaoh's daughter (a brilliant strategy by his mother to save her son's life). He was thus reared as an Egyptian prince. The first forty years of his life were spent in the environment of Egypt's splendor and power. Between Exodus 2:10 and 2:11, however, there is a silent gap of four decades. Only the book of Acts briefly says: "And Moses was instructed in all the wisdom of the Egyptians; and he was mighty in his words and works" (7:22). What were those words and works? What exciting events occurred during that first third of Moses' life? We long to know, but the Holy Spirit did not see fit to supply the information.

The Ark of the Covenant

The most revered item of furniture in Israel's sacred tabernacle was the Ark of the Covenant, that small wooden chest, overlaid with gold, which contained the tables of the Ten Commandments, a pot of manna, and Aaron's rod that had budded miraculously. What happened to the Ark? Sometime after the chest was placed in Solomon's temple (1 Kgs. 8:1–11), it simply vanished. Movies and television specials have speculated regarding its fate, but no one knows what happened to it. Surely a non-inspired literary genius would not have left the Ark's destiny shrouded in obscurity. Indeed, the apocryphal book of 2 Maccabees has Jeremiah hiding it in a cave until the time when God would restore his people (2:4–8). Men cannot resist the temptation to speak where God has been silent.

Joseph

Joseph of Nazareth was the foster father of Jesus, and Mary was his mother. The benevolent character of Joseph is tenderly revealed in Matthew 1. He was willing to endure the scorn of his peers by taking his pregnant betrothed into his home. What happened to him? He simply disappears from the New Testament record following that journey to Jerusalem when Jesus was twelve years old (Lk. 2:41ff; cf. Mt. 12:46).

Mary

And what of Mary? Surely she was one of the noblest women God ever made. Apparently she was in the care of the apostle John following the death of her son (Jn. 19:26–27). We find her in the company of the disciples following Jesus' ascension (Acts 1:14). But how did she eventually die? There is not a clue. What human biographer would have left these matters dangling?

Apostles

Is it not most unusual that there are no descriptions of the Lord's apostles in the New Testament, and, except for a few scant references (see Lk. 4:38; 1 Cor. 9:5), there is no information regarding their families.

Furthermore, where, after the establishment of Christianity, is there any mention of the evangelistic work of Andrew, Simon the Zealot, Thomas, etc.? The labors of most of the apostles are missing from the record. Who in the world, following common literary impulses, is going to pass over things of this nature? Finally, with the sole exception of James (see Acts 12:1ff), there is not a word as to how the apostles died.

John

The mission of John the Baptizer was to prepare the Jews for Christ. Accordingly, John immersed those who repented of, and confessed, their sins (Mt. 3:6–8). His baptism was "for the remission of sins" (Mk. 1:4), and those who rejected it were repudiating the very counsel of God himself (Lk. 7:30).

Unquestionably the Lord's apostles submitted to John's baptism, but where is the record of such? One can only infer it.

The Saints

When Jesus died, following his six hours of agony on the cross, the veil of the temple was torn in two from top to bottom, there was a tremendous earthquake, and, perhaps most shocking of all, the tombs in Jerusalem were opened, "and many bodies of the saints that had fallen asleep were raised; and coming forth out of the tombs after his resurrection they entered into the holy city and appeared unto many" (Mt. 27:52–53). Did these ex-corpses speak to folks on the street? What was the effect of this miracle upon the citizens of the city? What ultimately happened to those saints? Are we to be left hanging? Additionally, what was the impact of that severing of the temple's veil? There is not a word concerning the panic that must have seized the Jewish leaders.

Paul

The book of Acts is one of the great adventure narratives of the New Testament. It tells of the establishment and growth of Christianity. A major component of that expansion was the ministry of the brilliant zealot, Saul of Tarsus (later to become known as Paul, the apostle). Paul's conversion and his fruitful missionary campaigns are thrillingly detailed from Acts 9 onward. Towards the end of Acts, Paul is arrested as a result of Jewish harassment. Ultimately, he appeals his case to Caesar (the Supreme Court, if you will), and is taken to Rome. As the book of Acts concludes, Paul has been under house-arrest, daily chained to a Roman soldier, for two years. But Acts ends quite abruptly. When did Paul appear before Caesar (Acts 27:24)? What did he say? What effect was produced?

Luke

There is a considerable amount of extra-biblical evidence indicating that the author of the third Gospel was Luke, the physician (Col. 4:14). This view was "universally believed" by the middle of the second century. No one "speaks doubtfully on this point" (Plummer 1896, xvi). Moreover, both external and internal evidence suggests that the author of the third Gospel also penned the book of Acts. The Muratorian Canon (a fragmentary list of New Testament books from the late second century A.D.) states that Luke compiled "the Acts of all the Apostles" for "most excellent Theophilus" (see Acts 1:1; cf. Lk. 1:3). Luke was an associate of Paul on several of the apostle's missionary journeys, and during the dramatic voyage to Rome. This circumstance is reflected in the "we" segments of the book of Acts (16:10–17; 20:5–21:18; 27:1–28:16).

The character of Luke's writings reveals that he was a brilliant scholar and a devoted companion to Paul—to the very end of the great apostle's life (see 2 Tim. 4:11). And yet, as valuable as his contributions were, the New Testament student knows absolutely nothing of his background (e.g., where he was born, his educational training, his family associations, his conversion, etc.). Nor is anything known of his death. He is the only Gentile writer of the Bible (his literary contributions comprising about twenty-five percent of the New Testament), yet he is ever discreetly in the background. He is named in only three places in the entire New Testament (Col. 4:14; Philem. 24; 2 Tim. 4:11). Given the propensity of ordinary journalists, would any writer—who played such a prominent role in the affairs he chronicled—have so veiled himself? Surely, to the analytical person, this must suggest the superintendence of the divine Spirit of God.

What shall we make of these—and many other—puzzling omissions from the sacred text? Simply this: the Holy Spirit was the guiding hand behind the composition of the Bible. He incorporated into the sacred volume only such materials as were germane to the divine purpose. He did not cater to human curiosity. Thus, Bible inspiration is demonstrated as much by its exclusions as by its inclusions. The wide variety of evidence documenting the authenticity of the Holy Scriptures is truly profound.

Chapter 8

The Twelve Apostles—
an Argument for Inspiration

*"I speak as a man of the world to men of the world;
and I say to you, Search the Scriptures!"*
— John Quincy Adams (1767–1848)

There are two major areas in which one can argue for the divine inspiration of the Bible. One can appeal to the text of the sacred record itself, i.e., the information it contains. For example, one might argue for the heavenly origin of the data on the basis of such things as predictive prophecy, the amazing unity of the narratives as composed over a period of sixteen centuries, the uncanny accuracy of the text in a variety of areas, etc.

On the other hand, a formidable case may be argued for the Scriptures' sacred commencement on the bases of what the record does not contain, but should have, and almost certainly would have, if composed by writers who were guided strictly by human impulses.

For instance, in the chapter titled "When Silence Is Eloquent," we have observed that there is no description of the visual features of either God the Father or Jesus Christ. This is most curious, if not by divine design, for the writings of paganism are filled with the descriptions of false gods (cf. Baal in the Syrian monuments).

As noted earlier, when William Manchester wrote his acclaimed biography, *American Caesar—Douglas McArthur,* he referenced physical descriptions of the illustrious military commander on more than seventy pages. Yet in all the New Testament there is not a solitary sentence depicting the appearance of Jesus Christ. This is not coincidental!

THE APOSTLES

Aside from the Lord Jesus himself, there is no body of human characters in the history of Christianity more significant than the Lord's apostles—fourteen in total number, including Matthias (who replaced Judas) and Paul. This chapter will focus only on the original Twelve. Catalogs of the Twelve are found in four New Testament contexts (Mt. 10:2–4; Mk. 3:16–19; Lk. 6:13–16; Acts 1:13 [minus Judas Iscariot]).

These men accomplished the phenomenal task of planting the gospel throughout the antique world in less than half a century from the dawn of the Christian era (cf. Acts 17:6b; Rom. 10:18; Col. 1:6, 23). And yet, amazingly, there is such a minute body of information in the Gospel records concerning these men that the silence is deafening! Moreover, a good portion of the information highlights their flaws, rather than their virtue. The focus predominately is upon the apostles' mistakes, as they stumble along their way as students of the Master Teacher. The perceptive reader cannot but conclude that these circumstances do not conform to normal historical literary patterns.

The truth is, this circumstance constitutes a terrific argument for the view that the four Gospel accounts were not crafted by men under the passions of ordinary writers. Surely common historical interest begs for more information about these exceptional gospel pioneers. The restraint, we contend, can be explained reasonably in only one way—the supernatural guidance of the Spirit of God.

The original apostolic body of twelve were: Peter, Andrew, James, John, Philip, Bartholomew, Thomas, Matthew, James the son of Alphaeus, Thaddaeus [known also as Judas], Simon, and Judas Iscariot. Let us consider each of these.

Peter

Though Peter is the most prominent of the apostles in the ministry of Jesus, consider how frequently his weaknesses come to the forefront.

He is portrayed as one inclined to boast. He contended that he had left all to follow Christ and wanted to know what he would obtain for the bargain (Mt. 19:27). The fact that he claimed to speak for all the apostles may well have been presumptive.

His vulnerability was highlighted by the fact that he was one in need of special prayer by the Savior. In Luke 22:31 note the contrast between the plural "you," embracing all the apostles, and the singular "thee," focusing upon Peter in particular. Peter declared that while the other apostles might be offended in the Lord, he certainly would not be (Mk. 14:29–31).

His tendency to speak more than he had the faith to accomplish is demonstrated by the incident when he requested permission to walk on the tempestuous waves of the Sea of Galilee, yet began to sink when his faith failed; this called forth a rebuke from the Lord (Mt. 14:28–31).

His carnality and misguided zeal was revealed when he sought to defend Christ with the sword, severing a man's ear from his head, for which he was rebuked sternly for his impetuous effort (Mt. 26:52).

Peter shamefully denied that he knew Jesus when confronted by a maid in the temple courtyard, then again when accosted subsequently by Jewish authorities (Mt. 26:69ff;

Mk. 14:66ff; Lk. 22:55ff; Jn. 18:15ff). Some twenty-seven verses are consumed with "denial" narratives regarding the apostle. This was a significant breach of faith and courage.

Finally, there was the event in Antioch of Syria when Peter refused to eat with Gentiles, even though he had been shown by a miracle that he was not to regard non-Jews as unclean (Acts 10). In this act he stood condemned. His hypocritical influence affected even the generous Barnabas (Gal. 2:11ff; cf. Acts 4:36–37).

There is considerable exposure in the Gospel records of the weaknesses of the illustrious apostle—certainly unexpected from an ordinary journalistic vantage point. Especially is the case with reference to Mark's Gospel, since history indicates that Mark penned his narrative under the influence of Peter, as a number of early writers suggested (e.g., Papias, Clement of Alexandria, Tertullian, Origen, Eusebius, etc.).

Andrew

Andrew was the brother of Peter. The biblical information regarding him is meager indeed. He was instrumental in bringing Peter to the Lord—perhaps the most far-reaching effort for Christ of his life (Jn. 1:41–42). On the other hand, the New Testament text is also bluntly honest regarding him.

For example, although he was aware of Jesus' ability to perform miracles (cf. Jn. 2:1–11; 4:46–54; 5:1–9), nonetheless when the Lord encountered a hungry multitude of five thousand males (see the masculine "men," Jn. 6:10), and most likely an equal number of females, it was Andrew who said: "There is a lad here, who has five barley loaves, and two fishes: but what are these among so many?" He was slow to fathom his Lord's supernatural ability.

During the final week before Christ's death, certain Gentiles came seeking to see Jesus (Jn. 12:22). They first approached Philip, who then informed Andrew. Both Andrew and Philip reported the incident to the Lord. In the great plan of God, however, the offering of the gospel to the Gentiles must wait until after the Savior's death and the later establishment of the church (Acts 10ff). But neither Philip nor Andrew understood the heavenly schedule at this point.

Finally, Andrew was in the company of Peter, James, and John (the "inner circle" of Jesus' disciples), when several questions were asked of him as he sat on the side of the Mount of Olives (Mk. 13:3). They wished to know when the destruction of the temple would take place. They apparently felt that this would signal the "end of the world" as well. Their understanding of coming events was quite incomplete at this point, and the New Testament writers do not hesitate to reveal this fact.

James

The information regarding James, John's brother, is stunningly brief. He, along with his brother, John, were surnamed Boanerges, i.e., "Sons of thunder" (Mk. 3:17). The rash temperament suggested by the nickname certainly was displayed as these two brothers virtually exploded with anger when certain Samaritans refused lodging to the Lord and his disciples in Samaritan territory.

James and John asked Jesus if they should call down fire from heaven to consume these rebels (Lk. 9:54); and they received the Master's rebuke for their heated and unloving reaction. Little did they realize that the Samaritans would be some of the most eager recipients of the gospel (cf. Jn. 4:27–42; Acts 8:5–13).

Seized with a degree of ambition, the brothers sought places of distinction in the coming kingdom, most likely using their mother, who may have been a sister to Mary, to apply the pressure on the Lord (Mk. 10:35–37; cf. Mt. 20:20–21).

Finally, there is the scant mention of James' death. Only seven words in the Greek Testament are chosen by the Spirit of God to describe the death of the first martyr of the apostolic band! "And he [Herod] killed James the brother of John with the sword" (Acts 12:2). This literary restraint speaks loudly to him who has ears to hear!

John

The information regarding John is only slightly expanded from that of his brother. See the data mentioned above where the brothers acted jointly.

On one occasion John complained about a man who was casting out demons, but who had not been personally associated with the apostolic company. John informed the Lord that he and others "forbade" the man to continue in his benevolent teaching endeavor. The apostle had not concluded that the man could not have cast out demons except by Christ's authority. The Lord rebuked his disciple saying: "Forbid him not: for there is no man who shall do a mighty work in my name, and be able quickly to speak evil of me" (Mk. 9:38–39). John reflected a snobbish attitude unbecoming an apostle.

John, together with Peter, was sent to make ready the Passover supper which Christ would celebrate with the disciples (Lk. 22:8). Additionally, the apostle was charged with the care of Mary after the death of the Lord (Jn. 19:26–27).

When John and Peter arrived at the empty garden tomb on Sunday morning, and observed the grave clothes, John was the first to logically conclude the obvious, namely that Jesus had been resurrected from the dead (Jn. 20:8). His new "belief" on this occasion indicates that he had not believed (to some degree) thus far.

Philip

The sketch of Philip's activity is similar to Andrew's in some particulars. For example, Andrew brought Peter to Jesus, and

Philip sought out Nathanael and told him: "We have found him, of whom Moses in the law, and the prophets, wrote, Jesus of Nazareth, the son of Joseph" (Jn. 1:45). Nathanael resisted at first, because of the tarnished reputation of Nazareth, but Philip persisted: "Come and see."

Philip also was shortsighted regarding Christ's power to deal with the feeding of the vast multitude that followed him. Just as Andrew felt a little boy's lunch could not accommodate this throng (see above), even so Philip declared that not even two hundred denarii (the wages for about two hundred days' labor—cf. Mt. 20:2) would be sufficient to feed this throng (Jn. 6:5–7). The power of the Lord had not been factored into the equation.

Philip was the one who informed Andrew about the Greeks who wanted an interview with the Savior during the final days before the crucifixion. Both of them reported the Gentiles' request to the Lord, who tactfully pointed out that this was not consistent with the divine program.

Finally, in the concluding instructions that Jesus gave to the disciples prior to leaving the Passover supper, he had declared that he was the way, the truth, and the life: and no one would come to the Father except by him. A recognition of his own majesty and power should have been sufficient for the disciples, but their spiritual vision was obscured still.

Hence, Philip said: "Lord, show us the Father, and that will be sufficient"—suggesting, perhaps unintentionally, that the Lord himself was insufficient. With a tender rebuke, the Teacher replied: "Have I been with you [plural, the apostles] so long a time, and do you [singular, Philip] not know me, Philip?" (Jn. 14:8–9). The Lord then affirmed his deity; he, as a divine being, was a commentary on the Father (cf. Jn. 1:18b; especially "declared," the Greek word being the basis of our modern term "exegesis").

Bartholomew

There is nothing in the Gospel records regarding Bartholomew, except for the listing of this name in the apostolic catalogs. However, from about the ninth century onward it has been speculated that Bartholomew may be identified with Nathanael.

Nathanael is never mentioned in Matthew, Mark, and Luke; and Bartholomew is not referenced in John. Both Bartholomew and Nathanael are linked with Philip (though not in Acts 1:13), so it has been concluded that perhaps Bartholomew and Nathanael are the same person. The theory is intriguing, but the inferential conclusion is not provable. But why is there such a radical abbreviation of the sacred record regarding this apostle?

Thomas

There are three things noteworthy regarding Thomas. First, when Jesus declared his intention to go to Bethany where Lazarus had just died, the disciples knew it would be a dangerous journey (Jn. 11:8). They thus protested the trip, even though the Lord declared that the purpose of his mission was to "awake" Lazarus out of his "sleep," i.e., raise him from the dead (v. 11). Thomas proposes to the other disciples that they accompany the Teacher to his bloody destiny.

Two things may be said concerning his suggestion. First, it is one of courage; he is willing to die with the Lord if necessary. Second, however, this disciple obviously has little faith in Christ's declaration that he would raise Lazarus from his "sleep," which he clearly had identified as death (v. 14). He does not yet fathom the mystery of the power of the Son of God.

Then there was Thomas' complaint and question, as the Lord attempted to instruct and comfort the disciples before they left the upper room on the night of Christ's betrayal. The Savior knew their hearts were troubled about his sayings of leaving them (Jn. 14:1). Consequently, he promised that though he was going away, it was to prepare for them a place in his "Father's house."

He assured them that they "knew the way" to that reward. Thomas contradicted the Master, claiming, "[W]e do not know the way where you are going. How do we know it?" (v. 5). In essence Jesus responded, "I am the way. Everything I have taught you, all that you have seen in me—my supernatural power, the oral teaching, my perfect example, the chorus of divinely demonstrable truth—all this has been designed to show you the way!" Thomas was still straining to see through a fog of spiritual dullness.

On Sunday evening of the resurrection day, the Lord appeared to the disciples, but for some reason Thomas was not among the group (Jn. 20:19–24). Later, however, the others reported to Thomas that they had seen the resurrected Lord. At that point the "empirical" apostle declared that he would not believe in the resurrection: "Except I shall see in his hands the print of the nails, and put my finger into the print of the nails, and put my hand into his side, I will not believe" (Jn. 20:25).

Eight days later Jesus again appeared to the band of disciples; this time Thomas was there. The Lord passed right through the closed doors. After a brief greeting, he addressed Thomas directly, urging him to take the "print" test and chastised him for his faithlessness (thus revealing he knew of the previous week's conversation). The formerly skeptical apostle exclaimed, "My Lord and my God" (20:28). The testimony of "scientific Thomas" rings true across twenty centuries of history.

Matthew

Matthew is one of the celebrated apostles of Jesus, principally due to the document he penned under the guidance of the

Spirit of God, which has provided us with such rich information relating to the life of Christ. One would think that the sacred record would abound with information concerning this great man. We are thus shocked to learn that there are but two things the New Testament student knows about Matthew.

First, we know Matthew's occupation. He was a tax-collector, and when Jesus met him and invited him to discipleship he left his tax station and followed the Lord (Mt. 9:9; cf. Lk. 5:27–28). One must conclude that he was devoted to Christ; he was willing to sacrifice "all" on behalf of his Teacher (Lk. 5:28).

Of course there is considerable information that one can gather by studying the background of Palestinian tax officers, but that information is not collected from the data about the apostle himself. One thing we do know, as a tax collector—hence in the employment of the Roman government—he was a man despised by loyal Hebrews.

How very strange, then, that he should be selected to write a Gospel record, the design of which would be to convince Jews that Jesus of Nazareth was their promised Messiah! The credibility of the facts about Christ would override any negativity associated with the author. What powerful testimony this is to the integrity of the Gospel message!

Second, from Luke's narrative we find this passage. "And Levi made him [Jesus] a great feast in his house: and there was a great multitude of publicans and of others that were sitting at meat with them" (Lk. 5:29). It is clear that Matthew (Levi) was evangelistic. He put the Lord in contact with those among his associates who were hungry for the truth.

James the Son of Alphaeus

Nothing is known for certain about James the son of Alphaeus. There is no information about his call to follow the Lord, nothing of his occupation, his contributions to the cause of

Christ, etc. There is one spark of possibility. Since Matthew's father was named Alphaeus (Mk. 2:14), it is possible (though not provable) that Matthew and James were brothers. He remains in the biblical record a mystery to us—though not to God of course!

Thaddaeus

Thaddaeus is another of the apostles who remains in almost total obscurity. Matthew notes that his name also was Lebbaeus (10:3), and in Luke's writings he is characterized as "Judas the son of James" (Lk. 6:16; Acts 1:13), though he is carefully distinguished from "Judas" the traitor (Jn. 14:22).

The only situation concerning Thaddaeus, apart from the mere mention of his name, has to do with a question that he asked during that upper room meeting in connection with the last supper. Jesus had spoken of the fact that he would manifest himself to those who loved him and kept his com mandmcnts. This puzzled Thaddaeus, and he posed a question to the Savior: "Lord, how is it that you will manifest yourself to us, and not to the world?" (Jn. 14:22 ESV).

Clearly this apostle, together with the others (cf. Acts 1:6), still had a misconception of the nature of Christ's coming kingdom. They envisioned it as an earthly regime, reminiscent of the glorious days of David's reign. The idea was common among the Jews (cf. Jn. 6:15), and the disciples shared that view. Thaddaeus appears frustrated that Christ might not manifest himself openly as a reigning king.

It is noteworthy that Jesus did not answer the question directly. Rather, he simply encouraged Thaddaeus and the others to love him, and keep his word. In that event, both he and the Father would make their abode with them (14:23). With these words, Thaddaeus fades into the shadows of the Gospel records permanently.

Simon Zelotes

This Simon is another of the apostles of whose background information is virtually nil. Nothing is known of his parents, siblings, achievements, etc. Twice he is designated as Simon Zelotes (Lk. 6:15; Acts 1:13). In Matthew and Mark he is referred to as Simon Cananaean (not "Cananite" KJV), which term is an equivalent of Zealot—the former being Aramaic, the latter Greek. The word suggested a "devoted supporter."

The Zealots were a radical Jewish sect dedicated to the opposition of Roman rule of Palestine. They were in the forefront of the Jewish rebellion in A.D. 66, which resulted in the fall of Judaism by the Roman invasion four years later. These fanatics were violent and willing to fight their opposition to the death in the hope of Jewish independence.

It is an utterly amazing thing that Jesus brought together Matthew, the tax-collector, and Simon, the Zealot—two men who by disposition would be wholly antagonistic to one another. Only Christ would have done that; only he **could** have done it!

Judas Iscariot

Surely there was something good in Judas initially; otherwise, the Lord never would have chosen him and endowed him with supernatural ability (Mt. 10:5–8). Thus the common Calvinistic assertion that Judas was never saved is utterly void of merit. Whatever that good was, however, the New Testament does not reveal. There are four things—all negative—which must be noted regarding Judas (who incidentally, is always mentioned last in the apostolic catalogs).

First, he was a covetous man. When Mary, the sister of Lazarus, anointed Jesus' feet with precious ointment, Judas bitterly complained about it. After all, the ointment was worth the equivalent of almost a year's wages (cf. Jn. 12:3–5; Mt. 20:2). "What a waste!" he thought. His whining rationalization revealed two things: his disregard for the nature of Christ and his own covetous heart.

This money, he surmised, if not spent for precious ointment, might well have been deposited in the apostles' treasury, of which he was the caretaker (Jn. 13:29). And from that moneybag he was pilfering funds! His stingy heart manifested itself in sticky fingers; he was a thief! (Jn. 12:6). Exactly where, when, and how he began to go wrong, it is impossible to determine.

From base motives (far beyond the love of money) that fomented in his soul, he plotted and implemented the betrayal of his Master. He yielded to the influence of Satan (Jn. 13:2, 27), and identified Christ to the temple police (Jn. 18:2ff).

The betrayal of the Lord Jesus is recorded by each of the Gospel writers (Mt. 26:47–56; Mk. 14:43–52; Lk. 22:47–53; Jn. 18:1–11). It was the darkest transgression of human history.

One of the defining tragedies of redemptive history is the fact that Judas Iscariot could have genuinely repented of his sin, and received forgiveness had he desired such; but apparently he was too far gone to turn back. He punctuated his rebellion by a terminal exclamation point; he hanged himself, from which event he went to his "own place" (Mt. 27:3–5; Acts 1:25). [Note: The term "repented," mentioned in Matthew 27:3, was not a sorrow that produces a change of life; it was mere regret—void of any beneficent fruit.]

CONCLUSION

To a perceptive person, it will be obvious that the information contained within the four Gospel accounts has been carefully monitored. Only that which is absolutely relevant to the message of the cross has been included—whether such conforms to human wisdom or not.

After the death of Christ, and the establishment of the church on the day of Pentecost, only three of the Twelve are ever mentioned again—Peter, James, and John—and, as noted earlier, James is referenced only in the briefest fashion. This constitutes a strange circumstance in the annals of biographical history. Yet strange only in the view of those who are unacquainted with the purposeful restraint of inspiration.

The Scriptures are so rich that one could study them for a lifetime and still not mine the treasures that subtly lie beneath the surface. Bible investigation becomes richer and richer the longer one lives and studies.

Chapter 9

The Amazing Accuracy of the Bible— An Argument for Divine Inspiration

"A scientific theology is pointing out the footprints of the Creator to common sense. The brotherhood of man, the Fatherhood of God, is becoming the corner-stone of religion, as revealed in Christ, and as clearly traced in human history."
— James G. Blaine (1830–1893), U.S. Secretary of State

Horace (65–8 B.C.), a Latin lyric poet, wrote: "Sometimes even the noble Homer nods" (*Ars Poetica* I.359). Homer was the blind Greek poet of the eighth century B.C., so well-known for his works, the *Iliad* and the *Odyssey*. What Horace suggested was this: as accomplished as Homer was, he sometimes erred with reference to the facts of the incidents he mentioned.

More than a quarter of a century ago, the late B. C. Goodpasture, respected editor of the *Gospel Advocate* for some thirty-eight years, published an article in that journal titled, "Homer Sometimes Nods" (1970). The thrust of this fascinating essay was to show that human authors, regardless of their genius and skill, are fallible. Thus, in spite of their consummate care, they will "nod," or slip, on occasion.

By way of contrast, the writers of the biblical record never nodded. Even though many of them were not professional scholars (cf. Acts 4:13), nonetheless they wrote with astounding precision. The only reasonable conclusion the honest student may draw is this: their work was directed by the Spirit of God.

A poet once quipped: "To err is human." How very true. Humans do err; God does not. And that is why the careful student can clearly discern the difference between a document that is a mere human composition and one which was penned under the guidance of the infallible Creator of the universe.

LITERARY FLAWS—ANCIENT AND MODERN

Herodotus was a Greek historian of the fifth century B.C. Cicero called him "the father of history." He wrote nine books dealing with the Greek and Persian wars, together with a history of the customs and geography of those empires. In one of his writings, Herodotus claimed that oxen in Sythia grew no horns because it was too cold there (*The Histories* 4.29). He apparently had never heard of reindeer!

Aristotle, the famous Greek scholar of the fourth century B.C., was renowned for his knowledge. Yet he made some colossal speculative blunders. In his work titled *Parts of Animals*, he argued that within the human body man's soul is "lodged in some substance of a fiery character." He contended that the brain "is a compound of earth and water." He further suggested that sleep is caused by the blood flowing into the brain, thus making it heavy. This, he declared, "is the reason why drowsy persons hang the head" (Book II, Chapter 3).

Marcus Porcius Cato was a Roman statesman who died about the mid-second century B.C. His famous work *De Agri Cultura* (On Farming) has survived. In one passage (71) he gave a remedy for treating an ailing ox. It consisted of forcing down the ox a whole, raw hen's egg, followed the next day by a concoction of leek and wine. However, this treatment, in order to be efficacious, absolutely must be administered from a wooden vessel while both the ox and the administrator are standing (cited by Sarton 1959, 408).

It is obvious that the method of administration would have nothing to do with the curative value of Cato's concoction. But, such is the nature of human superstition.

Flavius Josephus was a Jewish writer who authored several works regarding the Hebrew nation—its fortunes and fates. Though he is considered a respectable historian for his day, he frequently slipped. For instance he declared that during the siege of Jerusalem (A.D. 70), a heifer, being led to sacrifice in the temple, gave birth to a lamb (*Wars of the Jews* 6.3).

Samuel Johnson was the author of the first bona fide English dictionary. He also produced *A Grammar of the English Tongue*. In that work the celebrated writer stated that the letter "H seldom, perhaps never, begins any but the first syllable" of a word. Regrettably, he had not noticed that "h" commences the second syllable in "perhaps." His humiliation must have been keen.

The famous poet, Lord Byron, wrote a magnificent composition he titled *The Destruction of Sennacherih*. In beautiful rhymc this literary masterpiece dramatically told of the devastating deaths of the 185,000 Assyrian soldiers who threatened Jerusalem in the days of Hezekiah, king of Judah. The poet slipped, though, because the rebel monarch Sennacherib was not destroyed when Jehovah's messenger smote that vast heathen camp. The king was several miles away at Lachish when the destruction occurred. He eventually returned to his home in the east and was slain by his own sons—in fulfillment, incidentally, of sacred prophecy (2 Kgs. 19:7, 36–37).

Adam Clarke was probably the most famous scholar produced by the Methodist Church. He spent forty years writing his famous *Commentary on the Bible*. As meticulous as he was, Clarke occasionally erred. For example, in commenting on Genesis 1:16, he suggested that the moon has streams and vegetation, and is inhabited by intelligent beings. Our modern space explorations have proved that speculation to be quite erroneous. Clarke also stated that Jewish historian Josephus never mentioned the Syrian soldier, Naaman. He was wrong, though, because Josephus asserted that the warrior who mortally wounded Ahab, by shooting an arrow randomly into the air, was Naaman (*Antiquities of the Jews* 8.15.5).

Alexander Cruden produced a very widely used concordance of the English Bible, a task for which he was well qualified by virtue of many years of Scripture study (even though, at times, he suffered from emotional illness). Yet, in his volume, *Explanations of Scripture Terms*, concerning the whale, Cruden wrote: "The [whale is the] greatest of the fishes that we know of" (1840, 366). He erred. Actually, the whale is a mammal, and not a fish at all.

The religion of Islam claims that the Qur'an is inspired of God. Clearly, however, it is not, for it is flawed by many examples of nodding. For instance, the Qur'an suggests that the human fetus results from "sperm" (no mention of an egg) that changes into "a clot of congealed blood," which then becomes bones, later to be covered with flesh (Sura 23:14). This is hardly an accurate description of fetal development.

The Book of Mormon is revered by millions of "Latter-Day Saints." It purports to be an infallible revelation from God given to Joseph Smith Jr. by an angel of the Lord. Whoever composed the narrative, however, nodded more than once (one is tempted to say he lapsed into a coma). For instance in Alma 7:10 it is said that Jesus Christ was born in Jerusalem. But, as every school child knows, the Lord was born in that "little town of Bethlehem" (Mic. 5:2; Mt. 2:1).

The Spirit of God makes no such blunders. Again, according to The Book of Mormon, a man by the name of Nephi was using a "compass" to find his direction in the sixth century B.C.

(1 Nephi 16:10; 2 Nephi 5:12). It is well known, of course, that the mariner's compass was not in use until at least a thousand years after the birth of Christ. This is a critical anachronism in Mormonism's "sacred" book.

Joseph Smith Jr. also taught that there are people living on the moon. According to Smith, they were six feet tall, dressed like Quakers, and had a lifespan of one thousand years (Huntington 1892, 263). Brigham Young, Smith's successor, when asked about this matter, concurred, suggesting that such beings lived on the sun as well (Young 1854–75, 271).

Mary Baker Eddy founded the "Christian Science" movement. She produced a book, *Science and Health with Key to the Scriptures*, which she claimed was co-authored by God. But Mrs. Eddy more than nodded when, in that volume, she wrote:

> Man is not matter, made up of brains, blood, bones, and other material elements . . . . Man is spiritual and perfect; and because of this, he must be so understood in Christian Science . . . . Man is incapable of sin, sickness, and death (1934, 475).

In spite of her denial of human mortality, she died December 3, 1910.

BIBLICAL ACCURACY

By way of glaring contrast, the holy writers of the biblical records never nodded. Their works are characterized by a razor-sharp accuracy that defies explanation save on the ground they were controlled by the Spirit of God. Consider the following factors.

The first two chapters of the Bible contain the divine record of the commencement of the universe, including the earth and its inhabitants. Though it was penned thirty-five centuries ago, there is not a syllable in this account that is at variance with any demonstrable fact of science. Any book on astronomy or earth science penned fifty years ago is already obsolete. And yet Genesis, simple and sublime, is factually flawless.

The Mosaic narrative asserts that the universe had a "beginning" (1:1), which is perfectly consistent with the Second Law of Thermodynamics. Contrast this with the Babylonian creation record known as *Enuma Elish*, which asserts the eternality of matter (Pfeiffer 1966, 226).

The Genesis record affirms that creation activity was concluded by the end of the sixth day (2:1–3). Science says, as per the First Law of Thermodynamics, that nothing is being created today.

No less than ten times Genesis 1 affirms that biological organisms replicate "after [their] kind." In passing we must note that modern pseudo-science (i.e., the theory of evolution) is dependent upon the notion that in the past organisms have reproduced after their non-kind! The biblical account, however, is in perfect harmony with the known laws of genetics.

The medical knowledge revealed in the Bible is truly astounding. It is well known, for instance, that medicine in the antique world was based upon myth and superstition. This was true in Babylon and Egypt.

For example the *Papyrus Ebers* (from the sixteenth century B.C.), edited by George M. Ebers in 1874, offered some very strange remedies for various illnesses. Here is a prescription for folks who are losing their hair:

> When it falls out, one remedy is to apply a mixture of six fats, namely those of the horse, the hippopotamus, the crocodile, the cat, the snake, and the ibex. To strengthen it, anoint with the tooth of a donkey crushed in honey (quoted by McMillen 1963, 11).

Even the Edwin Smith Surgical Papyrus, one of the more sophisticated examples of Egyptian medical "science," contains a spell for "transforming an old man into a youth of twenty."

In spite of the fact that Moses was reared in an Egyptian environment and "was instructed in all the wisdom of the Egyptians" (Acts 7:22), not one time did the great law-giver incorporate any of this magical mumbo-jumbo into the Scriptures. On the contrary, Moses was far ahead of his time in terms of medicine and sanitation. A careful study of Leviticus 13, with reference to certain skin diseases, reveals some rather modern techniques (e.g., the diagnosis of certain symptoms), treatment to lessen spread (e.g., disinfection), and quarantine. No other law code in the whole of ancient history came anywhere near rivaling these health regulations.

Consider, for instance, the fact that the "leper" was required to "cover his upper lip" (Lev. 13:45). Dr. J. S. Morton has noted: "Since the leprosy bacilli are transmitted from nasal drippings and saliva, this practice of having lepers cover their upper lips was a good hygienic policy" (1978, 255).

Concerning Moses' procedures for quarantining, Dr. William Vis has written:

> To show how far Moses was ahead of modern society we need only to remind ourselves that the word quarantine originated in the fourteenth century when the Italian ports of Venice and Genoa first refused admission to immigrants who might be harboring plague and required them to stay on board for forty days—hence the word quarantine. Even in the seventeenth and eighteenth centuries leprosy spread over southern Europe until the principles of Moses were re-enacted successfully (1950, 244).

As noted in an earlier chapter, when the *Encyclopedia Britannica* was first published, it had so many mistakes relative to American geography and topography that the publishers of the *New American Cyclopedia* issued a special pamphlet correcting the blunders of its British rival.

J. W. McGarvey once noted that when Tacitus wrote his celebrated work, *Germania*, which dealt with the geography, manners, customs, and tribes of Germany, it contained so many errors that many were inclined to doubt that this well-known Roman historian could have produced such a flawed volume (1956, 26–27). The *Encyclopedia Britannica* notes that "the geography is its weak point" (736).

The biblical writings contain literally hundreds of references to geography and topography relating to those lands which the prophets and apostles traversed. We are quite casual in our topographical allusions. Usually we speak of going "up" north and "down" south. For example, you might say you are going to travel from Atlanta up to Chicago, though Chicago is almost five hundred feet lower than Atlanta.

However the biblical writers are always precise when recording elevation references. One travels from Jerusalem (in the south) "down" to Antioch, some one hundred fifty miles to the north (Acts 15:1–2). Not once is there a geographical or topographical blunder in the sacred volume, in spite of the fact that the ancients did not possess the sophisticated instruments we have today.

Here is an amazing fact. In the book of Acts, the historian Luke mentions thirty-two countries, fifty-four cities, and nine of the Mediterranean islands (Metzger 1965, 171). There is not the slightest mistake in any of his references. Luke has been criticized over the centuries to be sure; his influence has increased, however, while his critics' credibility has decreased.

ALLEGED SLIPS

Over a span of many centuries, hostile critics of the Bible have charged the sacred writers with nodding. Time after time, however, when the true facts have come to light, the Scriptures have been vindicated. Reflect upon a few examples.

The Genesis record declares that while he was in Egypt, Pharaoh presented Abraham with some camels (12:16). Liberal writers disputed this. T. K. Cheyne wrote, "The assertion that the ancient Egyptians knew of the camel is unfounded" (1899, 1.634). Professor Kenneth Kitchen has shown, however, that "the extant evidence clearly indicates that the domestic camel was known [in Egypt] by 3,000 B.C."—long before Abraham's time (1980, 228).

On several occasions in the book of Genesis, it is recorded that Abraham and Isaac had associations with the Philistines (cf. Gen. 21 and 26). Liberal scholars consider these references to be anachronistic (details from a later age inappropriately inserted into the patriarchal account). H. T. Frank characterizes the allusions as "an historical inaccuracy" (1964, 323).

It has been shown, however, that "Philistine" was a rather generic term and that there is no valid reason to doubt that these groups were in Canaan before the arrival of the main body in the early twelfth century B.C. (Unger 1954, 91; Archer 1962, 266; Harrison 1963, 32). Harrison says that the archaeological evidence "suggests that it is a mistake to regard the mention of the Philistines in the patriarchal narratives as an anachronism" (362).

Elsewhere, this writer has catalogued no less than twenty major slips with which the biblical writers have been charged (Jackson 1988). Each of these has evaporated with the passing of time and the exhumation of evidence.

Yes, even the noble Homer may nod; those guided by the Spirit of God, however, never did. You can trust the Bible!

And here is a crucial point: if the Bible proves to be reliable in hundreds of matters that are verifiable, why should it not be trusted in issues in the spiritual realm that, from the very nature of the case, are beyond human verification, e.g., issues pertaining to redemption from sin?

The author acknowledges his indebtedness to the lamented B. C. Goodpasture for the idea from which this chapter sprang, and for a few of the examples that illustrate the concept developed (1970, 322, 325).

Chapter 10

Are the Scriptures Verbally Inspired?

"I have always believed in the inspiration of the Holy Scriptures, whereby they have become the expression to man of the Word and Will of God."
— Warren Harding (1865–1923)

In logic, there is a principle called the Law of the Excluded Middle. Simply stated, it is this: a thing either must be, or not be. A line is either straight, or it is not. There is no middle position.

Applied to the Bible, one therefore must declare: the Scriptures are inspired of God, or they are not inspired of God. If the writings of the Bible are not inspired of God, then they are the mere productions of men, and as such would merit no religious respect; in fact, in view of their exalted claims, they would merit only contempt.

Paul, an apostle of Christ, wrote: "Every scripture is inspired of God, and profitable for teaching, for reproof, for correction, for instruction in righteousness: that the man of God may be complete, furnished completely unto every good work" (2 Tim. 3:16–17). The Bible asserts its own inspiration—of this there is no doubt. But to what extent does the sacred volume claim inspiration? This is a question that has perplexed many.

SOME POPULAR BUT FALSE THEORIES

Some have suggested that the Bible is "inspired" only in the sense that other great literary productions are inspired. That is, they all are simply the results of natural genius, characteristic of men of unusual ability. Such a notion must be rejected immediately since: (a) it makes liars of the biblical writers who claimed the Holy Spirit as the ultimate source of their documents (2 Sam. 23:2; Acts 1:16); and (b) it leaves unexplained the mystery of why modern man, with his accumulated learning, has not been able to produce a comparable volume that has the capacity to make the Bible obsolete.

Others have claimed that only certain portions of the Scriptures are inspired of God. We often hear it said, for example, that those sections of the Bible that deal with faith and morals are inspired, but that other areas, particularly those accounts which contain certain miraculous elements, are merely the productions of good, but superstitious and fallible men.

Again, though, such a concept is not consistent with the declarations of the divine writers. They extended inspiration to every area of the Scriptures, even emphasizing, in many instances, those very sections that modernists dub as nonhistorical, mythical, etc., for example: Mt. 12:39–40; 19:4ff.; Lk. 4:27; Jn. 3:14–15. See the chapter, "Jesus Christ Versus Modernism."

Too, the allegation has been made that the Bible is inspired in "sense," but not in "sentence." By that, it is meant that in some sense the Scriptures are of divine origin, but that the very words of the Holy Book are not to be construed as inspired. Such a view is nonsensical. If the words of the sacred narrative are not inspired, pray tell what is inspired? Is the binding? The paper? The ink? The truth is, if the words of the Bible are not inspired of God, then the Bible contains no inspiration at all!

VERBAL INSPIRATION

What do we mean when we speak of the "verbal inspiration" of the Holy Scriptures? Frank E. Gaebelein has suggested that a sound view of inspiration holds that:

> the original documents of the Bible were written by men, who, though permitted the exercise of their own personalities and literary talents, yet wrote under the control and guidance of the Spirit of God, the result being in every word of the original documents a perfect and errorless recording of the exact message which God desired to give to man (1950, 9).

In his classic work, *Theopneustia—The Plenary Inspiration of the Holy Scriptures*, L. Glaussen, professor of systematic theology at Oratoire, Geneva, defined inspiration as:

> that inexplicable power which the Divine Spirit put forth of old on the authors of holy Scripture, in order to their guidance even in the employment of the words they used, and to preserve them alike from all error and from all omission (n.d., 34).

Let us take a closer look at 2 Timothy 3:16. The Greek text says: "All scripture is God-breathed." Something within this context is said to be "God-breathed." What is it? All Scripture. The term "scripture" (*graphe*) denotes that which is written. But it is the words of the biblical text that are written; hence, the very words of the Bible are God-breathed! No one can appeal to 2 Timothy 3:16 as evidence of Bible inspiration without, at the same time, introducing the concept of verbal inspiration. The truth is, the doctrine of the verbal inspiration of the Scriptures is abundantly claimed throughout the sacred canon. Consider the following examples.

Thus Says the Lord

More than 3,800 times in the Old Testament, the claim is made that the Scriptures are the word (or words) of God. For instance: "And Jehovah said unto Moses, Write this for a memorial in a book" (Ex. 17:14). David declared: "The Spirit of Jehovah spoke by me, and his word was upon my tongue" (2 Sam. 23:2). God instructed the prophet Jeremiah, "Behold, I have put my words in your mouth" (Jer. 1:9). The Scriptures are exalted as the Word of God some 175 times in Psalm 119 alone!

Jesus and the Old Testament

Jesus Christ certainly endorsed the concept of verbal inspiration. He affirmed that neither "one jot nor one tittle" would pass away from the law "until all things be accomplished" (Mt. 5:17–18). The jot was the smallest Hebrew letter, and the tittle was a tiny projection on certain Hebrew characters. Professor A. B. Bruce noted: "Jesus expresses here in the strongest manner His conviction that the whole Old Testament is a Divine revelation, and that therefore every minute precept has religious significance" (1956, 104).

The Lord frequently made arguments based upon the text of the Old Testament, wherein he stressed very precise grammatical points. His argument for the resurrection from the dead in Matthew 22:32 depends upon the present tense form of a verb—"I am [not "was"] the God of Abraham." Within the same context, Christ quoted Psalm 110:1, showing that David, speaking in the Spirit, said, "The Lord said unto my Lord . . ." (Mt. 22:41ff.). Again, the emphasis is on a single word. Jesus (affirming his own deity) asked the Pharisees why David referred to his own descendant, the promised Messiah, as Lord. Not recognizing the dual nature of the Messiah (i.e., as man, he was David's seed; as deity, he was David's Lord), they were unable to answer. Had Christ not believed in the inspired words of the Old Testament, he hardly could have reasoned as he did (see also Jn. 10:30ff).

The Lord's Promise

Jesus promised his apostles that the words of their gospel declaration would be given them. He told them: "But when they deliver you up, be not anxious how or what you shall speak; for it shall be given you in that hour what you shall speak" (Mt. 10:19). And, note Luke's parallel that they were not to "meditate beforehand" how to answer their antagonists (Lk. 21:14). That has to involve their very words!

Inspired Writers

It is quite clear that the penmen of Scripture were conscious of the fact that they were recording the words of God. Paul wrote: "I received of the Lord that which I also delivered unto you" (1 Cor. 11:23). What he had received from the Lord came in the form of words. Again, "This we say unto you by the word of the Lord" (1 Thes. 4:15). "When you received from us the word of the message, even the word of God, you accepted it not as the word of men, but, as it is in truth, the word of God, which also works in you that believe" (1 Thes. 2:13). When Philip preached in Samaria, those people to whom he spoke had heard "the word of God" (Acts 8:14).

In a remarkable passage, Paul asked: "For who among men knows the things of a man, except the spirit of the man which is in him?" He means this: "You cannot know what is in my mind until I, by my words, reveal to you what I am thinking." That is the apostle's illustration. Here is his point. "Even so the things of God none knows, save the Spirit of God . . . . which things [i.e., the things of God] we also speak, not in words which man's wisdom teaches, but which the Spirit teaches; combining spiritual things with spiritual words" (1 Cor. 2:11–13). There is not a more comprehensive statement of verbal inspiration to be found anywhere in the holy writings. The mind of God has been made known by means of the inspired words of those representatives whom he chose for that noble task.

"Scripture"

The biblical writers considered one another's productions to be inspired of God. In 1 Timothy 5:18, Paul writes: "For the scripture says: You shall not muzzle the ox when he treads out the corn. And, The laborer is worthy of his hire." In this passage, the apostle has combined Deuteronomy 25:4 and Luke 10:7, and classified them both as "scripture." Similarly, Peter refers to Paul's epistles as "scripture" in 2 Peter 3:15–16.

MECHANICAL DICTATION—A STRAW MAN

Whenever you hear someone accusing advocates of verbal inspiration of believing in "mechanical dictation," most likely you are dealing with a theological liberal. The notion of "mechanical dictation" (i.e., that the Bible writers were only "recorders," or impersonal "word-processors," hence, their cultural and personality factors did not enter into their works) is not the concept taught by most conservative Bible scholars. Certainly, Paul's writings differ in style from those of John, etc. But that does not negate the fact that after God used the individual writers of Scripture, in the final process only the exact words that he wanted in the text appeared there!

HAS TRANSMISSION DESTROYED INSPIRATION?

"But suppose," someone wonders, "the Bible was verbally inspired initially. Hasn't the transmission of the text across the centuries caused a corrupt degeneration of the original documents, so that the 'verbal inspiration' has been virtually destroyed?" Not at all. The text of the Bible—both Old and New Testaments—has been preserved in a remarkable fashion. For example, after years of scientific research in connection with the text of the Old Testament, professor Robert Dick Wilson, who was thoroughly acquainted with forty-five languages, stated that "we are **scientifically certain** that we have substantially the same text that was in the possession of Christ and the apostles" (1929, 8; emphasis added). See the chapter on "Radical Criticism and the Old Testament."

Evidence for the textual reliability of the New Testament is no less impressive. Scholars are now in possession of more than five thousand Greek manuscripts (in part or in whole) of the New Testament, and some of these date to the early part of the second century A.D. It has been estimated that textual variations concern only about one one-thousandth of the entire text (see Gregory 1907, 528). Transmission, therefore, has not destroyed verbal inspiration. See the chapter on "Radical Criticism and the New Testament."

DOES TRANSLATION NULLIFY INSPIRATION?

Since the Holy Scriptures originally were penned in Hebrew, Aramaic, and Greek, and since the original documents have been translated into many languages, some are concerned that the translation process has destroyed the Bible's initial inspiration. But there is no need for concern over this matter so long as accurate translation has been done. When a word is translated precisely from one language into another, the same thought or idea is conveyed; thus, the same message is preserved.

That translation need not affect inspiration is evinced by an appeal to the New Testament itself. In the third to second centuries B.C., the Hebrew Scriptures were translated into Greek. This version, which was begun in Alexandria, Egypt, is known as the Septuagint (abbreviated as LXX). The fact is, Jesus Christ himself, and his inspired New Testament writers, frequently quoted from the Septuagint translation of the Old

Testament Scriptures! For example, in Matthew 22:32, Christ quoted from the Septuagint (Ex. 3:6), and of that passage said: "Have you not read that which was spoken unto you by God?" (22:31). A translation from Hebrew to Greek did not alter the fact that the message remained the word of God!

It also might be observed that scholars generally agree that the Septuagint is not as reliable a translation as is the Hebrew text of the Old Testament. Yet in spite of this reality, the New Testament frequently quotes it. However, as one author observed:

> The writers of the New Testament appear to have been so careful to give the true sense of the Old Testament, that they forsook the Septuagint version whenever it did not give that sense (Horne 1841, 1.312).

The fact is, when a New Testament writer was quoting from the Greek Old Testament, the Holy Spirit sometimes led him to slightly alter the phraseology to give a more accurate sense. Thus, inspiration was still preserved though a less-than-perfect translation was being used. See the chapter on "How New Testament Writers Used the Old Testament in Their Teaching."

The Scriptures are the verbally inspired Word of God. This view has been defended by reverent students of the Holy Writings for multiplied centuries. Fritz Rienecker noted that the Jewish

> rabbinical teaching was that the Spirit of God rested on and in the prophets and spoke through them so that their words did not come from themselves, but from the mouth of God and they spoke and wrote

in the Holy Spirit. The early church was in entire agreement with this view (1980, 301).

Let us therefore exalt the Holy Scriptures as the living word of God (Heb. 4:12), and acknowledge them as the only authoritative source of religious guidance.

Chapter 11

The Miracles of Christ versus Modern Miracles

> *"My dear children, I am very anxious that you should
> know something about the History of Jesus Christ.
> For everybody ought to know about Him."*
> — Charles Dickens (1812–1870)

The Gospel accounts record more than three dozen specific miracles that Jesus of Nazareth performed during his ministry. In addition, there are frequent general references to a number of other signs that Christ did while he was on Earth (see Jn. 20:30–31, et al). The miracles of Jesus are crucial to the validity of Christianity. C. S. Lewis has well noted:

> All the essentials of Hinduism would, I think,
> remain unimpaired if you subtracted the [alleged]
> miraculous, and the same is almost true of
> Muhammadanism, but you cannot do that with
> Christianity. It is precisely the story of a great
> Miracle. A naturalistic Christianity leaves out all
> that is specifically Christian (1947, 83).

The Lord performed a great variety of wonders. For example, he showed his power over nature when he calmed a storm (Mt. 8:23–27). He also was able to manipulate material objects supernaturally. For instance, he transformed water into wine (Jn. 2:1–11) and multiplied loaves and fish (Jn. 6:1–14). Christ exhibited his authority over disease when He healed a man born blind—a feat that never had been observed in the entire history of the world (Jn. 9:1–7, 32). He even raised the dead. Lazarus had been a corpse four days when Jesus bade him come forth from his tomb (Jn. 11:39–44).

But were the miracles of Christ authentic? Infidelity begins with the *a priori* (i.e., without examination or analysis) assumption that the supernatural does not exist; therefore, Jesus did not perform true miracles. But this is not an honest approach to the issue. The question is: what does the evidence of history indicate? Are there sufficient historical data to warrant the reasonable deduction that Christ did effect certain "signs" that cannot be explained upon any natural basis? This issue really comes down to two significant points. First, what does the ancient documentation indicate about the nature of the Lord's miracles? Second, is the historical record credible?

CHARACTERISTICS OF JESUS' MIRACLES

There are a number of tell-tale traits characteristic of the miracles of Christ which, if we accept the descriptions of them presented in the New Testament, give them an aura of credibility. First, the wonders that Jesus did were subject to sense perception. The water that the Lord changed into wine could be tasted (Jn. 2:9). Thomas could feel the wounds in the hands and side of the resurrected Lord (Jn. 20:27). The restored ear (amputated by Peter) of the high priest's servant could be seen (Lk. 22:51). The signs of Jesus' ministry were in the form of objective demonstrations, not subjective speculations,

Second, the miracles of Christ were performed in the presence of a wide variety of witnesses. There were male and female, educated and uneducated, friends and foes, etc. The wonders were done in the synagogues, in the public streets, during the great festivals, etc. When the Lord multiplied the loaves and fish, possibly some ten thousand people witnessed the event (see Jn. 6:10). Repeatedly, the miracles were said to be done in the presence of great crowds (Mt. 4:23ff; Mk. 3:7ff; Jn. 5:8ff).

Third, the signs of Christ were independent of any secondary causes. By this we mean that there is no possible way to explain these phenomena upon any naturalistic basis. Neither medical treatment nor mental suggestion, is sufficient to explain how a man congenitally blind could have his sight restored (Jn. 9:1–7), or how a man, dead four days, could come out of his grave (Jn. 11:39).

Fourth, the miracles of Christ produced instantaneous results and their effect was complete. When the Lord healed Peter's mother-in-law, she rose up and "immediately" served others (Lk. 4:39). A certain woman, who had suffered from hemorrhaging for twelve years, was healed by Christ and "immediately her bleeding stopped" (Mk. 5:29). Though Lazarus had been "sick" (Greek *astheneo*, "weak, feeble") prior to his death (Jn. 11:1–6), when Christ raised him from the dead he was able to come forth from the tomb of his own strength, even though he was bound hand and foot with grave clothes (11:44). He came back, not merely to life, but to vigorous life!

Fifth, there is not the slightest bit of evidence that Christ ever failed in attempting to work a miracle. His enemies never once accused him of such. The New Testament makes it plain: his success rate was always one hundred percent. "He cast out spirits with a word, and healed all who were sick" (Mt. 8:16; cf. 12:15). Some claim that Mark 8:22ff is an example of Christ being unable to effect an instantaneous and complete cure of a blind man. Such, however, is not the case. This might be called a two-stage miracle. J. W. McGarvey has commented:

> Jesus adopted this method of cure to give variety to the manifestations of his power by showing that he could heal in part and by progressive steps, as well as by his more usual method of effecting a perfect cure at one word. This cure was not less miraculous than others, but rather more so: for it was really the working of two miracles, each effecting instantaneously all that was intended by it (1875, 314).

Sixth, the miracles of Christ always were characterized by a stately dignity; they never smacked of the bizarre. Moreover, they uniformly evinced a worthy motive. They never were performed to satisfy the personal needs of the Lord; rather, they always were in the ultimate interest of others. Contrast this, for example, with the ancient Catholic legend regarding "Saint" Eligius who was said on one occasion to be shoeing a horse that would not stand still. To circumvent the problem, he simply took off the leg, shod the foot, and restored the limb—the horse being none the worse for the procedure. Eligius thus became the "patron saint" of blacksmiths!

Seventh, the signs of Jesus were not denied by his contemporaries, or by others for many years beyond the first century. For example, the Pharisees—pronounced enemies of Christ—conceded that he was casting out demons; they rationalized, however, and suggested that these deeds were done by the power of the prince of demons (Mt. 12:24). That argument was demolished, though, when the Lord pointed out that were such the case, Satan actually would be divided against himself! Note the frustrated testimony of the chief priests and Pharisees in John 11:47: "What do we? for this man doeth many signs." Additionally, as Thomas Horne has observed, while the facts were too recent to be disputed, the post-apostolic enemies of Christianity—e.g., Celsus, Porphyry, Hierocles, Julian, and others—admitted that Christ did some inexplicable wonders. They merely characterized them as magic and, of course, denied the divine commission of him who performed them. However, "to whatever cause they ascribed them, their admission of the reality of these miracles is an involuntary confession that there was something preternatural in them" (1841, 1.103).

Finally, we may note that not one time do we have the record of a disciple of Jesus Christ defecting and then doing an exposé of the "fakery" involved in the Savior's miracles. Judas, who betrayed the Lord, had every opportunity to do this. He was in the inner circle of disciples, even as treasurer of the apostolic band (Jn. 12:6). Surely, over a span of three-and-a-half years, if Christ had been perpetrating a hoax, Judas would have known it. And he would have provided such information to the Jewish authorities. But he never did. In fact, as is well known, he brought back the pieces of silver and confessed: "I have sinned in that I betrayed innocent blood" (Mt. 27:4). Is this the testimony of a person, on the verge of suicide, concerning one known to be a charlatan? Hardly.

IS THE HISTORICAL RECORD RELIABLE?

Since we were not present at the dawn of the first century to actually see the miracles of Jesus, we obviously are dependent upon historical records for our faith in their validity. Can we trust the testimony of those who claimed to have seen the miracles of Christ?

Let us consider the credibility of the four writers of the Gospel accounts. Two of these, Matthew and John, were apostles of Christ who were with him on virtually a daily basis for three-and-a-half years. They were eyewitnesses to the deeds of the Lord. Mark, who wrote as a protégé of Peter (see the comment of Irenaeus [ca. A.D. 140–203], *Against Heresies* III, i, 1), likely records the testimony of that eminent apostle, and perhaps writes from some firsthand knowledge as well. Finally, Luke, admittedly a first-rate historian, had "traced the course of all things accurately from the first" (Lk. 1:3). Aside from the presumptions of skeptical bias, there is no reason to question these records. These men firmly and harmoniously declared that Jesus of Nazareth performed many miracles, thus authenticating his claim of being the Son of God (see Jn. 20:30–31). If their narratives are to be rejected, upon what ground will such be done? There are but a few possibilities.

Were these sincere and intelligent men who were simply ignorant of the actual facts? Were they deluded simpletons incapable of judging the events they observed? Or were they dishonest hucksters desirous of perpetrating a deception? Actually, none of these theories harmonizes with the evidence—and evidence is the only thing that matters. What are the facts?

First, one cannot argue that they were uninformed of the first-century circumstances. They were there. Hence, they were in a much better position to assess the situation than modern infidel critics—two millennia removed from the scene.

Second, there is no justification for suggesting that they were rattle-brained enthusiasts who were undependable as historians. In recording these phenomenal events, which they personally witnessed, they wrote with a calmness and a dispassionate demeanor that utterly defies explanation.

Third, their documents are precise in countless historical details. When they are demonstrated to be accurate in such a variety of ways, why should it be assumed that they are incorrect in their narratives concerning the signs of Jesus?

Fourth, the fact that the Gospel writers are so harmonious in their testimonies regarding the Lord's miracles argues for the accuracy of their accounts. (Note: though the Gospel narratives sometimes supplement one another, they never contradict. The fact is, the differences reflected by the various authors evince a lack of collusion.)

Fifth, their writings indicate a scrupulous honesty that makes the productions extremely credible. For example, Matthew, with incriminating candor, declared that when the Lord was arrested "all the disciples [that includes John] left him, and fled" (Mt. 26:56).

Sixth, the integrity of the Gospel writers is evinced by the fact that they were willing to suffer the consequences of their testimony. They had nothing to gain (and much to lose, from a physical-material vantage point) by insisting that Jesus performed genuine miracles. They suffered the hatred of their contemporaries. They were subjected to torture and even death, not merely for emotionally-charged beliefs, but for their testimony concerning the miracles that they personally witnessed; yet they never recanted. This level of dedication passes the highest test of authenticity.

When all the facts are in, and when they are analyzed in the light of honest objectivity, the conclusion is clear. Jesus actually did perform miracles, and thus was who he claimed to be—the Messiah, the Son of God.

MODERN "MIRACLES"

But how does one explain the alleged "miracles" of this age? In the first place, we are not obligated to defend, as divine, an event simply because it may have certain elements that are difficult to explain. There are many illusions which magicians perform that I cannot explain; they do have natural explanations, however, and are not miracles. That aside, there are several possible bases for so-called modern miracles. As an example, let us focus upon the acts of supposed "faith healings."

First, some instances of "faith healing" are pure fakery. Consider the case of Peter Popoff, alleged miracle-working cleric of Upland, California. Popoff, who claimed the supernatural ability to give revealed information about people in his audiences (in conjunction with "healing" them), was receiving such information through a tiny hearing aid, via messages being transmitted by his wife from backstage. Prominent magician, James Randi, exposed the entire affair on nationwide television (1987, 139–181). Randi also demonstrated that Popoff was providing rented wheelchairs for people who could actually walk; then, at his services, he was pronouncing them "healed."

Second, some "miraculous cures" are claimed by people who honestly believe that God has healed them. The fact is, however, they had nothing really organically wrong with them. Their ailment was psychosomatic. This means that though some bodily feature actually was affected, the real root of the problem was mental or emotional; hence, by mere suggestion a cure might be provided. It has been estimated that some fifty-five percent (or more) of the patients applying for medical treatment in the United States suffer from psychosomatic illnesses. In fact, Dr. William S. Sadler has written:

> It is generally believed by experienced physicians that at least two thirds of the ordinary cases of sickness which doctors are called upon to treat would, if left entirely alone, recover without the aid of the doctor or his medicine (1929, 15).

Taking advantage of this type of sickness, the faith-healer, in an atmosphere of hysteria and feverish emotionalism, produces some phenomenal "cures." But there is absolutely nothing miraculous about such cases. A physician in Toronto, Canada, investigated thirty cases in which Oral Roberts claimed a miraculous healing took place; he "found not one case that could not be attributed to psychological shock or hysteria" (Randi 1987, 288). Dr. Sadler affirmed that after twenty-five years of sympathetic research into faith-healing, he had not observed a single case of an organic disease being healed.

It is commonly known that an African witch-doctor can literally command a believer in voodooism to die, and within the prescribed time, the victim will expire. This evinces the powerful command of the mind over the body. Surely no one will claim, though, that the witch-doctor has "the Spirit of God."

Third, another explanation for some so-called faith cures is a phenomenon known as spontaneous remission. Spontaneous remission is an unexpected withdrawal of disease symptoms and an inexplicable disappearance of the ailment. It occurs in about one out of every eighty thousand cancer patients. Joseph Maycrle of Bremerton, Washington had exploratory surgery; it was discovered that he was consumed with cancer. His physicians gave him only a few months to live. Months sped by and his disease utterly vanished. There was nothing miraculous about it. According to newspaper accounts, Mr. Mayerle, a bartender, made no claim to faith, prayer, or a "miracle cure." Would not a faith-healer have delighted in taking credit for that case?

Fourth, it must be admitted that since physicians are but human, they can and do make mistakes, and sometimes wrongly diagnose a case. Some of these situations are seized upon by modern "miracle-workers" and a supernatural aura is attributed to them.

There is one final point of this discussion that needs to be pressed with great vigor. There is no alleged "miracle" being performed today by Pentecostals, or those of similar "Christian" persuasion, that cannot be duplicated by various other cults and "non-Christian" sects. Those who practice Christian Science, Mormonism, Transcendental Meditation, Yoga, Psychic Healing, Scientology, New Age Crystal healing, etc., claim the same type of "signs" as the Pentecostals. In fact, more than twenty million Americans annually report mystic experiences (including healing) in their lives (Harris 1989, 64).

Since the Scriptures clearly teach that the purpose of miracles, as evinced in biblical days, was to confirm the message proclaimed, hence, to validate the Christian system, do the multiple alleged examples of miracle-workings indicate that the Lord has authenticated all of these contradictory systems? Think of the implication of that in light of Paul's affirmation that God is not the Author of confusion (1 Cor. 14:33).

There is abundant evidence that there were genuine miracles performed by Jesus Christ and his divinely appointed followers of the first century; but there is no proof whatsoever that such wonders are being duplicated today.

Chapter 12

Jesus Christ versus Modernism

---

*"Christianity is a reality, not an appearance. Were it a myth
devised by cunning imposters, it would have come to
naught before this. It has done more to fraternize the races
than all human systems of religion together. The Bible is the
supreme over all books. Besides it there is none other. Its
Divine truths meet the wants of a world-wide humanity."*
— Francis M. Cockrell (1834–1915), U.S. Senator

"**M**odernism" is the name of the procedure that proposes
to re-interpret certain historical data in the Bible. This
misinterpretation purports to be in better harmony with the
era of modern "scientific" criticism. Anything, therefore, of a
miraculous nature is considered untenable. Any extraordinary
event must be divested of the miraculous and viewed in terms
of "natural phenomena." In the expression coined by radical
theologian Rudolf Bultmann (1884–1976), the biblical record
must be "demythologized" (Harvey 1964, 67).

The vocabulary of the modernist abounds with such
terms as "myth," "legend," "fable," "parable," and "folklore."
If this method is valid, the writers of the Bible scarcely can be
considered dependable in anything they wrote; and frankly,
often were guilty of nothing less than dishonesty.

It is not without paramount significance that Jesus Christ himself endorsed many of the most disputed narratives in the Old Testament, and in a way that clearly demonstrates he acknowledged them as historically reliable, literal accounts. It is therefore a matter of who is accurate—the Son of God or modernists.

THE CREATION

The book of Genesis states that Jehovah formed man from the dust of the earth and animated him with the breath of life. With a rib and flesh from Adam's side, woman was fashioned. The theory of evolution alleges that originally there was a non-sexual blob of non-living substance that spontaneously generated life, and from that asexual matter two genders evolved. A popular Bible commentary describes the Mosaic record of the creation events as "parables" with the echoes of Canaanite "Baal" mythology (Mays 1988, 88, 93).

But Jesus did not subscribe to such a modernistic view. He declared: "Have you not read, that he who made them from the beginning made them male and female" (Mt. 19:4). Moreover, the term "made" in the Greek Testament is an aorist tense form, suggesting definite acts of creation—not a gradual development that would have been conveyed by an imperfect tense format.

THE FLOOD

The great flood of Noah's day is recorded in Genesis 6–8. Because of man's wickedness, a tremendous deluge engulfed the earth and all humanity was destroyed, with the exception of the eight persons within Noah's ark (1 Pet. 3:20). Typically, the skeptic scoffs at the biblical record. One writer says:

> Legends of a universal flood are found in almost every part of the world. There can be little doubt

that where they have not borrowed from alien traditions they go back to some natural event, local in its extent. A universal flood would of course be a physical impossibility. . . . The myth of the Flood, it may be assumed, was like the creation myth, ultimately carried to Palestine (Buttrick 1952, 537).

Christ taught just the opposite. He said: "For as in those days which were before the flood they were eating and drinking, marrying and giving in marriage, until the day that Noah entered into the ark, and they knew not until the flood came, and took them all away" (Mt. 24:38–39).

THE FATE OF SODOM

Because of strife involving his herdsmen, Lot, the nephew of Abraham, took up residence in Sodom. The cities of the plain were terribly corrupt (homosexuality was the besetting sin), and eventually God vowed to destroy them—which he did with fire and brimstone out of heaven (Gen. 19:24). Of this event a Jewish modernist comments:

We may assume, then, that in its original form, the Sodom and Gomorrah story was an independent narrative, unconnected with Abraham and his family. The Bible has once again adopted the nucleus of a popular saga to rework it in accordance with its own ethico-religious purposes (Sarna 1960, 142–143).

Notwithstanding such reckless claims, the Savior declared:

Likewise even as it came to pass in the days of Lot; they ate, they drank, they bought, they sold, they planted, they built; but in the day that Lot went out of Sodom it rained fire and brimstone from heaven, and destroyed them all (Lk. 17:28–29).

Further, the account of Lot's wife "turning into a pillar of salt" is considered by some to be fiction. D. J. Wiseman cites C. Westerman as contending that "the metamorphosis of [Lot's] wife, unique in the OT, resulted from the transgression of a magic taboo" (Bromiley 1986, 172). Others have asserted that the story of Lot's wife was suggested merely by a geological oddity in the region. Josephus had written that Lot's wife "was changed into a pillar of salt; for I have seen it, and it remains at this day" (*Antiquities of the Jews* 1.11.4).

These speculations aside, the Lord Jesus warned: "Remember Lot's wife" (Lk. 17:32). What else is there to remember about this woman, except that dramatic incident in Genesis 19? To thrust the account into the fiction mold is to reflect seriously upon Christ's credibility.

THE PLAGUES

One of the more disputed events in Old Testament history is the record of the plagues upon Egypt, as chronicled in the book of Exodus. One skeptic depicts the situation in this fashion. "The plague stories are a legend or myth used by the Israelite community in its celebration of the Passover rite" (Harrelson 1964, 83).

The final plague involved the death of the firstborn throughout Egypt. The Israelites, in order to escape this judgment, were commanded by the Lord to kill a lamb and smear its blood on the doorposts and lintels of their houses that the Destroyer might "pass over" their firstborn. The slain lamb was a "type" of the shedding of Jesus' blood (1 Cor. 5:7).

Near the commencement of his ministry, John the Baptizer introduced Jesus as "the lamb of God that takes away the sin of the world" (Jn. 1:29). Christ accepted that designation, thus acknowledging that he was the anti-type of the Passover lamb. Thereby, he endorsed the historicity of the tenth plague, thus, by implication, the other nine as well.

THE MANNA

While the children of Israel sojourned in the wilderness of Sinai, Jehovah gave them bread to eat; it was known as "manna." The Lord declared: "I will rain bread from heaven for you" (Ex. 16:4). They ate it for forty years (v. 35). The provision was miraculous. Since modernism rejects the supernatural, they must conjure up some naturalistic explanation for the "bread." A common view represents it in this fashion:

> In the early summer several types of desert trees and shrubs, notably the tamarisk, exude a sweet sticky substance such as this appears to have been. It drips to the ground, crystallizes and turns white. The comparison which likens the manna to hoarfrost and the observation that it tasted "like wafers made with honey" (verse 31) show that this natural substance was the origin of the manna story (Buttrick 1952, 952).

Contrast this with the words of the Lord Jesus: "Your fathers ate manna in the wilderness, and they died. This is the bread [a reference to himself] that comes down out of heaven that a man may eat thereof, and not die" (Jn. 6:49–50; cf. v. 58). Jesus referenced history, not mythology.

THE BRAZEN SERPENT

Because of discouragement in the wilderness, the people of God yielded to temptation and spoke against the Lord. Accordingly, Jehovah sent fiery serpents among the people and "they bit the people" (Num. 21:6). Confessing their sin, the Hebrews sought deliverance, and according to the instruction of the Lord, a bronze serpent was erected upon a standard that all who looked thereupon in faith might be healed. Modernists repudiate this incident. One writer explains the narrative like this:

> In the East serpents are often regarded as having healing power. In that case the P [priestly] writers told the story of Moses making the serpent in the wilderness to provide a suitable explanation of how the serpent came to be in the Temple at all, and to show that Yahweh, and not the serpent, was the true healer (Davies et al. 1955, 149).

Christ did not consider the account to be a manufactured story in order to explain an event that occurred in Hezekiah's day (2 Kgs. 18:4). He said: "And as Moses lifted up the serpent in the wilderness, even so must the Son of man be lifted up; that whosoever believes may in him have eternal life" (Jn. 3:14–15). Was the Lord's prophetic utterance of his crucifixion grounded upon an event that never even occurred? How shameless they are who would indict the Son of God.

JONAH AND THE GREAT FISH

Jonah was a prophet of God, commissioned to preach a message of repentance to the citizens of Nineveh, a task which he hardly relished since these were a pagan people. Accordingly, he attempted to flee from his duty. But the Lord sent Jonah to "school" for three days in the belly of a great fish. He graduated the third day with honors!

This historical record has been ridiculed countless times. A singular quotation will illustrate the point. The late Edgar J. Goodspeed, former professor at the University of Chicago, wrote: "If people would recognize it as fiction, they might get more from its meaning, which was never more needed than today" (1946, 149).

The question is, therefore, is the book of Jonah fact or fiction? And whose word carries more weight—that of professor Goodspeed or Jesus Christ?

When certain false teachers pressed Christ for a miracle (after having had ample opportunity to evaluate his signs already), the Lord chastised them as follows:

> There shall be no sign given it [the current generation] but the sign of Jonah the prophet: for as Jonah was three days and nights in the belly of the sea-monster [Greek text]; so shall the Son of man be three days and three nights in the heart of the earth (Mt. 12:39–40).

Thus it stands; if modernists are correct, then either: (a) Christ was unaware of the nature of Old Testament literature, hence, was ignorant of the facts of history—in which case he was not the all-knowing Son of God (cf. Col. 2:3), or (b) he knew these controversial cases were mere mythological metaphors which were never intended to be taken literally, yet he dishonestly portrayed them as historical events to a naïve people whom he felt would not perceive the difference which, again, nullifies his claim of being the Savior of unimpeachable character (Jn. 8:29; 14:6).

Is it not strange that Christ's enemies, desperate as they were to find flaws in his teaching and character, never once raised objections on the grounds that he was misrepresenting the nature of these cases we have cited previously from the Old Testament?

Little wonder that the Savior could press his adversaries: "Which of you can convict me of sin?" (Jn. 8:46). Jesus endorsed, as historically credible, the most controversial events of the Old Testament record. How pitiable is the person who thinks he can do otherwise.

Chapter 13

Modernism's Assault on Biblical Miracles

> *"But Thou art true, Incarnate Lord!*
> *Who didst vouchsafe for man to die;*
> *Thy smile is sure, Thy plighted Word*
> *No charge can falsify."*
> — William Wordsworth (1770–1850)

The design of miracles in biblical times was to establish as true the claim and/or message of the one demonstrating the supernatural power. At the beginning of his ministry, Jesus performed miracles to confirm his affirmation that the kingdom of God was near. Later, his claim of being the Son of God was shown to be reliable by the signs that he did (Jn. 5:19–29). When the apostles proclaimed that Jesus was the promised Messiah, their message was verified by the mighty works they demonstrated (see McGarvey 1910, 353ff). Any attack upon the miracles of the New Testament, therefore, is an assault upon the claims and authority of Christ himself. The liberal who rejects the biblical miracles likewise repudiates the Savior.

MODERNISM'S APPROACH TO MIRACLES

The modernist rejects miracles on the supposition that they are unscientific. The late professor J. Gresham Machen, a conservative scholar who taught at Princeton Theological Seminary, described this situation in the following way:

> Science, it is said, is founded upon the regularity of sequences: it assumes that if certain conditions within the course of nature are given, certain other conditions will always follow. But if there is to be any intrusion of events, which by their very definition are independent of all previous conditions, then, it is said, the regularity of nature upon which science bases itself is broken up. Miracle, in other words, seems to introduce an element of arbitrariness and unaccountability into the course of the world (1923, 101).

The Christian denies, of course, that miracles are arbitrary. They are not intrusions into nature. Nature, admittedly, and necessarily, proceeds according to a set of natural laws. Moreover, these laws indicate a Law-giver. There is nothing at all unreasonable in concluding that the Law-giver might, consistent with his own purposes, suspend natural laws and/or subject them to the workings of higher laws. Professor G. H. Clark expressed this point quite well:

> When . . . one adopts a view of the world as God's creation, and when God is regarded as a living, acting, personal Being, the appropriateness of miracles depends upon God's purposes. In such a theistic world-view, where God desires to have some converse with mankind, the occurrence of miracles is no longer an anomaly (1975, 249).

It is the ambition of the modernist to emasculate the supernatural events of the Bible of their miraculous nature. Rudolf Bultmann, who was skeptical of the historical reliability of the Gospel accounts, called the process "demythologizing" the New Testament. What he proposed to do was to separate the chaff of myth from the reality of truth in the New Testament documents. What really happens, of course, is that these theological infidels simply filter the Bible through their own biased minds, accepting what they deem to be consistent with modern "science" and rejecting all else. Historical evidence is flung to the wind. It is as if it does not exist.

However, modernistic attacks upon the miraculous elements of the New Testament often tax the credulity of the inquiring student much more than a simple faith in the incredible power of Almighty God. As we cite examples of the liberal approach to a few of the miracles of Christ, it will become apparent how distant such viewpoints stray from the available inspired data.

In the following cases, I am going to direct the reader's attention to the testimony of noted Scottish scholar, William Barclay, and his approach to the miracles of Christ. He attempted to dismiss a number of them as perfectly natural events, erroneously interpreted as supernatural by those who are naïve and inept at seeing the true picture. Yet, not even he could escape the conclusion that some of Jesus' signs are impossible to dismiss. Note his testimony:

> It is claimed that certain miracles of Jesus are susceptible of a perfectly natural explanation. That is true. In the raising of Jairus's daughter all three gospel-writers who tell the story agree that Jesus said that the little girl was not dead but asleep. . . . But when all is said and done along that line, it is quite impossible to rationalize **all** the miracles.

There will always remain a stubborn residue beyond the mind of man to understand or to explain (1976, 13–14; emphasis in original).

We will, therefore, "analyze" some of Professor Barclay's "analyses," and see whether they survive.

JAIRUS'S DAUGHTER

A certain ruler had a young daughter (twelve years old) who was seriously ill, even at the point of death. The gentleman sought out Christ and petitioned him to come and restore the child to life. Jesus followed him to his residence in the company of his disciples, as well as a crowd that pursued them. On the way, the company was approached by messengers from the ruler's house who informed the father that his daughter had died. While some languished under the conviction that all hope now was gone, the Lord uttered words of comfort, encouraging them not to fear, but to have faith in what he could do. Cryptically, the "great Physician," declared, "She is not dead; only asleep." Of course the skeptics laughed. Dismissing all others except family members and close friends, the Savior took Peter, James, and John and entered the room where the sweet girl's body lay. He then addressed the corpse: "Little girl, arise" (ESV). Immediately the girl arose and walked (Mk. 5:42).

Let us consider the following basic facts of the case as set forth in Matthew, Mark, and Luke's records (Mt. 9:18–19; Mk. 5:21ff; Lk. 8:40ff): (a) The little girl's father, a ruler—not an ignorant bumpkin—came to Christ, begging him, "My daughter is even now dead: but come and lay your hand upon her, and she will live" (Mt. 9:18). Mark's account, which is the most extensive (a third longer than Matthew's), adds another detail. The ruler reported that the child was "at the point of death" (5:23). Some claim a discrepancy in the two records.

A fair approach would suggest that Mark, speaking comprehensively and literally, represents the ruler's anticipation of the child's imminent death as he left to find Jesus, while Matthew, abbreviating the record, reflects the father's fearful conviction that by the time he arrives, she is dead. Such literary condensation, in both ancient and modern literature, is not at all uncommon (cf. Mt. 8:6; Lk. 7:2). (b) That the child was actually dead, and not in a coma, is evidenced by the fact that multiple persons brought the news to the ruler that the girl in fact was dead (Mk. 5:35; Lk. 8:49). A funeral entourage was assembled already, with musicians and mourners (Mt. 8:23; Mk. 5:38). Luke, a physician (Col. 4:14), and first-class historian who had collected the facts (Lk. 1:2–3), emphatically declared that when Jesus instructed the maiden to arise, "her spirit returned and she rose up immediately" (Lk. 8:55; cf. Gen. 35:18; Jas. 2:26).

When the Savior said, "The damsel is not dead, but is sleeping" (Mt. 9:24; Mk. 5:39; Lk. 8:52), he spoke figuratively, in anticipation of what he was about to do. Though she was literally dead, Jesus viewed her as already alive again; thus her body, in a manner of speaking, was merely sleeping, for it would "awaken" momentarily in the bloom of health! Christ knew what he could do and would do! He therefore used extraordinary language to express his purpose. To interpret the text otherwise is to be wholly irresponsible and reveal a subversive motive.

FEEDING THE MULTITUDE

Each of the Gospel narratives contains the account of the miraculous feeding of a great multitude as the Lord taught near the city of Bethsaida on the northeastern shore of the Sea of Galilee (cf. Mt. 14:13–21; Mk. 6:32–44; Lk. 9:10–17; Jn. 6:1–14). Upon hearing of the death of John the baptizer, the Savior departed by boat to a place of solitude. The crowds anticipated his destination and pursued in haste. Christ was moved with compassion; he taught them and healed their sicknesses throughout the day. The twelve disciples urged the Master to send the crowds away from this deserted place so that they might obtain food and lodging in nearby villages. The Lord, though, received from a boy five barley loaves and two fish, and therewith he fed five thousand men (in addition to women and children) to their complete satisfaction. Afterward, twelve baskets full of fragments were gathered up.

A classic example of the liberal approach to miracles is seen in Barclay's assessment of this incident. The former professor of divinity and biblical criticism at the University of Glasgow, wrote:

There are three ways in which we can look at this miracle.

(a) We may look at it as a simple multiplication of loaves and fishes. That would be very difficult to understand; and it would be something that happened once, and which never in this world repeated itself; but if we regard it that way, then let us be content, but let us also not be critical and condemnatory of anyone who feels that he must find another way. [In other words, be tolerant of the liberal approach, which rejects it as a miracle.]

(b) Many people have seen in this miracle a sacrament. They have felt that those who were present received only the smallest morsel of food, and yet with that food were strengthened for their journey and were content. They have felt that this was not a meal where people sat and glutted their physical appetite; but that it was a meal where they ate the spiritual food of Christ.

(c) There are those who have seen in this miracle
     something which is perfectly natural, and yet
     which in another sense is a real miracle, and
     which in any sense is very precious. [Don't you
     just love the way modernists speak of the "natu-
     ralness" of the supernatural? It becomes increas-
     ingly obvious that Barclay's use of the term
     "miracle" is not at all consistent with the biblical
     usage.] Picture the scene. There is the crowd; it is
     late; and they are hungry. But was it really likely
     that the vast majority of that crowd would set out
     across the lake without any food at all? Would
     they not take something with them, however lit-
     tle? Now it was evening and they were hungry. But
     they were also selfish. And no one would produce
     what he had lest he had to share it and he himself
     had not enough. Rather than share their scanty
     provisions they kept them in their wallets. Then
     Jesus took the lead. Such as He and His disciples
     had, He began to share with a blessing and an
     invitation and a smile. And thereupon all began
     to share, and before they knew what was happen-
     ing, there was enough and more than enough for
     all (1957, 113–114).

In a startling display of infidelity, Barclay has brutally
ravaged the New Testament record. Those who believe in the
reliability of the biblical accounts have no difficulty at all in
regarding the event as a supernatural multiplication of loaves
and fish—viz., a real miracle. Such a view is much easier to
harmonize with the Gospel narratives than the fantastic
alternatives suggested by Barclay. Let us carefully analyze his
two substitute theories in light of the Scripture accounts.

The "Pinch" Theory

The curious view that each person in this crowd received only a "sacramental" pinch is remarkably at variance with the recorded facts. Consider the following details as recorded in the Gospel accounts. (a) The crowd was tremendously large; since the men alone numbered five thousand, the multitude of men, women, and children would have been considerably greater. (b) According to the divine record (and that is all we have to go on), a minute amount of food was the source of this bountiful meal; it was the small lunch of a small boy. (Note: in the Greek Testament, both "fishes" and "lad" are diminutive, meaning a small lad with his little lunch.) (c) Yet remarkably, the entire multitude was said to have been "filled." "Filled" is from the Greek *empiplemi*, which means to "fill full, satisfy." (d) Philip, one of the Lord's apostles, had complained that two hundred pennyworth (about six months' wages for a working man) would not be enough to buy sufficient food for such a large crowd, even if each took only a "little" (Jn. 6:7). It almost seems as if the Holy Spirit anticipated the "pinch" argument. (e) Moreover, twelve full baskets remained—more than the initial amount! The "sacramental pinch" theory, therefore, simply does not fit the New Testament data.

The "Greed" Theory

If anything, this position is even more incredible than the first. It is suggested that in reality, the people had food but had concealed it. They were greedy. What a baseless assumption and unwarranted charge against these first-century folks. In response, consider the following. (a) The disciples, who were in a better position to know what happened than some modern skeptic, said: "They have nothing to eat" (Mk. 6:36). (b) The Scriptures specifically indicate that many in the multitude had left their villages in haste (Mk. 6:33); and likely, therefore, without the necessary time for the preparation of food. (c) It is difficult to see how the distribution of one small boy's lunch could have been of sufficient prominence to precipitate a sharing among the thousands present, who, according to Barclay, were inclined to selfishness anyway. (d) Finally, there is that inexplicable twelve baskets full. Sharing could hardly account for that.

The miracle stands!

WALKING ON THE WATER

The incident of Jesus walking on the surface of the Sea of Galilee is recorded by three of the Gospel writers—Matthew (14:24–36), Mark (6:47–56), and John (6:16–21). Jesus had crossed to the eastern side of the Sea of Galilee. After the miracle of feeding the multitude with the loaves and fish, Christ retired to a nearby mountain for solitude and prayer, and the disciples departed across the lake in a boat. They were about halfway across the sea (Mt. 14:24), about three or four miles from shore (Jn. 6:19). It was between three and six a.m. (Mk. 6:48), and the unpredictable sea, recessed in the Jordan Valley (approximately six hundred feet below sea level), became tempestuous.

Presently, the Lord approached the tossing vessel. Each of the writers declared that he was "walking on" the water. The Greek preposition that describes the Savior's relationship to the water is *epi*, "on, upon,"—not "in" or "beneath the surface" of the water. This is important to remember. Professor Wuest once called attention to the significance of this.

> The preposition *epi* when used with the genitive case means "contact." John 6:19 reports our Lord as walking upon the sea. *Epi* with the genitive [case] is used here. Our Lord's sandals actually had contact with the surface of the sea, as our shoes have contact with the hard pavement upon which we walk (1946, 71; emphasis added).

It would be best to say that *epi* is usually rendered "on" or "upon." File this away momentarily.

Now assemble the following. This Master encountered the disciples about half way across the sea. The sea is about one hundred sixty-five feet deep at its maximum. He was walking "upon" the surface of the sea. These are the indisputable facts of the case.

Again we will consider the rationalization of the distinguished Professor Barclay for an example of a bizarre approach to the sacred text. He begins with his usual attempt to disarm the reader in view of the radical interpretation he will pose.

> This is one of the most wonderful stories in the Fourth Gospel, and it is all the more wonderful when we press behind it to the original meaning of the Greek and the original incident, and when we find that it really describes, nor some extraordinary miracle, but a simply incident in which John found, in a way that he never forgot, what Jesus was like (1956a, 210).

The esteemed scholar then says that what the Greek actually means is that "Jesus was walking on the seashore" (212). He cites John 21:1 where the preposition *epi* is rendered (and correctly so) "at" (ASV) the sea, or "by" the sea (ESV). He thinks this establishes the fact that Jesus was merely walking on the beach. The preposition *epi* is found in the New Testament some 219 times with the genitive. In the common version, it is rendered "on" or "upon" 109 times. It is translated "at" (as in John 21:1) six times, and this is because the context requires it. The utter folly of Barclay's egregious misinterpretation can be illustrated by the following paraphrase parody.

And when the disciples saw him walking on the beach, they were troubled, saying, "It is a ghost!"; and they cried out for fear. But instantly Jesus spoke to them, saying "Be of good cheer; it is I; be not afraid." And Peter answered him and said, "Lord, if it is you, invite me come unto you upon the beach." And he said, "Come." And Peter went down from the boat, and walked upon the sand to come to Jesus. But when he saw the wind, he was afraid; and beginning to sink [in the sand], he cried out, saying, "Lord, save me." And immediately Jesus stretched forth his hand, and took hold of him, and said unto him, "O you of little faith, why did you doubt?" And when they were gone up into the boat [which was now on the beach], the wind ceased (Mt. 14:26–32).

If I may borrow from Barclay's vocabulary, "wonderful!"; wonderful indeed! It is "full of wonder" that anyone could so massacre the sacred text of the word of God and expect reasonably intelligent people to be gullible enough to fall for it!

These rationalistic theories, when carefully considered, are found exceedingly barren. Let it be stressed again—faith in the power of God is not nearly so imposing as some of the modernistic views that are calculated to subvert the Scriptures.

Chapter 14

The Vocabulary of Biblical Criticism

"The Bible is no mere book, but a Living Creature,
with a power that conquers all that oppose it."
— Napoleon Bonaparte I (1769–1821)

Approaches that men take regarding the Bible vary radically. Several terms have been coined to depict the divergent viewpoints that are entertained with reference to these divergent concepts, and the careful student would do well to familiarize himself with the vocabulary common to such issues.

Biblical study may be viewed in terms of four major categories—critical, historical, exegetical, and theological. Let us give brief consideration to each of these areas.

CRITICAL STUDY

Critical study pursues several aspects of biblical concern. It addresses which books do or do not belong in the volume of sacred literature. What is the evidence for such in terms both of internal and external considerations? What is revealed in the actual text of the Bible itself, and what is the testimony of history as to the sifting process that distinguishes the genuine from the spurious? This approach deals with such issues as authorship, date of writing, circumstances that precipitated the composition, the audience addressed, and specific subjects surveyed.

HISTORICAL STUDY

The historical approach attempts to integrate the biblical text into the flow of the ancient past. The early period of human existence, the selection and isolation of the Hebrew people as a distinct nation, and their unique role in the divine scheme of redemption are of paramount importance. The influence of various nations upon Israel, and the Hebrew impact upon others, are crucial to the understanding of Scripture. The birth and life of Jesus Christ, as well as the establishment of his spiritual regime, are integral elements of biblical appreciation.

EXEGETICAL STUDY

The term "exegesis" derives from a compound Greek term literally signifying "to lead out." The original word is rendered "declared" in John 1:18, where it is indicated that the incarnate Christ, in a manner of speaking, functioned as a "commentary," thus "leading forth" the meaning of what God is like as viewed in human form (cf. Phil. 2:5ff). The Son of Man became the "exegete" of the divine nature.

With reference to the text of the Bible, legitimate exegesis accepts the testimony of the biblical writers as empowered by the Spirit of God (Mt. 22:31; Acts 1:16; 1 Cor. 2:13; 2 Tim. 3:16–17; 2 Pet. 1:21). The true exegete, therefore, studies the words, phrases, and clauses of sacred Scripture with a determined resolution to know the precise will of God, and make application of it to his life.

THEOLOGICAL STUDY

Legitimate theology begins with the premise that "all scripture is inspired of God" (2 Tim. 3:16) and is, therefore, harmonious.

The consistency of divine revelation implies that sources of information dealing with a similar theme may be gathered and systematized into a useful body of information for the enlightenment of the student and the enhancement of his journey to heaven. The careful scholar recognizes that the revelation will be progressive, i.e., with the passing of time (from the Old Testament era to the New Testament period) the information becomes more comprehensive and transparent (cf. 2 Tim. 1:10). In the final analysis, therefore, it is profitable to study the Bible thematically to ascertain the Mind of God on a particular subject.

RADICAL CRITICISM

Clearly there is value in employing legitimate principles of "historical criticism" in order to determine the authenticity of ancient documents. By this process early scholars were able to distinguish the genuine books of the Bible from apocryphal (spurious) works. Sometimes this process is classified as "lower criticism."

With the passing of time (eighteenth and nineteenth centuries), however, the disposition and methodology of the "critical" procedure became radically altered. In Europe certain scholars began to argue that many errors, both deliberate and unintentional, had corrupted the biblical documents. This ideology became known popularly as "higher criticism." This school of thought operated on the premise that the Bible is not the inspired word of God, but merely an ancient body of literature that could and should be treated as any antique piece of writing because it was characterized by all the frailties of human composition. Such humanistic approaches to the Scriptures are variously labeled as "radical criticism," or "destructive criticism." Other descriptive terms have been employed as well, e.g., "modernism" or "liberalism." Elsewhere in this work, see the chapter on "Destructive Criticism and the Old Testament."

LIBERAL THEOLOGY

"Liberal theology" grew out of a combination of highly presumptive attitudes. One was a resistance to authority. The liberal theologian is "suspicious of authority" and labors under the illusion that man is more autonomous than he is subservient. "Freedom of thought" became a catchphrase that empowered a rebellion against the older conviction of a static and infallible revelation of God as codified in the documents of Scripture.

The former "orthodoxy" came to be viewed as irrational, and gave way to the "refreshing relevance" of human "freedom" and independent "religious experience." Thus the authoritative Christ evolved into a mere figure of "love," and the biblical books a collection of principles containing pockets of time-tested truth, but certainly not a book of divine law.

MODERNISM

"Modernism" is yet another term that was coined to define a decided departure from the Bible's claim of divine authority. While both liberalism and modernism share a common bond, many would distinguish the two in some particulars. Some would contend that all modernists are liberals but not all liberals are modernists. Modernists would be viewed as the more radical, though in reality they are both cut from the same rationalistic cloth. Their difference is perhaps one of degree, and not of kind.

What is the prevailing sense of modernism? The history of "Christendom" for the past twenty centuries has been characterized by cycles. One of those recurring cycles is that of theological modernism. Modernism is a determined effort on the part of those who have lost their personal faith in the divine origin of the Holy Scriptures to convince others of their impoverished views. For more than a century, modernism,

in a very concerted fashion, has gnawed at the vital organs of
the "Christian" movement. Following are some of the traits
of theological modernism.

Modernism and the Nature of God

Modernism repudiates the biblical description of the nature
of God. The God of the Old Testament is seen as a hateful deity
of vengeance, and thus is rejected. Albrecht Ritschl (1822–89),
for example, rejected the biblical affirmations regarding
Jehovah's holiness and wrath and viewed the Lord solely as a
being of love. This view ignores the justice of God, disdaining
the proposition that Jehovah will punish the rebel.

Modernism and the Creation Account

Modernism attacks the scriptural account of creation, suggesting
that the Mosaic record is simply an ancient "myth" (cf. Simpson
and Bowie 1952, 460ff). It denies that man has fallen from his
holy estate; rather, it asserts that humanity has actually ascended
from a brutish past (via the evolutionary process) to its current
status. Lutheran theologian Helmut Thielicke declared that
he was not embarrassed to confess that his grandfather was a
monkey and his great-grandfather a tadpole.

Modernism and Higher Criticism

Modernism adopts the "higher critical" attitude towards the
Bible, that ignores the testimony of Scripture itself. For example, it is claimed that Moses did not author the Pentateuch,
as both Old and New Testament evidence indicate; rather,
supposedly, the first five books of the Bible are but a compi-
lation of certain documents that are code-named J, E, P, D—
the initials signifying "Jehovah," "Elohim," "Priestly," and
"Deuteronomic"—designations for the alleged authors or
editors who lived at a much later period of history.

Modernism and Biblical History

Modernism contends that the Bible, as an historical record, is not trustworthy. Advocates of this viewpoint do not hesitate to assert that the Scriptures contain a host of errors of a considerable variety. They believe that the basis of the biblical record is an ancient legendary tradition that is fraught with self-contradiction and a mixture of historical and scientific errors.

Modernism and Miraculous Events Recorded in Scripture

Modernism seeks to "de-mythologize" the Scriptures. Anything of a miraculous nature must be rationalized away as having a natural explanation, perhaps inexplicable from the modern vantage point. According to this ideology, for example, Jesus did not walk upon the waves of the Sea of Galilee; instead, he was merely strolling in the shallow surf near the coast, and the disciples, from a distance, imagined he was upon the surface of the sea. See the chapter, "Modernism's Assault on Biblical Miracles."

Modernism and Ethics

Modernism asserts that human conduct is not to be regulated by a "rule book," e.g., the Bible. Instead, one must personally make decisions on ethical issues, letting subjective "love" be the guiding principle in various situations. Joseph Fletcher's school of "situation ethics" has propagated this hedonistic ideology and such has been widely adopted by society. This ideology is occasionally known also as "contextual ethics."

Modernism and the Foundations of Faith

Modernism would plunge its rationalistic dagger into the very heart of the Christian system. For example, the New Testament affirmation that Jesus is the Son of God, born of a virgin, is rejected upon the premise that the supernatural birth was but "a symbol, expressing the confession" that

Jesus was a disclosure of the divine will. Neither was Christ raised bodily from the dead; the "resurrection" is not to be interpreted literally. Rather, one is "to live as if Christ were our contemporary," rather than endorsing the foolish notion that a first-century corpse was resuscitated from its tomb (cf. Harvey 1964, 153, 249).

There are, of course, additional modernistic traits that might be included, but these will suffice for the moment. It hardly needs to be pointed out that "modernism" is actually but another term for infidelity.

Theological modernism was technically set forth in the writings of such men as F. D. E. Schleiermacher (1768–1834) and A. Ritschl (1822–89). Later it was popularized in the works of men like Harry Emerson Fosdick (1878–1969). Fosdick, an American Baptist minister, authored some thirty books, including, *The Modern Use of the Bible* and *A Guide to Understanding the Bible*. He was significantly influential in the liberal movement that now ravages modern Protestantism. Many religious movements, to greater or lesser degrees, have been influenced by the insidious ideology of modernism.

FORM CRITICISM

Form criticism, as pertains to the Gospels, rejects the idea that Matthew, Mark, Luke, and John were actually written by the men whose names have been associated with the sacred books for many centuries—virtually from the apostolic age. Rather, this quasi-scholastic theory is based upon a "layered" concept of evolutionary document development. It begins with the presupposition that ancient writers commonly collected stories, legends, wise sayings, so-called miracle stories, etc. Subsequently these bits of data were arranged, supplemented, edited, etc., until ultimately a finished product resulted. It is a procedure that starts with a set of preconceived assumptions, and then fashions the New Testament documents into that mold. Form criticism generally repudiates the concept of the verbal inspiration of the Scriptures, and goes so far in some cases as to deny the professed apostolic authorship of some New Testament books, e.g., 1 Timothy, 2 Timothy, Titus, and 2 Peter.

The Two-source Theory

One category of form criticism is known as the two-source theory. This view alleges that the four Gospel narratives were not independently composed under the guidance of the Holy Spirit by Matthew, Mark, Luke, and John. The motive behind the concept is an attempt to explain the similarities and differences between the Gospel records, as if these varying details could not have been the result of each writer's thematic development under the guidance of the Spirit of God. The common view is that Mark wrote the first record and Matthew and Luke copied from him. Further, it is alleged that they likewise borrowed from a document called "Q" (which some allege derives from the German term, *Quella*, i.e., "source"). For a further discussion of this matter, see the chapter, "Radical Criticism and the New Testament."

PSEUDONYMOUS LITERATURE

The term "pseudonymous" derives from original roots that signify a "false name." There are ancient books that profess the authorship of great names (associated with both Old and New Testament eras) that obviously are false in attribution. For example, The Book (or books) of Enoch (I Enoch, II Enoch—late B.C. to early A.D.) have nothing to do with the Old Testament prophet of the same name. Neither does the Gospel of Peter, or the Gospel of Thomas bear any relationship to the apostles of Christ who bore those names.

Liberal critics, however, do not hesitate to classify some of the biblical books as pseudonymous. It is alleged, for example, that Moses did not write the Pentateuch (as both Christ and the New Testament writers indicated); rather, a core of early teaching was edited over the centuries that incorporated legends, folklore, and possibly Mosaic reminiscences, ultimately dating from the ninth to fourth centuries B.C. Also Isaiah, Daniel and other works similarly are alleged to be significantly pseudonymous. Literary surgery is likewise performed on certain New Testament books.

Churches of Christ are not without their own "critical predators" who assault the credibility of the biblical documents. A one-volume commentary from Abilene Christian University Press (Abilene, Texas) typically espouses "standard critical conclusions (multi-source Pentateuch, multiple Isaiahs, two-source hypothesis for the Synoptic Gospels)" etc., states Mark Hamilton, the editor-in-chief of the project (Hamilton 2006, 200–201).

Carl Holladay (a professor at Methodist-affiliated Emory University) contends that the books of Colossians, 1 Timothy, 2 Timothy, and Titus are post-Pauline, and 2 Peter likewise is pseudonymous, being classified as "transparent fiction"—an expression he apparently borrowed from Bauckham (see: Hamilton 2006, 196; Holladay 2005, 516; cf. Bauckham 1983, 134).

In his commentary on 2 Peter, Burton Coffman has an excellent essay titled: "Excursions on NT Criticism." It is a clear and forceful expose of the baseless presuppositions upon which the house-of-cards of higher criticism has been constructed. The ironical thing is, the same ACU Press that publishes Coffman's commentaries has now become the purveyor of the rankest forms of "critical" garbage. James once asked: "Does the fountain send forth from the same opening sweet and bitter water" (Jas. 3:11)? Apparently the "fountain" in Abilene does.

Literary criticism, properly employed, is a helpful tool to the devout Bible student. Egregiously abused, as so often is the case, it becomes a weapon of infidelity that guts the sacred library, leaving it a soul-less literary graveyard.

Chapter 15

Radical Criticism and the New Testament

> *"Mark you this, Bassanio:*
> *The devil can cite Scripture for his own purpose.*
> *An evil soul, producing holy witness,*
> *Is like a villain with a smiling cheek,*
> *A goodly apple rotten at the heart."*
> — William Shakespeare, *The Merchant of Venice*

Most of the New Testament books have been attacked by radical critics at some time in the past—some more than others. The bases of such criticisms generally fall into two categories. First, it is alleged that there is not sufficient external evidence to warrant the acceptance of these documents as being what they claim, i.e., the work of an apostle or otherwise inspired person. Second, a common contention is that the writings contain contradictions, inconsistencies, unusual vocabulary, stylistic peculiarities, anachronisms, etc. We will briefly survey some of these matters.

THE SYNOPTIC RECORDS

To speak of the "Synoptic" Gospels is to refer to the writings of Matthew, Mark, and Luke. "Synoptic" means "to view together," the term being used of the first three Gospels due to their similar approach to Jesus and his ministry. John's Gospel is unique.

Many writers contend that two of the synoptic writers were less than original in their compositions. It is claimed that at least Matthew and Luke copied heavily from Mark and also from a fictional document called "Q," a symbol for the hypothetical "source" that supposedly lay behind both Matthew and Luke's Gospel narratives. There is no real evidence that such a document ever existed, though the idea has gained popularity over the past two hundred years and is vigorously advocated among liberal writers.

Here is one author's assessment of the matter:

> It is widely accepted that Mark's Gospel is prior to the others and that both Matthew and Luke made use of it. Matthew indeed made it his framework, adding supplements from his own private material and from a source [Q] which contained many of our Lord's sayings. Luke used this same source [Q] in combination with his own material (Ward 1978, 62).

Regarding this theory, the following brief observations may be made.

First, conservative scholars contend that the two-source view is assumptive and supported by no solid evidence, but is based merely upon the inferences of its advocates.

Second, it was influenced significantly by the theory of evolution, i.e., that the simple produces the more complex—a premise not supported by fact and frequently undergirded by the opposite order (cf. Thiessen 1955, 110–111).

Third, the theory was birthed in the early 1800s and is wholly unknown in the writings of the "church fathers."

Fourth, while Luke acknowledged his own investigation of eyewitness reports, and that he had "traced the course of all things accurately from the beginning" (Lk. 1:2–3), it is going much too far to suggest this text reflects the "stages" of form criticism as advocated by modern critics (cf. Carson, Moo, and Morris 1992, 20). As Barbieri observed, while the Gospel writers "may have used different sources" (e.g., genealogical records), "this is not what critical scholars mean when they talk about sources. Most critical scholars view the 'sources' as extensive writings which were joined together by skilled editors to produce their own accounts" (1983, 13). With reference to Luke's statement (1:2–3):

> It is evident that he is alluding to other documents than the Gospels we possess, both because he speaks of the writers as "many," in a tone scarcely consistent with the respect due to apostolic records, and because a comparison of the four Gospels leads to the conclusion that he could not have had any of the three others before him when he drew up his narrative (M'Clymont 1893, 26–27).

Fifth, no "Q" document has ever been discovered. If Matthew and Luke were so enthralled with "Q," and the early church so captivated thereby, why wasn't this crucial, more original source preserved?

Sixth, the Matthew, Mark, Luke, John document sequence is the order preserved in the vast majority of the ancient manuscripts and versions. Were these early lists unaware of the priority of Mark?

Seventh, the two-source theory flies "in the face of the testimony of the early Christian writers who had been in touch with the apostles or those instructed by them. The issue is history versus theory, facts versus presuppositions" (Foster 1971, 69). Foster's work on form criticism and the two-source theory (1971, 59–123) is must reading for the serious New Testament student.

Eighth, the utter confusion of the source critics, even those of a more conservative disposition, is evidence of the serious weakness of this theory. Note this concession:

> The two-source theory has been **appropriately dethroned** from the status of being an "assured result of scholarship." Nevertheless, properly nuanced, the two-source theory remains the best general explanation of the data (Carson, Moo, and Morris 1992, 32; emphasis added).

"Dethroned" yet the "best explanation"! What nonsense!

Ninth, the absolute conglomerate of confusion, in terms of who copied what from whom, is, in itself, a devastating reflection of the subjectivity of this relatively recent hodgepodge of critical quackery.

Tenth, since Matthew was an apostle of Christ, and Mark was not, why would it seem reasonable that the apostle would have needed to copy so extensively from Mark and "Q"? And why is there this insatiable passion to seek for sources simply because there are certain percentages of parallels or differences in the Gospel records? While it unquestionably is the case that a Gentile writer like Luke could have sought information from those who knew Mary, in the composition of the birth narrative regarding Jesus, or consulted genealogical records of Jesus' ancestry, why would it be necessary for either Matthew or Luke to significantly plagiarize either Mark or the elusive "Q"? Was the Holy Spirit orchestrating this affair? There are many things about the two-source theory that simply do not make sense.

THE GOSPEL OF JOHN

The Gospel of John has overwhelming support as a document produced by John the apostle near the end of the first century. Irenaeus (ca. 130–200 A.D.), for example, who knew Polycarp (ca. 69–155 A.D.), a disciple of John's, wrote that: "John, the disciple of the Lord, who also leaned upon his breast, did himself publish a Gospel during his residence at Ephesus in Asia" (*Against Heresies* III.1). The solitary exception appears to have been a heretical group of Asia Minor, called the Alogi, who attributed the Gospel account to a Gnostic false teacher named Cerinthus. In his famous work, *Ecclesiastical History* (ca. A.D. 324–325), Eusebius declared: "But of the writings of John, not only his Gospel, but also the former of his epistles, have been accepted without dispute both now and in ancient times" (3.24.1).

When the radical critics began to develop their theories regarding the fourth Gospel, they asserted that the document was not written until the mid-second century, and so could not have been composed by the apostle John. However, the John Rylands Papyrus Fragment (P51), published in 1936, and dated ca. A.D. 135:

> necessarily implies several previous decades for the writing, copying, and circulation of the fourth gospel as far as the Egyptian hinterland, where the fragment was discovered. Other very early papyri containing the text of John confirm the implication of the Rylands Fragment (Gundry 1981, 99).

ACTS OF THE APOSTLES

Liberal critics of the Bible have frequently alleged that Acts is not a reliable document from the standpoint of history. F. C. Baur (1792–1860) of Germany popularized this view more than a century ago. This notion, however, has been thoroughly discredited.

Sir William Ramsey (1851–1939), a British scholar, initially questioned the historicity of Acts, but after years of literally digging up the evidence in archaeological explorations, Ramsey became convinced that Acts was so remarkably accurate in its details that the whole of it must be considered trustworthy. He wrote:

> I had read a good deal of modern criticism about the book, and dutifully accepted the current opinion that it was written during the second half of the second century by an author who wished to influence the minds of people in his own time by a highly wrought and imaginative description of the early Church. His object was not to present a trustworthy picture of facts in the period about A.D. 50, but to produce a certain effect on his own time by setting forth a carefully coloured account of events and persons of that older period. He wrote for his contemporaries, not for truth (1979, 37–38).

After much investigation, though, Ramsey wrote:

> The present writer takes the view that Luke's history is unsurpassed in respect of its trustworthiness. At this point we are describing what reasons and arguments changed the mind of one who began under the impression that the history was written long after the events and that it was untrustworthy as a whole (1979, 81).

J. B. Lightfoot (1828–1889) was one of the greatest scholars of his day. Fluent in seven languages, he made vast contributions to the literature of the New Testament. In one of his works defending the supernatural character of the New Testament, he said of the book of Acts:

> [N]o ancient work affords so many tests of veracity; for no other has such numerous points of contact in all directions with contemporary history, politics, and topography, whether Jewish, Greek, or Roman (1889, 19–20).

In more recent times, Henry J. Cadbury, the liberal scholar of Harvard University, authored a volume titled, *The Book of Acts in History*, in which he introduced many examples of the amazing accuracy of Luke's second letter to Theophilus.

Luke records an abundance of details, and this allows the careful student to check the ancient historian for credibility. For instance, the physician-historian mentions thirty-two countries, fifty-four cities, and nine Mediterranean islands. In addition, he alludes to ninety-five different people, sixty-two of which are not mentioned by any other New Testament writer. Twenty-seven of these are unbelievers, chiefly civil or military officials (Metzger 1965, 171–172). The book of Acts will definitely stand the test of historical examination.

SOME EPISTLES OF PAUL

The epistles of Paul have not escaped the jaded analyses of the hostile critics. We will cite but a few examples as illustrations of the arrogance of those who would buck the tide of history.

Colossians

Rudolf Bultmann (1884–1976) and others of his ilk began to assert that Paul was not the actual author of Colossians. The expression "deutero-Pauline" began to be employed to describe the epistle. The contention, now popular among radical critics, is that Paul had a connection with the book, but some unknown disciple of Paul's actually penned the letter. This view, utterly void of objective evidence, has grown in liberal circles for the last half century. This theory, then, ultimately forces one to the conclusion that the writer was a liar who misrepresented the truth when he claimed Pauline authorship in the opening line (1:1), and subsequently reaffirmed that authorship (1:23; 4:18—"I Paul . . ."). Holladay, with his own subjective critical surgery, contends that the differences between Colossians, and non-disputed Pauline letters, "are too great—at all levels—for the letter as we have it to have been written by Paul," at least in the sense in which he wrote Galatians or 1 Thessalonians (2005, 394). Elsewhere see our discussion on the so-called "pseudepigraphical" literature of the New Testament, in our chapter "The Vocabulary of Biblical Criticism."

The Pastorals

The term "pastoral" is a relatively modern expression, used of 1 Timothy, 2 Timothy, and Titus because of the emphasis in these letters on church administration. Radicalism more vigorously disputes Paul's authorship of these books than that of any of the apostle's other letters. From our commentary, *Before I Die—Paul's Letters to Timothy and Titus*, we take the liberty of incorporating the following material.

1 Timothy

Was Paul actually the author of this document, as claimed (1:1), or was some later writer, who forged the apostle's name to the letter, the real author? One modern writer says: "[T]he Pastorals, in large part at least, are pseudonymous; they belong to a later generation than Paul" (Gealy 1955, 343–344). Holladay quips: "Of all the letters attributed to Paul, the Pastorals are the least likely to have come directly from the pen of Paul himself" (2005, 421). Again, Holladay waves his magic wand of "language, style, and outlook," that segregates the Pastorals from the genuine epistles of the apostle. Supposedly the words are related to Paul's "spirit," but the text did not flow from his pen (2005, 423).

Aside from a couple of early heretical critics (e.g., Marcion and Tatian—late second century), whose bias against Paul's teaching was obvious, the Pauline authorship of 1 Timothy was not significantly disputed until the early part of the nineteenth century. There is ample evidence, both internally and externally, for the integrity of the letter.

Internally, the "fingerprints" of Paul are all over the epistle. For instance, who, but Paul, would have designated himself as a former "blasphemer," "persecutor," one who was "injurious," and still had the pangs of conscience to view himself as the "chief" of sinners (1:13, 15; note the "I am" of v. 15)? Additionally, there is the generous reference to personal names. These allusions are easily checkable and would not have been carelessly introduced by a forger.

Ancient external testimony is powerful as well. Externally speaking, several of the patristic writers appear to quote from, or refer to, this epistle. Ignatius (ca. A.D. 35–107) seems to refer to 6:1–2 (*Epistle to Polycarp* iv). Polycarp (ca. A.D. 69–155) reflects the language of 6:7, 10 (*Epistle to the Philippians* iv). The *Epistle of Barnabas* (ca. A.D. 70–100) seems to allude to 3:16 (xii), and Athenagoras (second century) appears to borrow Paul's expression "light unapproachable" from 6:16 (*A Plea for the Christians* xvi). Clement of Alexandria (ca. A.D. 150–215) quotes 6:20–21, and attributes it to "the apostle" (*Stromata* II.xi). He also cites "Paul" as the author of 4:1, 3, in his opposition to those who are anti-marriage (III.vi). Tertullian (ca. A.D. 160–220) refers to 1:18; 6:13, 20 as authored by "Paul" (*On Prescription Against Heretics* I).

Recent scholarship has noted that though some modern scholars question the authenticity of 1 Timothy (along with 2 Timothy and Titus), this fledgling view "does not correspond to any widely held opinion in antiquity" (Carson, Moo, and Morris 2005, 374). Mounce observes that all three documents "were widely accepted as authoritative and Pauline" by the end of the second century (2000, lxiv).

2 Timothy

As was the case with 1 Timothy so is it with 2 Timothy. The Pauline authorship of this document was scarcely disputed (except by a very few early heretics, e.g., Marcion and Tatian), until the early nineteenth century. Generally speaking, the same arguments employed against the genuineness of 1 Timothy are recycled for an indictment of Paul's second letter to his friend as well. A number of the patristic writers cite 2 Timothy with the same authority as they do the undisputed books of the New Testament.

For example, Clement of Rome, Ignatius, Polycarp, Justin Martyr, etc., cite the book. All three of the so-called "pastoral" epistles are listed in the Muratorian Canon (a catalog of the New Testament books dating from the late second century), and in the Old Latin and Old Syriac versions—in all manuscripts and versions, and in the same order as in our present New Testaments. Second Timothy has twenty-three personal references to Paul. Both internal and external evidence clearly establishes that Paul was the author of this document.

Titus

Did Paul actually write this epistle to Titus? Ever since the days of Johann Eichhorn (1752–1827), liberal critics have disputed the Pauline authorship of both the letters to Timothy and to Titus. Modernism varies in its approach to the authorship issue. The most radical of the radicals allege that Paul had nothing to do with these letters; rather, supposedly they were penned by anonymous, second-century writers. The more moderate modernists allow that some fragments were authored by Paul, but an editor(s) pieced the material together, combined with his own insertions. However, with a wide range of evidence, conservative writers forcefully contend for the strictly Pauline authorship.

In terms of external evidence, Clement of Rome (ca. A.D. 96) cites the book of Titus in 3:1; 2:10 (*Epistle to the Corinthians* ii, xxvi). Similarly, Ignatius seems to reference 1:14; 3:9 (*Magnesians* viii). Justin Martyr (A.D. 100–165) appears to allude to 3:4 (*Dialogue with Trypho* xlvii). Tertullian quotes 3:10–11 and declares that these are the words of Paul to Titus (*Prescription Against Heretics* vi).

It has been noted that the book of Titus is "included in all manuscripts, versions, and lists of the Pauline Epistles without exception" (White 1956, 76). "By the end of the second century they [Timothy and Titus] are firmly fixed in every Christian canon in every part of the empire and are never doubted by anyone until the nineteenth century" (Fee 1988, 23).

The internal evidence for genuineness is equally compelling. The multiple citations of personal names and places—matters easily open to examination in the days of late-apostolic era—provide a sense of authenticity. Forgers avoid such details like a plague. One of the chief problems to some is the modification of vocabulary in Timothy and Titus, from some of the apostle's other writings. But, as one writer has observed:

> vocabulary and turn of phrase can form no basis of argument in such a brief text. Vocabulary depends upon subject matter, and style can be a matter of transient mood, time at the writer's disposal, the audience addressed, and many other matters (Blaiklock 1972, 69).

An attorney, for example, may write three letters: one to a client regarding legal matters, another to a friend discussing a recent fishing trip, and a third to his wife who is away from him on a trip. The vocabulary and style will vary considerably in the three compositions. There is no historical or logical reason to deny that Paul wrote this letter.

SECOND PETER

> Every book in the New Testament is challenged by some one, as indeed the historicity of Jesus Christ himself is and the very existence of God. But it is true that more modern scholars deny the genuineness of II Peter than that of any single book in the canon.

So wrote A. T. Robertson in the introduction to Second Peter, as found in his *Word Pictures in the New Testament* (1930–33, VI.139). Nonetheless, the noted scholar, after careful consideration of all factors, concluded that "the Epistle is what it professes to be," namely a document penned by the apostle himself (144).

The external evidence for the genuineness of 2 Peter is not ample compared to that of the other New Testament books, but that is not to say it is insufficient. There are probable allusions to 2 Peter in the writings of the "church fathers" from the time of 1 Clement (A.D. 95) to that of Hippolytus (A.D. 180). Origen, near the beginning of the third century, refers to 2 Peter six times and identifies it as "scripture." The discovery of the third century Papyrus 72, which contains 2 Peter, demonstrates that the work was accepted in Egypt at a very early period (Green 1980, 13ff).

By the fourth century this letter had been debated vigorously by the scholars of the antique world—who were much closer to the evidence than the radicals of the today's society—and it was accepted throughout most of the ancient world, being acknowledged as genuine by both the councils of Hippo and Carthage. Professor Green notes how significant this was in view of the fact that spurious books were being rejected, e.g., the Epistle of Barnabas, 1 Clement, etc. (15). There are some logical reasons as to why 2 Peter took a bit longer to receive church approval, but ultimately did, while several other obviously spurious documents, with Peter's name falsely attached, were readily rejected. Even Jospeh Mayor, who disputed the authenticity of 2 Peter, was compelled to say that if one had only the external evidence, he would be inclined to concede that the epistle was genuine (1979, cxxiv).

Some scholars, based largely upon certain internal, subjective considerations (involving style and vocabulary use), cast 2 Peter into the mold of a work that falsely bears Peter's name. Holladay asserts: "The early church rightly saw Petcrine authorship of the letter as an easily recognizable, **transparent fiction**," but nonetheless embraced it as a work associated with the apostle (2005, 516; emphasis added). Different "styles" are said to characterize the two letters attributed to Peter.

The "style" argument was addressed as early as the time of Jerome (ca. 342–420), who suggested that such may have been due to the apostle's use of different transcribers (see 1 Pet. 5:12; cf. Rom. 16:22; 1 Cor. 16:21; Gal. 6:11; Col. 4:18; 2 Thes. 3:17). One must ever keep in mind that the Holy Spirit was overseeing the composition so that the inspiration and integrity of the sacred words (2 Tim. 3:16–17) remained intact. Even Mayor admitted that "there is not that chasm between them [the two epistles] which some try to make out" (1979, civ), and the style argument was his main reason for rejecting Peter as the author of the second letter!

That aside, a compelling case may be made for the similarity of vocabulary between 1 and 2 Peter; for example there are terms common to both letters but rarely found elsewhere. Note: "precious" (1 Pet. 1:7, 19; 2 Pet. 1:1); "virtue" (1 Pet. 2:9; 2 Pet. 1:3); "supply" (1 Pet. 4:11; 2 Pet. 1:5); "love of brethren" (1 Pet. 1:22; 2 Pet. 1:7); "behold" (1 Pet. 2:12; 3:2; 2 Pet. 1:16); "without blemish . . . without spot" (1 Pet. 1:19; 2 Pet. 3:14). Observe also parallel references to "the end of the age" (1 Pet. 1:5; 4:7; 2 Pet. 3:3, 10); "prophecy" (1 Pet. 1:10–12; 2 Pet. 1:19ff; 3:12); the flood (1 Pet. 3:20; 2 Pet. 2:5; 3:6), etc. Moreover, as one scholar has observed, "words used by the writer [of 2 Peter] are used almost exclusively by Peter in the Acts of Apostles," e.g., "obtained," "godliness," "unlawful," "day of the Lord" and, "wages of iniquity." "These [similarities] would seem to indicate that the speaker in Acts is the man who wrote this letter" (McNab 1954, 1143–1144).

Finally, there is this matter. The writer begins the letter with the declaration that it is the work of "Simon Peter, a servant and apostle of Jesus Christ" (1:1). It contains his affirmation that Christ specifically foretold the apostle's death (1:13–14; cf. Jn. 21:18ff). The author asserts that "we were eyewitnesses of [Jesus'] majesty" in the "holy mount" (1:16–18)—a reference to the events of the transfiguration. The "we" would include Peter, along with James and John—the latter two clearly being excluded as the authors (cf. Mt. 17:1ff).

If one contends that 2 Peter was written in the late first or early second century A.D., as Professor Holladay alleges, then the undeniable conclusion must be that the real author lied in his initial affirmation, together with the supporting historical allusions, when he attributed the composition to Peter, the apostle. If the book commences with deception, how would one know that anything in the document is trustworthy? There were early pseudo-writings attributed to Peter, e.g., the Gospel of Peter or the Apocalypse of Peter, but the character of the spurious documents was vastly inferior to that of 2 Peter (Hillyer 1992, 11).

British scholar David Wheaton has observed that the "pseudepigraphical" theory raises an important moral problem (1970, 1250). Paul himself condemned such a procedure (2 Thes. 2:2; 3:17). How could the early church acknowledge this book as canonical when it is characterized by multiple false attributions, and yet it lays such stress on holiness and truth? (1:3–4, 12; 3:11, 17). There is nothing more inconsistent than radical criticism!

There have been many able defenses of the genuineness of this work. Gundry confidently contends:

> Despite modern doubt, then, we may accept the final verdict of the early Church that shortly after the Apostle Peter wrote his first epistle and shortly before his martyrdom in A.D. 64, he wrote this second epistle which bears his name (1981, 335).

Thiessen firmly asserted that "the Christian earnestness, apostolic tone, and autobiographical allusions make it impossible to believe that the Epistle is spurious" (1955, 289).

Chapter 16

Destructive Criticism and the Old Testament

*"As our knowledge of nature and her laws has increased, so has
our knowledge of many passages of the Bible improved."*
— Matthew Fontaine Maury (1806–1873)

Dr. Richard E. Friedman, a professor of Hebrew and comparative literature at the University of California (San Diego), has attracted considerable publicity in recent years with his radical claim that Baruch, Jeremiah's scribe (Jer. 36:4), authored much of the Old Testament. Friedman's book, *Who Wrote the Bible?*, argues—on the basis of language analysis, structure, and the style of the book of Jeremiah (all subjective criteria)—that there are remarkable similarities between this document and several other Old Testament books.

He has concluded that not only was Baruch the author of Jeremiah's prophecies, but also major portions of other Old Testament books (e.g., parts of Deuteronomy, Joshua, and the books of Kings and Chronicles.) Moreover, the professor opines that no serious scholar today accepts Moses as the author of the Pentateuch (the first five books of the Old Testament). He suggests these documents were probably compiled in

Babylonia during the fifth century, by weaving together the work of two or three other authors.

Dr. Friedman's approach to the Old Testament is typical of the liberal twist of mind that has seized many religious teachers in the so-called scholastic community. It is fraught with ignorance—eclipsed only by arrogance—and is diseased with dishonesty.

HIGHER CRITICISM

The expression "higher criticism" has to do with the study of sources, times, and the authorship of ancient literary documents. Many of the biblical "higher critics" have been grossly influenced by German rationalism. Accordingly, they have been "destructive" in their approach to the study of the Bible. Their investigations have proceeded along lines buttressed with biased presuppositions that are grossly inaccurate, and which have been repeatedly and thoroughly discredited by reputable scholars.

Let us consider some of the bases upon which the destructive critical theories rest.

Higher Critics Deny the Miraculous

There is a denial of the miraculous elements of Scripture that results from naturalistic assumptions. The Bible is viewed as merely a collection of myths and legends. The accounts regarding the creation, the fall of man, the flood, etc., are, with a proverbial wave of the hand, dismissed from the realm of factual history. We are patronizingly told that these "charming stories" contain lessons for us, but are not to be understood as literal history. One writer, for example, has explained the Genesis record of creation as "something that never was, but always is." Such is the typical nature of modernistic mumbo-jumbo.

A classic example of this sort of perspective is found in *The Broadman Bible Commentary*. Therein Adam, the first man, is treated as a mere symbol of mankind, rather than as an historical person. Joseph Callaway of the Southern Baptist Theological Seminary writes: "If we rob Adam of his symbolic meaning and simply literalize him, then we reduce him to one historical individual for the anthropologist to study." Professor Callaway goes on to suggest that if this is our view of Adam, in reality, "We have lost man!" (1973, 47–48). Consistent with the foregoing suppositions, therefore, is the notion that there can be no such thing as "predictive prophecy" (since this would involve a miracle). No Old Testament character could have foretold the details of particular events—many years before their actual occurrence.

Characteristic of this mode of thought was the statement of Professor A. B. Davidson:

> The prophet is always a man of his own time, and it is always to the people of his own time that he speaks, not to a generation long after, nor to us (1902, 118).

Noted scholar J. A. Alexander of Princeton was quite correct when he observed that about the only matter upon which the critics really agree is that there simply "cannot be distinct prophetic foresight of the distant future" (1953, 24).

Consider this example: since the book of Daniel contains clear statements as to the fate of certain empires (e.g., Babylonian, Medo-Persian, Greek, etc.), it is alleged that the narrative could not have been penned by Daniel; rather, the document supposedly was authored by some unknown scribe of the inter-biblical era (ca. 167 B.C.).

Porphyry, a pagan philosopher of the late third century A.D., was the first to deny the genuineness of Daniel's prophecies. He wrote fifteen books against Christianity, the twelfth of which was intended to depreciate the predictions of the inspired

Daniel. But, as Jerome, an ancient scholar (ca. A.D. 348–420), once noted, such oppositions to the prophecies are:

> the strongest testimony of their truth. For they were fulfilled with such exactness, that to infidels the prophets seemed not to have foretold things future, but to have related things past (quoted by Newton 1831, 202).

A denial of Old Testament prophecy, of course, flies directly in the face of Jesus Christ. Without belaboring the point, we merely mention that the Lord affirmed the Old Testament prophets spoke and wrote about him (cf. Lk. 24:44; Jn. 5:39, 46–47). The destructive critics would indict Jesus as being a victim of the ignorance of his day—or else nothing more than a dishonest charlatan.

Evolutionary Influences

The higher critics, considerably influenced by Darwinism, assume that the biblical narratives developed along evolutionary lines. Harry Emerson Fosdick, a radical modernist, wrote:

> We know that every idea in the Bible started from primitive and childlike origins and, with however many setbacks and delays, grew in scope and height toward the culmination of Christ's Gospel (1924, 11).

It is argued, for example, that material which appears technical must be assigned a late date—even if a great variety of evidence reflects an earlier period of composition. Julius Wellhausen (1844–1918), a prominent leader in the critical movement, contended that the Israel of Moses' day could not have possessed a code containing the complicated civil and social laws that are reflected in the Pentateuch. Accordingly, the law necessarily must have arisen at a later date.

The discoveries of archaeology, however, have demolished that allegation. A number of law codes have been exhumed from the ancient past, i.e., the Sumerian systems of Ur-Nammu (ca. 2050 B.C.) and Lipit-Ishtar (ca. 1850 B.C.), the Akkadian laws of Eshnunna (ca. 1950 B.C.), and the code of Hammurabi (ca. 1792–50 B.C.). These systems, which were several centuries before Moses, were as technical as the Hebrew code (though the Mosaic Law is morally superior by far; Jackson 1999, 43).

It might be noted further that liberals of an earlier generation maintained that Moses could never have authored the Pentateuch, since the art of writing was unknown in his day. Never mind that the Bible clearly indicates otherwise (cf. Ex. 17:14). The claim was made that writing was invented only at about the time of David (ca. 1000 B.C.). Archaeological discoveries, of course, have long since dissolved such misguided charges (Jackson 1988, 30–32).

In his fascinating book, *History Begins At Sumer*, the late Dr. Samuel Noah Kramer, America's foremost Sumerologist, has shown in great detail that civilization, complete with schools, writing, etc., was an established fixture in the Mesopotamian world more than a thousand years before Moses was born!

But here is an important point that highlights the lack of integrity on the part of the critics: evidence for early writing was known already in the time of Wellhausen, but it was ignored in deference to the sacrosanct theory!

Reading Between the Lines

Based upon supposed literary "strata," or sources, critical theorists, through "comparative studies" (again, a highly subjective and speculative concept), have dissected certain biblical books according to alleged authors, times, etc.

The well-known Graf-Wellhausen school of thought, for instance, divides the Pentateuch into four basic documentary sources called J, E, P, and D. These segments supposedly represent Jehovistic, Elohist, Priestly, and Deuteronomic origins. For example, because certain divine names (e.g., "Jehovah," or "Elohim" [God]) are used in various portions of the Pentateuch, the critics assumed that such patterns must imply a variety of sources.

These scholars are totally dominated by the ideology that differences necessitate multiple authors. Such a notion is utterly ridiculous, and it has been demonstrated to be fallacious time and time again.

There now are known to exist numerous documents of antiquity—admittedly unified literary productions—which employ the use of alternate names as a form of stylistic relief. Kenneth A. Kitchen, of the School of Archaeology and Oriental Studies at the University of Liverpool, has discussed this matter in considerable detail in his book, *Ancient Orient and Old Testament* (1966, 120–125). He says that "major variations in style" are "universal in ancient texts whose literary unity is beyond all doubt" (125).

Professor Kitchen further declares that:

> even the most ardent advocate of the documentary theory must admit that we have as yet no **single scrap** of external, objective, i.e., **tangible**, evidence for either the existence or history of "J," "E," or any other alleged source-documents (23).

Even certain liberals have been forced to admit that the JEPD hypothesis is really without merit. For example, Umberto Cassuto, late professor at the University of Jerusalem, authored a work, *The Documentary Hypothesis*, in which he confessed the main arguments for this theory are "without substance."

He declared that the system is an edifice "founded on air," and that it is "null and void" (1961, 5, 100, 101).

Moses H. Segal, Professor Emeritus at the Hebrew University in Jerusalem, has written:

> [W]e must reject the Documentary Theory as an explanation of the composition of the Pentateuch. The theory is complicated, artificial, and anomalous. It is based on unproved assumptions. It uses unreliable criteria for the separation of the text into component documents (Otten 1965, 179).

There simply is no support for the documentary theories of the higher critics, and there is much evidence against them. A couple of examples should help clarify this matter.

HIGHER CRITICISM AND THE PENTATEUCH

The first five books of the Old Testament are designated as the Pentateuch. For many centuries these documents were generally regarded by Jews and Christians alike as the work of Moses. In relatively modern times (seventeenth century onward), the Mosaic authorship has been disputed by radical critics, though there is scarcely any unanimity among them as to time, place, or number of authors allegedly involved in the composition of these books. This fact alone reveals the weakness of this theory. Consider the following facts.

First, there is a smooth historical connection between the first five books of the Old Testament. In Genesis, there is a steady movement from the creation account, to the call of Abraham, to the arrival of Jacob's family in Egypt. Exodus, which relates Israel's deliverance from Egypt and the nation's reception of the Law, is connected to Genesis by the transitional conjunction "now these" (1:1 ASV), suggesting a continuation of the previous document. See also Leviticus 1:1 and

Numbers 1:1 (as reflected in the ASV), that contain similar verbal-form connections (cf. with 2 Kgs. 1:1; 2 Chron. 1:1).

Leviticus discusses the worship system (priestly regulations, etc.), while Numbers surveys the Hebrews' sojourn in the wilderness of Sinai. More than one hundred fifty times in the book of Numbers, God is said to have spoken to and/or through Moses. Deuteronomy sets forth the rehearsal of the Mosaic Law to the generation about to enter Canaan. The Pentateuch is not a discombobulated collection that is void of historical continuity.

Second, the critical Documentary Hypothesis is woefully at variance with the testimony of Jesus and his inspired New Testament penmen. The Lord rebuked the Jews for rejecting his identity, saying: "If you believed Moses, you would believe me; for he wrote of me. But if you believe not his writings, how will you believe my words?" (Jn. 5:46–47).

Elsewhere, referring to Exodus, Christ asked: "Have you not read in the book of Moses, in [the passage about] the bush, how God spoke to him . . .?" (Mk. 12:26). The expression, "law of Moses," is used by Luke to embrace the entire Pentateuch (24:44; cf. 16:31). Note also this question from Christ to the Jews: "Did not Moses give you the law?" (Jn. 7:19). No New Testament passage provides the slightest suggestion otherwise.

Peter, quoting from Deuteronomy, said, "For Moses truly said . . ." (Acts 3:22). In one of his defenses, Paul sums up the whole Old Testament under the expression, "the law of Moses" and "the prophets" (Acts 28:23; see also Rom. 10:5; 2 Cor. 3:15).

The foisting of the Documentary Hypothesis upon the Pentateuch is utterly without justification and an affront to the Lord Jesus Christ and the evidence within the New Testament. It is a reflection of "loose" souls who have been swayed by modernistic teachers.

HIGHER CRITICISM AND THE BOOK OF ISAIAH

The book of Isaiah receives its title from its illustrious author, Isaiah, the "prince of the prophets," who was probably the most renowned of the literary prophets of Old Testament fame. In Hebrew his name is *Yesha-Yahu*, meaning "Jehovah is salvation," a designation which actually sets forth the tone of this great document's message.

Isaiah, the son of Amoz (1:1), lived in Jerusalem with his "prophetess" wife and at least two sons (7:3; 8:3). He prophesied during the reigns of four kings of Judah—Uzziah, Jotham, Ahaz, and Hezekiah—for a period of some forty to sixty years, in the latter half of the eighth century B.C. (ca. 739–683 B.C.). His ministry occurred, therefore, some two centuries after the division between the kingdoms of Israel and Judah. His prophetic labors were concentrated in and around Jerusalem, while his contemporary, Micah, worked in the surrounding countryside (cf. Mic. 1:1). There is an ancient tradition that asserts that Isaiah ended his life in martyrdom—being sawn asunder in the reign of the evil king Manasseh. Could Hebrews 11:37—"they were sawn asunder"—be an allusion to this? No one knows for sure, but it certainly is possible.

Background of the Book

The years of Isaiah's ministry were characterized by both political and religious turmoil. The Northern Kingdom of Israel was dredging deeper and deeper into idolatry, despite the valiant efforts of prophets like Hosea and Amos, who sought to effect a return to the Lord (cf. Hos. 1:1; Amos 1:1). Israel would fall to the Assyrian Empire in 722/21 B.C., that pagan nation being used as the instrument of Jehovah's wrath to punish his people for their rebellion (cf. Isa. 10:5ff). It had appeared (from the human vantage point) that the Southern Kingdom might also succumb to Assyria, but Jehovah intervened and punishment upon Judah was delayed for awhile.

The dominant political power of Isaiah's day was Assyria, and this empire's oppression was felt in Palestine. Tiglath Pileser III (745–727 B.C.) had extracted heavy tribute from Menahem, king of Israel (cf. 2 Kings 15:17–22). In 733 B.C., he invaded the Northern Kingdom and deported many Israelites (2 Kings 15:29). The following year, Damascus, the capital city of Syria, fell under his assault. Shalmaneser V, son and successor of Tiglath Pileser, also invaded Israel. Samaria was besieged for three years, finally crumbling in 722 B.C., under the hands of Shalmaneser and his brother, Sargon II (Jackson 1988, 35–37).

During the reign of King Hezekiah (716–687 B.C.), Judah joined a coalition against Assyria led by Tyre and Egypt. Accordingly, in 701 B.C., Sennacherib, son of Sargon II, invaded Palestine. The account of his campaign against Judah is recorded in 2 Kings 18:13–19:37, and in Isaiah 36–37. Forty-six Judean cities were sacked and thousands of prisoners were taken. Jerusalem was threatened as well, but through the petitions of Hezekiah and Isaiah, the holy city was saved due to a great destruction that Jehovah visited upon the Assyrian army.

As Assyria loomed on the eastern horizon, so Egypt was a mighty force to the south. Judah was thus sandwiched between two powerful pagan forces. Languishing in the shadows of these ever-threatening empires, Judah was inclined to form alliances for her protection (cf. Isa. 30:1ff; 31:1ff; 36:6). The Lord's people desperately needed to learn, therefore, that "Jehovah is salvation"—protection derives from him, not from human military alliances. This point is forcefully stressed in this great book.

The social and religious conditions in Judah during Isaiah's ministry were in a sad state of disarray. It was an economically prosperous period, thus creating conditions that allowed considerable wealth for some, yet poverty for others. Corrupt government, land-grabbing, extortion, etc., were the order of the day. Luxury and laziness settled like a warm blanket over many. Drunkenness and sexual immorality were common. Too, pure religion was fading rapidly. Rather than influencing their neighbors with the lofty concept of the one, true, and holy God, the Hebrews were playing the harlot with the idolaters of that region. Pagan superstition and idol worship had invaded them like a plague. Moral and religious convictions were only a veneer. Even the leaders of the people were given to lust, greed, and drunken feasts. A careful survey of 2 Kings 15–20 will reveal the political, moral, and religious rot that engulfed the Jews of that era. The task of the true prophet in such a time would be difficult indeed, but Isaiah was equal to the assignment! When the Creator needed a man for this hour, the prophet was there with the noble response, "Here am I; send me" (Isa. 6:8).

The Unity of the Book

In relatively recent times the book of Isaiah has been embroiled in controversy concerning its authorship. Because of their infidelic bias against the concept of predictive prophecy, the so-called higher critics have doubted that Isaiah authored much of the narrative. T. K. Cheyne contended, for example, that scarcely any lengthy passage anywhere in the book could be the sole work of Isaiah. He alleged that the prophet's words would have been modified by editors in subsequent centuries (1899, 2.2193). In fact, Cheyne, and others of similar persuasion, have suggested that some eighty percent of the book cannot be credited to Isaiah.

Modern critics have generally supposed that the book of Isaiah falls into three parts. First Isaiah (chapters 1–39) contains the nucleus of Isaiah's ethical teaching, together with added supplements. Second Isaiah (40–54) allegedly was written by some unknown scribe in Babylon about 549–538 B.C. Finally, Third Isaiah (55–66), likewise anonymous, was penned in the fifth century B.C.

The denial of Isaiah's authorship of chapters 40–66 is based largely upon three assumptive premises. It is claimed that: (a) The historical background indicates that this section was written during and after the Babylonian captivity. (b) The major divisions supposedly reflect differences in style. (c) The theological emphases of the various sections differ. These claims are highly subjective and speculative, and, as a matter of fact, will not stand in the light of honest investigation. There is much evidence to support the unity of the entire book of Isaiah.

Internal Evidence

The internal evidence for the unity of the book of Isaiah may be summarized as follows:

First, there are historical indications within the book which place chapters 40–66 before the Babylonian captivity (see 40:9 and 62:2, where Jerusalem and other cities are still standing). It should be noted, though, in harmony with his intended purpose, Isaiah sometimes thrusts himself forward in spirit to the time of the captivity to give emphasis to his message. The critics ignore his prophetic stance. Moreover, in 6:11–13, a section admitted by all to be from Isaiah, there is a prophetic description of the captivity and return. The prophet even named his first son Shear-Jashub, which meant "a remnant shall return" (7:3). If the prophet's revelatory ability can be recognized in this early portion of the book, there should be no objection to the same gift that is evidenced later in the document.

Second, the argument based upon alleged stylistic differences is highly subjective. The fact is, language similarities are found throughout the narrative. The "highway" terminology is employed in the different sections (cf. 11:16; 19:23; 35:8; 40:3; 62:10). The expression "the Holy One of Israel," a title for God, is found only thirty-two times in the Bible. Twelve of these are in Isaiah chapters 1–39, and fourteen are in chapters 40–66. Arguments of a similar nature could be multiplied many times over (Martin 1985, 1030).

Third, analogous prophetic admonitions in the various portions of the book indicate that the same social and moral problems are being addressed. For example, the Jews' hands were "full of blood" (1:15), indeed, "defiled with blood" (59:3). Compare also 10:1–2 with 59:4–7.

Fourth, in the latter sections of the book, allegedly written in the Babylonian and post-Babylonian era, there are numerous references to Judah's idolatry (cf. 40:19; 44:14; 57:4ff; 65:2–4), and yet, it is well-known that the Hebrews did not practice idol worship after the fall of Jerusalem! This is demonstrated by the fact that though the post-Exilic prophets, e.g., Haggai, Zechariah, Ezra, Nehemiah, and Malachi, addressed a variety of other sins, they never mentioned idolatry. This is a clear indication that the latter portions of this book were not written during the Babylonian era.

Fifth, language symbolism in the latter segments of the book is drawn from geographical features that relate to Palestine, not Babylon. Note, for instance, that these idol-worshippers were slaying their children "in the valleys, under the clefts of the rocks" and "among the smooth stones of the valley" (57:5–6), which is descriptive of the torrent streams in Canaan, but not of the lazy canals in the flat alluvial soil of Babylon.

Gleason Archer Jr. was correct when he declared:

> There is not a shred of internal evidence to support the theory of a Second Isaiah, apart from a philosophical prejudice against the possibility of predictive prophecy (1962, 607).

External Evidence

In addition to the above, there are external evidences for the unity of the book of Isaiah.

First, for ages the unity of the book was accepted by Jews and Christians alike. The critical theories are only a couple of hundred years old. Even liberal writer A. B. Davidson admitted: "For nearly twenty-five centuries no one dreamt of doubting that Isaiah, the son of Amoz, was the author of every part of the book that goes under his name" (Robinson 1954, 59).

Second, there is no indication in the Septuagint (a Greek translation of the third century B.C.) that the book had a multiple authorship.

Third, the discovery of the Dead Sea Scrolls (1947), that contain an Isaiah manuscript, argues against the Deutero-Isaiah, etc., theories. For example, chapter forty (allegedly the commencement of Second Isaiah), begins on the very last line of a column which contains chapter thirty-eight, verse nine, through chapter thirty-nine, verse eight. Noted scholar Oswald T. Allis observed: "Obviously the scribe was not conscious of the alleged fact that an important change of situation, involving an entire change of authorship, begins with chapter 40" (1950, 40).

Fourth, the New Testament quotes more from the book of Isaiah than all other prophecies combined. There are 308 quotations from, or references to, Isaiah in the New Testament, and these involve forty-seven of the sixty-six chapters. The prophet is cited by name twenty-one times, and all three of the so-called divisions are credited to him. For example, in John 12:37–41, the apostle quotes from Isaiah chapter fifty-three and chapter six in the same breath, citing Isaiah as the author of both passages, even joining the two quotations together by saying, "Isaiah said again . . ." (12:39). It is impossible to deny the unity of Isaiah without reflecting upon the integrity of the New Testament record.

Finally, we might ask if Isaiah did not author the material in chapters 40–66 of that ancient work, just who did? It is incredible that the Hebrews would not have preserved their names, in view of the Jews' careful handling of the Scriptures. In some of the ancient Scripture collections, the books of Ezra and Nehemiah were bound together, yet the authorship of these two books was never confused. That such a gross tragedy should mysteriously occur in the case of the book of Isaiah is inexplicable. The case for the unity of the document is overwhelming!

A LEGAL TEST OF THE CRITICAL THEORY

The methodology of the higher critics was highlighted some years ago by an interesting case that proceeded through the Canadian and British court systems. The entire affair is set forth in G. M. Price's work, *Modern Discoveries Which Help Us To Believe* (1934, 57–58). Here are the facts:

A lady named Florence Deeks brought a suit in the Ontario courts against H. G. Wells and his publisher, the Macmillan Company. Allegedly, Wells had plagiarized a manuscript which Deeks had submitted to these publishers, and from which she claimed Wells had borrowed extensively in his celebrated book, *Outline of History*.

The defendants denied the charge, affirming that Wells's work had been done in England, and he had never seen Miss Deeks's manuscript. When the case went to court, Deeks employed D. A. Irwin, MA, PhD, professor of Old Testament language and literature at the University of Chicago, as an expert to show, in detail, the many ways in which her manuscript and Wells's book resembled one another.

Professor Irwin was delighted to oblige Miss Deeks, since, as he boasted, "this is the sort of task with which my study of ancient literature repeatedly confronts me, and I was interested to test out in modern works the methods commonly applied to those of the ancient world."

The legal test, however, was a devastating blow to the "critical" procedure. The judge dismissed the case, characterizing the analyses of Professor Irwin as "solemn nonsense." The jurist further said: "His [Irwin's] comparisons are without significance, and his argument and conclusions are alike puerile." In a word, the so-called critical method was judged to be just plain silly!

But the case was appealed to the Superior Court of Ontario, and then finally to the Judicial Committee of the Privy Council of England, the highest legal body of the British Empire. The judges announced that Dr. Irwin's arguments were "almost an insult to common sense," and they decried the "utter worthlessness of **this kind** of evidence."

HIGHER CRITICISM AND A PARODY

In order to expose the utter folly of the so-called critical methods, J. W. McGarvey authored (in 1893) a parody titled, "A Literary Analysis of an Ancient Poem." The hilarious satire throws a floodlight upon the absurdity of the critical ideology. The well-known poem, analyzed by Professor McGarvey, reads as follows:

> Old Mother Hubbard went to the cupboard,
> > To get her poor dog a bone.
> When she got there, the cupboard was bare,
> > And so the poor dog had none.

Pursuing the same sort of methodology as that employed by those who dissect the Bible into its alleged literary sources, Professor McGarvey presented the following parody of this nursery rhyme. (Note: we have paragraphed McGarvey's composition for easier reading.)

> In the uncritical ages of the past, this poem was believed to be the composition of a single person—a

very ancient English woman by the name of Goose. Whether we should style her Mrs. Goose, or Miss Goose, we have no means of deciding with certainty, for the stories which have come down to historical times concerning her are mostly legendary. It might be supposed that the title "mother" would settle this difficult question; but, as in certain convents of our day, venerable spinsters are styled Mother, so may it have been in the days of Goose.

But, leaving this interesting question as one for further historical inquiry, we turn to the poem itself, and by applying to it the scientific process of literary analysis, we find that the document did not originate, as our fathers have supposed, from a single author, but that it is a composite structure, at least two original documents having been composed within it by a Redactor. This appears from the incongruities between the two traditions which evidently underlie the poem.

One of these traditions represents the heroine of the poem, a venerable Mrs. Hubbard, as a benevolent woman, who loved her dog, as appears from the fact that she went to the cupboard to get him some food. If we had the whole story, we should doubtless find that she did this every time the dog was hungry, and as she surely would not go to the cupboard for the dog's food unless she knew there was some in the cupboard, we can easily fill out the story of her benevolence by assuming that she put something away for the dog when she ate her own meals.

Now, in direct conflict with this, the other tradition had it that she kept the dog "poor"; for he is called her "poor dog"; and, in keeping with this fact, instead of giving him meat, she gave him nothing but bones. Indeed, so extreme was her stinginess toward the poor dog that, according to this tradition, she actually put away the bones in the cupboard with which to mock the poor dog's hunger. A woman could scarcely be represented more inconsistently than Mrs. Hubbard was by these two traditions; and consequently none but those who are fettered by tradition, can fail to see that the two must have originated from two different authors.

For the sake of distinction, we shall style one of the authors, Goose A, and the other, Goose B. In these two forms, then, the traditions concerning this ancient owner of a dog came down from prehistoric times. At length there arose a literary age in England, and then R [Redactor] put together into one the accounts written by the two gooses, but failed to conceal their incongruities, so that unto this day, Mother Hubbard is placed in the ridiculous light of going to the cupboard when there was nothing in it; of going there, notwithstanding her kindness to her dog, to tantalize him by getting him a mere bone; and to cap the climax, of going all the way to the cupboard to get the bone when she knew very well that not a bone was there.

Some people are unscientific enough to think, that in thus analyzing the poem, we are seeking to destroy its value; but every one who has the critical faculty developed can see that this ancient household lyric is much more precious to our souls since we have come to understand its structure; and that, contradictory as its two source documents were, it is a blessed thing that, in the providence of God, both have been preserved in such a form that critical analysis is capable of separating and restoring them (1910, 34–36).

There have been many efforts across the centuries to destroy the integrity of the biblical record. Some attacks come from militant skeptics—who make no apology for their in-your-face assaults. Other efforts are more subtle. They issue from those who profess a friendship with the Scriptures, but who, in reality, are enemies as deadly as the rabid atheist. The conscientious Christian need not be distracted by their fanciful dreamings.

Chapter 17

How New Testament Writers Used the Old Testament in Their Teaching

> *"If God and His Word are not known and received, the devil and his works will gain the ascendancy. If the evangelical volume does not reach every hamlet, the pages of a corrupt and licentious literature will."*
> — Daniel Webster (1782–1852)

Older Bible scholars were fond of saying, "The New is in the Old concealed; the Old is by the New revealed." In this clever declaration they underscored the precious unity that binds together the two major divisions of the Bible.

One of the perplexing problems the Bible student encounters is exactly how the writers of the New Testament used quotations from the Old Testament as they made their proclamations and defenses of the gospel of Christ. Some critics have charged they were unethical, illogical, and erroneous, often misusing the Old Testament texts they cited. The accusation is false and it reflects more upon the critic than upon the sacred writers.

The Old Testament information incorporated into the New Testament documents is considerable. One scholar declared that some 295 separate references to the Old Testament are found in the new; these occupy some 352 New Testament passages. He further noted, however:

> If clear allusions are taken into consideration, the figures are much higher: C. H. Toy lists 613 such instances, Wilhelm Dittmar goes as high as 1,640, and Eugen Huehn indicates 4,105 passages reminiscent of Old Testament (Nicole 1958, 138).

Walter Kaiser thinks a more realistic approach would be to note the "introductory formulas" used by the New Testament writers that formalize the relationship between the Old Testament passages and their use by the New Testament writers. Citing H. M. Shires, he says that 239 New Testament passages are taken from 185 different Old Testament sources. If one includes "unacknowledged quotations," along with "rewording or paraphrasing" cases, there would be about 1,604 New Testament citations of 1,276 Old Testament texts (Kaiser 1985, 2–3). It is estimated that about ten percent of the New Testament has been taken from the Old Testament—either by direct quotations or general allusions.

Our versions of the Old Testament are based mostly upon what is called the Masoretic Text. The name is derived from a Hebrew term that signifies "traditionalist," which suggests the rigorousness with which the Jewish scribes sought to preserve the texts at their disposal. The discovery of the Dead Sea Scrolls in 1947, which thrust our knowledge of the Old Testament Scriptures back some one thousand years, revealed how faithfully the Hebrew text had been preserved and handed down. An example pertaining to the book of Isaiah is remarkable:

> Even though the two copies of Isaiah discovered in Qumran Cave 1 near the Dead Sea in 1947 were a

thousand years earlier than the oldest dated manuscript previously known (A.D. 980), they proved to be word for word identical with our standard Hebrew Bible in more than 95 per cent of the text. The 5 per cent variation consisted chiefly of obvious slips of the pen in variations in spelling (Archer 1964, 19).

To cite a specific example of the accuracy, one may compare the Masoretic text of Isaiah 53 with the same text in the Dead Sea Scrolls—and remember, the two are separated in time by approximately ten centuries.

> Of the 166 words in Isaiah 53, there are only seventeen letters in question. Ten of these letters are simply a matter of spelling, which does not affect the sense. Four more letters are minor stylistic changes, such as conjunctions. The remaining three letters comprise the word "light," which is added in verse 11, and does not affect the meaning greatly. . . . Thus, in one chapter of 166 words, there is only one word (three letters) in question after a thousand years of transmission and this word does not significantly change the meaning of the passage (Geisler and Nix 1986, 263).

A major version cited by the New Testament writers was the Greek translation (Septuagint—signified by LXX). This edition of the Old Testament was produced by Jews in Egypt in the third century before Christ.

LITERARY TECHNIQUES

In considering this theme of how the New Testament writers employed the Old Testament documents, two important preliminary points should be understood.

First, ancient writers did not use the literary devices common to our modern language, e.g., quotation marks, ellipsis periods, etc. Thus, their methods may be ambiguous to the modern reader who is unable to appreciate the literary modes of the past. But the writings of the New Testament authors were perfectly consistent with the stylistic practices of the world in which they lived, and even, to a significant degree, with the accomplished writers across the ages. Johnson catalogued an impressive array of evidence from the Greek classics establishing this point (1896, 92ff).

Second, the Holy Spirit, who inspired both Testaments, had the perfect right to employ quotations from the Old Testament as he willed. The quotations might be from either the Hebrew-Aramaic text, or from the Greek translation. The New Testament writers might make their own translation, or quote in whole or in part from an Old Testament text. They could cite passages precisely, or in an amended fashion—consistent with the divine purpose. The fact is, meanings that are more obscure in the Old Testament may more readily come to light by the Spirit's rendition in a New Testament context.

Scholars are not always agreed on the precise manner in which the New Testament writers are quoting or adapting the Old Testament texts in new settings. In his work, *Introduction to the Old Testament in Greek*, H. B. Swete contended that the major source of New Testament quotations was taken from the LXX (1914, 381–403). On the other hand, the United Bible Societies Greek text appears to suggest that the majority were derived from the Hebrew Scriptures. In their index of some 350 quotations from the Old Testament, only seventy-three are identified as coming from the LXX (cited by McLay 2003, 38).

An older writer, T. H. Horne (1780–1862), in his *Introduction to the Critical Study and Knowledge of the Holy Scriptures* (1841, vol. 2, part 1, chapter 4), suggested the following classifications.

Hebrew Text—(a) quotations exactly agreeing with the Hebrew (62); (b) quotations nearly agreeing with the Hebrew (62); (c) quotations agreeing with the Hebrew in sense, but not in words (23); (d) quotations that give the general sense, but which abridge or add to it (12); (e) quotations taken from several passages of Scripture (5); (f) quotations differing from the Hebrew but agreeing with the LXX (6); (g) quotations in which there is reason to suspect a different reading in the Masoretic Text, or that the apostles understood the words in a sense different from usual lexical definitions (16); (h) passages in which the Hebrew seems corrupted (8); (i) passages that are not quotations proper, but mere allusions (7).

Greek Text—(a) quotations agreeing almost verbatim with the LXX (74); (b) quotations from the LXX with some variation (47); (c) quotations agreeing with the LXX in sense, but not in precise wording (32).

Other—quotations which differ from both the Hebrew and the Septuagint, and may be taken from other translations, are merely paraphrased, or given a new translation by the inspired writers (23).

We introduce this material mainly for illustrative purposes to show that the cataloging is far from an exact science. Some of the classifications listed by Horne seem inconsistent or at least puzzling.

THE HEBREW TEXT

Matthew 2:15—"Out of Egypt did I call my son"—is directly from the Hebrew. In the LXX, the term is "children," not "son." Since the ultimate focus of the text is upon Christ, the Hebrew, by the use of the singular form, reflects a more appropriate usage.

In Matthew 8:17 the inspired apostle quotes Isaiah 53:4. Regarding the coming Messiah, the prophet wrote that he "took our infirmities and bare our diseases." On the other hand, the LXX has Isaiah saying, "He bears our sins and suffers for us." Matthew appeals directly to the Hebrew because Jesus "is speaking of miracles of healing," a fact which is obscured by the LXX (Johnson 1896, 26).

Note this prophecy from Isaiah: "Behold, my servant, whom I uphold; my chosen, in whom my soul delights: I have put my Spirit upon him; he will bring forth justice to the Gentiles" (42:1). The translators of the LXX did not translate; rather, they presented an interpretation that missed the messianic emphasis. Thus, in citing this text, Matthew goes back to the Hebrew text for the most part; he follows the LXX only in verse four, where he alters "law" to "name," thus emphasizing that the "name" of Jesus was fraught with the authority of law!

THE GREEK TRANSLATION

Professor Franklin Johnson wrote: "The quotations of the New Testament are not usually exact translations of the Hebrew; the majority of them are drawn from the Greek version called the Septuagint" (1896, 1). Not infrequently a New Testament writer will quote the LXX instead of the Hebrew because he is making a special point that the Greek amplifies.

The author of Hebrews quotes from the LXX in a prophecy pertaining to Christ. The New Testament says, "[A] body you did prepare for me" (Heb. 10:5b); while the Hebrew has it, "My ears you opened" (Psa. 40:6b). The New Testament use of the text stresses the incarnation of the eternal Word (cf. Jn. 1:1), while the Hebrew emphasizes the willingness of Jesus to listen obediently to his Father's instructions (cf. Jn. 8:29). The texts complement one another.

Consider the case in Luke 4, where Jesus returned to his home town of Nazareth. As his common practice was, he went to the synagogue on the Sabbath. The Lord stood up to read and an attendant delivered unto him the Isaiah scroll. He unrolled the scroll and read from chapter 61:1ff.

> The Spirit of the Lord is upon me, Because he anointed me to preach good tidings to the poor: He hath sent me to proclaim release to the captives, And recovering of sight to the blind, To set at liberty them that are bruised, To proclaim the acceptable year of the Lord (Lk. 4:18–19).

The text cited is from the prophet's message in chapter sixty-one (in the LXX), but also with the insertion of a line from chapter fifty-eight. The citation in Luke 4:18–19 flows as follows—61:1a, b, d; 58:6d; 61:2a; with 61:1c and 62:2b, c omitted. Thus chapters sixty-one and fifty-eight are linked by common words and ideas (Evans 1980, 73).

Here is a significant point for reflection. The Isaiah scroll of the synagogue was written in Hebrew. Most likely, as Jesus read from that Hebrew manuscript, he translated the message into the Aramaic dialect, the common spoken language of the Hebrews—most no longer using the older Hebrew. Nonetheless, when Luke, under the guiding hand of the Spirit of God, recorded the message, he rendered the text from the Greek translation! This demonstrates two important points. First, translation does not destroy the inspiration of the original. Second, the importance of the LXX in presenting the message of the gospel is clearly illustrated.

In 1 Peter 3:10–12 there is the following:

> For, He that would love life, And see good days, Let him refrain his tongue from evil, And his lips that they speak no guile: And let him turn away from evil, and do good; Let him seek peace, and pursue it. For the eyes of the Lord are upon the righteous, And his ears unto their supplication: But the face of the Lord is upon them that do evil.

This text is from Psalm 34:12–16 [33 LXX]. It basically follows the LXX but Peter has made some variations to conform to his usage of the text. One writer has described it as follows:

> Peter's quote skillfully rephrased the Septuagint, which fairly represents the Hebrew: "What man is he that desireth life and loveth many days, that he may see good?" (Ps. 34:12). He made the picture more intense by dropping the rhetorical question and stressing the dominating desire that character- izes the life he commended. That alteration enabled him to change from the second to the third person singular imperative in setting forth the activities that should characterize such a life (Hiebert 1984, 216).

COMBINED TEXTS

Occasionally a New Testament writer will combine multiple Old Testament texts without any formal notification of such. For example, in discussing the apostasy of Judas and his replacement in the apostolic office, Peter said: "For it is writ- ten in the book of Psalms . . ." (Acts 1:20). He then quotes from Psalm 69:25 and 109:8, combining the two citations into one grand affirmation.

At the commencement of Mark's Gospel, he quotes from the Old Testament: "Behold, I send my messenger before your face, who shall prepare my way; the voice of one crying in the wilderness, make ready the way of the Lord, make his paths straight." Mark says this is "written in Isaiah." Actually verse two is from Malachi, and verse three is from Isaiah, but Mark combines quotations on the same theme, and gives prominence to Isaiah because he was recognized as the chief of the prophets.

INSPIRED EMENDATIONS

Sometimes a New Testament writer, under the guidance of the Spirit, will deliberately change an Old Testament text, reflecting a departure from both the Hebrew and the LXX.

In Malachi 3:1, "Jehovah of hosts" declares that a special messenger (John the Baptizer) will prepare the way "before me." Since John was preparing the way for Christ, would it not follow that the "Jehovah" of this context was Christ himself?

On the other hand, the speaker, "me" (in the first person), appears to be distinguished from "the Lord" who is coming to "his" (third person) temple. To further complicate this grammatical "maze," there is the fact that when Malachi 3:1 is quoted in the New Testament (Mt. 11:10; Mk. 1:2; Lk. 7:27), in each instance Isaiah's first person, "me," is changed to "you" (second person—"thee," "thy," KJV, ASV), thus differing from both the Hebrew and Greek versions.

Matthew, Mark, and Luke, each under the guidance of the Holy Spirit, have altered the text deliberately to make the application of the prophecy find its fulfillment in Christ. There are two possibilities from which one might view this matter, and neither necessarily excludes the other.

First, with the coming of Christ there was a sense in which the Father had come (see Jn. 14:9). Jesus was the "image of the invisible God" (Col. 1:15), the "very image of his substance" (Heb. 1:3). Actually, the mission of the two was "one" (Jn. 10:30).

On the other hand, it is imperative that we acknowledge that Jesus himself may be designated appropriately as "Jehovah," since the name depicts a self-existing, eternal one; and Christ is precisely that (Isa. 9:6; Mic. 5:2; Jn. 1:1). In fact, there are several Old Testament texts that refer to Jehovah, but in which Jesus clearly is the object of the name (see Isa. 40:3; 44:6; cf. Isa. 8:13 with 1 Pet. 3:15). How utterly amazing are the prophecies of the Bible—a genuine proof of its inspiration!

In Romans 11:25ff, Paul argues the case that if Israel is to be saved, such will have to be through Christ. He cites Old Testament prophecy to prove his point (Isa. 59:20ff). The quotation basically is taken from the LXX. Where the Hebrew indicates that, "a Redeemer will come to Zion"; the LXX has it, "for the sake of Zion." Yet Paul, following neither text precisely, changes the wording to "out of Zion." The apostle's point may be this: while it is true that the Redeemer's mission is "to," i.e., "for the sake of" Zion, the Jews should take pride in their historical role, because the Messiah also came "out of" Zion (cf. Jn. 4:22).

When one understands the flexibility the New Testament writers had, under the guidance of the Spirit of God, the variations in the use of Old Testament quotations are not an insurmountable problem. The challenge is to find why the respective texts (i.e., the Hebrew or Greek) were selected (if possible), or why changes were made. And what a wonderful challenge that is, for nuggets of precious truth lie hidden there to be discovered and treasured.

SUBSTANCE SUMMARIES

Some Bible critics have charged the Sacred Volume with error in that they claim that some writers appeal to Old Testament cases to establish their theological points, when their alleged "proof texts" do not appear anywhere in the Hebrew Scriptures. A few examples that are employed to illustrate this criticism are as follows.

It is contended that Matthew represents Jesus as growing up in Nazareth "that it might be fulfilled which was spoken through the prophets, that he should be called a Nazarene" (2:23), when in reality there is no such specific prophecy of this nature in the Old Testament.

But clearly Matthew is not claiming to cite a specific Old Testament text. His reference to the "prophets" (plural) argues against this narrow focus. The apostle seems to be using Nazareth (a very despised community—cf. Jn. 1:46) as an example of the hateful and wretched treatment that would be afforded the Lord (cf. Psa. 22; Isa. 50:6; 53:1ff; Zech. 11:12–13; 12:10; 13:1, 7). It is apparent that Matthew summarized the substance of several Old Testament texts that suggested the sort of spiteful treatment the Messiah would have to endure (cf. Jackson 2002).

In John 7:38 Jesus declared: "He who believes on me, as the scripture has said, from within him shall flow rivers of living water." Here the Lord speaks of those blessings that will result from the influence of the Holy Spirit. The fact is, however, there is no isolated Old Testament text that contains these words. There are many Old Testament passages that describe the blessings associated with the beneficent nature of water. Isaiah declared, "You shall be like a watered garden, and like a spring of water, whose waters fail not" (58:11; cf. 12:3; Prov. 18:4; Amos 5:24; Rev. 22:17). Summary examples such as these are common among both ancient and modern writers, and do not constitute any problem to the reasonable student.

PARAPHASE

A paraphrase reflects an author's intention to reference a previous text, conveying, however, the sense of the passage, rather than the exact sentence structure.

For instance, in 1 Peter 3:14–15, the apostle writes: "Be not afraid of their terror, neither be troubled, but sanctify the Lord God in your hearts." Professor Fairbairn declares "there can be no doubt" but that the apostle has adopted the language of Isaiah 8:12–13, "but he does not profess to quote what had been written by the prophet." Rather, he "reproduces the passage" quite freely, i.e., the substance of the divine exhortation, rather than with verbal precision (1859, 391). As an inspired apostle of Christ, under the guidance of the Spirit, he had every right to so adapt the original text.

QUOTATIONS THAT ILLUSTRATE

It is occasionally the case that a New Testament writer will reference an Old Testament passage, not because the latter is a direct fulfillment of the former, but because the Old Testament text in some way illustrates a lesson being conveyed by the New Testament writer.

In Isaiah 52, Jehovah, through the prophet Isaiah, rebukes the kingdom of Judah. Because of its apostasy, the nation was being taken into captivity (and for no outwardly discernable reason); thus, the heathen enemy claimed that the Hebrews' God was unable to save them. They exulted in this theory, and as a result, the name of God (i.e., the Person himself) was being blasphemed continually (v. 5). It was a shameful spectacle indeed.

In his letter to the Romans, Paul borrows this language to illustrate the corruption of the Jews of his own day, and the disgrace their conduct generated among the Gentiles. They had a written revelation from God (the Law), but ignored it in their lives. The Gentiles knew of the Hebrews' claim of being the unique people of God, yet the pagans observed Israel's gross wickedness; erroneously, they charged the Lord with the responsibility for such.

The Jews were not without culpability for this blasphemy against God, and they would not escape punishment just because of their unique relationship with Jehovah. Thus, Paul uses the corruption of Israel, six centuries earlier, to illustrate that the nation had hardly changed in its rebellious ways, and it was not exempt from punishment (Rom. 2:24ff).

In verse seven of chapter fifty-two, Isaiah describes the "beautiful feet" of the one who announces the "glad tidings" that the Jewish captives are to be "returned" from slavery to Zion. Paul lifts this phraseology to illustrate the "beautiful feet" of those who proclaim the gospel of Christ, thus providing an avenue to deliverance from an enslavement greater than any political bondage (Rom. 10:15). There is little doubt, however, that the Spirit of God, by the use of this language through the prophet Isaiah, anticipated the gospel age. And this leads us into another classification.

DUAL APPLICATIONS

There are some texts in the literature of the Old Testament that are strictly Messianic, i.e., they have exclusive reference to the coming Messiah, and no one else. For example, Isaiah 7:14 constitutes a prophecy of the virgin birth of Jesus; it contains no reference to a maiden of the prophet's day, with an accommodative application to Mary (contrary to the views of many otherwise "conservative" scholars). There has never been a virginal "conception" aside from the mother of the Lord.

Isaiah 53, with reference to the slaughtered "lamb," is not an allusion to the persecutions endured by the Jewish nation, as alleged by some Jewish writers. The New Testament writers appeal to this text about thirteen times, with the application being to Christ alone.

There are some Old Testament prophetic texts, however, that have an initial application to an ancient situation, but an ultimate fulfillment in a New Testament setting. A recognition of this interpretative principle will exonerate the New Testament writers of the ignorant and/or malicious charge that they carelessly, or worse, deliberately distorted, the Old Testament prophecies to make their case for the validity of Christianity—a case they were unable to make honestly!

As mentioned in another chapter, a clear example illustrating this is found in the final days of Christ's earthly ministry. Jesus, at the last supper, referred to the treachery of

Judas when he said, "He that eats my bread lifted up his heel against me" (Jn. 13:18). The Savior declared that this heinous act "fulfilled" Scripture.

The full text is found in the book of Psalms. "Yes, my own familiar friend, in whom I trusted, who did eat of my bread, has lifted up his heel against me" (41:9). According to the superscription, the Psalm is attributed to David (though superscriptions are not an infallible guide to authorship). Many of the circumstances depicted in the song do parallel events that occurred in the life of Israel's king. It is certain that at times close friends betrayed him. For more on this see, the chapter "The Old Testament in the Gospel of John."

It is interesting that Christ quotes a portion of the psalm in John 13:18, with the application to Judas Iscariot. That the psalm, as a whole, cannot refer to Christ is evidenced by the author's confession of sin (v. 4); that it must, in some sense, be applicable to the Lord is apparent from the fact that Jesus so cites it. Are we to suppose that the Savior wrested the passage and gave it a meaning entirely alien to the context?

It is important to observe how selectively Jesus appealed to the text. He omits the phrase, "whom I trusted" (v. 9a), for the Lord never trusted Judas, knowing from the very "beginning" of his ministry "who it was that should betray him" (Jn. 6:64). Though there was a primary application of the psalmist's language to his own circumstances, the Son of God indicated that this caliber of treachery reached its zenith (ultimate fulfillment) in the traitorous conduct of Judas.

Psalm 69 has a number of Messianic allusions. While the song took its rise out of events in David's experiences (cf. Acts 1:16; Rom. 11:9), and certainly had immediate application to him (cf. v. 5), the Holy Spirit also foretold some of the circumstances associated with the ministry of Christ. (a) The Messiah would be "hated without cause" (v. 4; Jn. 15:25). (b) Zeal for God's house would consume him (v. 9a; the disciples were reminded of this text when Jesus cleansed the temple; see John 2:17). (c) David suffered the wrath of those who reproached God (v. 9b); similarly, to an even greater degree, Christ suffered the reproaches of God-haters (Rom. 15:3). (d) In his persecution, David was given gall and vinegar for food (v. 21—perhaps the language is metaphorical), while Christ was tormented literally with these noxious items (Jn. 19:29). (e) David declared that justice demanded that the "habitation" of his enemies should be made "desolate" (v. 25); the Holy Spirit, through David, saw an ultimate fulfillment in the replacement of Judas, the betrayer of Christ, with a new apostle (Acts 1:20a).

Again we must insist that we absolutely dispute those who contend that New Testament writers frequently misused the Old Testament by lifting passages (such as these) from their contexts and applying them to situations to which they had no original design. Such a concept reflects upon the inspiration of the New Testament writers. Is it not possible that the omniscient Holy Spirit, who guided David's record of his reflections concerning his enemies, could have also foreseen that similar hateful conduct would be directed toward the Son of God, and so adapted the language of the prophet to be a prophetic precursor to the sufferings of Christ? Have the critics never even considered this possibility? Moreover, since Christ quoted from these psalms, applying them to himself, dare we charge the Lord with a glaring breach of the rules of acceptable interpretation?

HISTORICAL REFERENCES

There are numerous passages in the New Testament that illustrate how the writers appealed to the Old Testament in making very important theological and practical points. Those inspired men referred to historical persons, places, and events of the Old Testament era, sometimes generally without necessarily citing a specific text, at other times alluding to particular events, though without citing any explicit passage.

In his letter to the saints in Rome, Paul writes: "For whatsoever things were written aforetime were written for our learning, that through patience and through comfort of the scriptures we might have hope" (15:4). This passage clearly affirms the value of the Old Testament Scriptures, even for us today.

We are not, of course, under the Law of Moses as a legal system, bound by its unique requirements, e.g., the offering of animal sacrifices, annual commemorative celebrations, and Sabbath observances. Nonetheless, the Christian profits immeasurably from a consideration of the thirty-nine books of the Old Testament canon.

From that narrative one learns much of the nature of God himself, e.g., his power, wisdom, and holiness. The Lord's creative activity of our universe is sketched. There is a defining of sin (cf. Rom. 7:7ff), and the devastating nature of the consequences of rebellion against the holy God is emphasized (cf. 1 Cor. 10:6, 11). There also is the history of Jehovah's unfolding plan of human redemption; this is a major point of emphasis in the plan of sacred revelation.

[Note: As this book was about to go to press, I gained access to a volume just published, *Commentary on the New Testament Use of the Old Testament*, edited by G. K. Beale and D. A. Carson, with contributions by a number of additional scholars. I had ordered the book with great anticipation, and doubtless it might have assisted somewhat in the composition of the present chapter. However, my initial survey of the book has left me with a less than enthusiastic feeling for the ambitious work. Though the writers doubtless would classify themselves as "conservative," it is clear to me that to a degree these men have been influenced by the unfounded presuppositions of radical criticism. An example is observed in one of the initial entries in the book. Craig Bloomberg, a professor of New Testament at the Denver Theological Seminary, argues against the view that Isaiah's "virgin" passage (7:14) referred primarily to Jesus, contrary to the apostle Matthew's explicit testimony (Mt. 1:21). Rather, Bloomberg contends that, "the most probable interpretation is that Isaiah's prophecy refers to his own son" (Beale and Carson 2007, 4). He concedes that a "handful of very conservative scholars insist on seeing solely a messianic prophecy here," but he argues otherwise. Obviously he does not consider himself as one of the "very conservative" expositors of biblical literature. I picked up other hints of liberal compromise in this volume as well.]

Chapter 18

The Old Testament in the Gospel of John

---

*"I cannot too greatly emphasize the importance and value of
Bible study—more important than ever before in these days
of uncertainties, when men and women are apt to decide
questions from the standpoint of expediency rather than
of the eternal principles laid down by God, Himself."*
— John Wanamaker (1838–1922), U.S. Postmaster General

The theme of John's magnificent Gospel record is stated
near the end of this remarkable document. The apostle
contends that the "signs" documented in his book are for the
purpose of establishing that Jesus of Nazareth is the "Christ,"
i.e., the appointed Old Testament Messiah, and the "Son of
God," i.e., one who is deity in nature (20:30–31).

The unique way in which the sacred writer, under the
guidance of the Holy Spirit (16:13), developed his material is
a fascinating study within itself. Interestingly, John's Gospel
embraces approximately only thirty days out of the 1,260 days
of the Lord's personal ministry (McGarvey 1956, 35).

While Matthew's record is directed primarily to the Jews,
Mark's to the Roman populace, and Luke's for the benefit of
the Greeks, John's account is cosmopolitan in scope. It cuts

across nationalistic lines and goes to the heart of all sincere souls seeking truth. It has been hailed as "the most amazing book that ever was written" (Hendriksen 1953, I.3). At the same time, if we may borrow a phrase from Sidlow Baxter, "the pens, brains, theories and prejudices" of hostile critics have combined their futile and dubious talents in an attempt to obscure the "splendor of this most precious Gospel" (1966, 301).

In this study our attention will be focused upon one theme—John's use of the Old Testament in the presentation of his case for Christ.

In the Greek New Testament edited by Aland, Black, Martini, Metzger, and Wikgren, fourteen texts are cited in John's Gospel that are taken from the Old Testament. Three of these are identified as coming from the Greek version (LXX); a number of scholars would expand the influence of the LXX in the Gospel of John beyond these three. A survey of these texts is fascinating. In addition to the passages that cite specific Old Testament texts, there are more generic references that provide what one might call a "substance summary" that perhaps involves several Old Testament passages.

JOHN 1:23—ISAIAH 40:3

The apostle records the dialogue between certain Jewish priests and Levites as to the nature of John the Baptizer's identity (1:19–22). The wilderness preacher denied that he was the Messiah, Elijah, or "the prophet" (cf. Dt. 18:15). Affirmatively, then, he declared: "I am the voice of one crying in the wilderness; Make straight the way of the Lord" (v. 23). There are several important points to make here. John does not hesitate to identify himself as the one who fulfills the prophecy of the harbinger of Christ. (See also: Mt. 3:3; Mk. 1:2–3; LK. 3:4–6).

First, basically, the text is taken (with some abbreviation) from the Greek version (LXX) of the book of Isaiah (40:3).

This demonstrates that a translation does not destroy inspiration. The Septuagint was the common version in that day, even for the Jews. Moreover the fact that the apostle John abbreviated the text reveals that the Holy Spirit, consistent with his own purpose, could direct a biblical writer to alter the text without any compromise of integrity (cf. Jn. 1:23 with Mt. 3:3). Abbreviations or alterations of the text by an inspired spokesman were employed frequently (Lenski 1943, 223), thus demonstrating that the Holy Spirit had control of his own words in a variety of biblical settings.

Second, John attributes the Old Testament text to "Isaiah the prophet." This stands in contradistinction to the allegations of modern critics, who contend that chapters forty and onward were composed by writers other than Isaiah, the son of Amoz (Isa. 1:1). Modern "scholarship" is arrogant enough to allege that it knows more about authorship than an apostle of Jesus Christ.

Third, the use of the term "prophet" is clear validation of the ability of certain inspired men to foretell the future, and Isaiah was among the prophets. In that Old Testament book of 1,292 verses, no fewer than 754 (59%) deal with future events (Payne 1973, 278), and some 129 of these are Messianic in thrust.

Fourth, the wilderness voice was to prepare the way for the coming of the "Lord" (Greek, *kurios*; Hebrew, *Yahweh*), identified also as "God" (*theos*). Inasmuch as the baptizer's mission was to prepare the way for Christ (vv. 24ff), this is certain testimony of the divine nature of Jehovah-God, Jesus.

JOHN 2:17—PSALM 69:9

Near the commencement of his ministry, Jesus was in Jerusalem at the time of the Jewish Passover. He observed the crass commercialism that was taking place in the temple (*hieron*—the entire temple complex; here, one of the outer courts). The Lord drove out the animals being sold as sacrifices, and overturned the moneychangers' tables. This incident is not to be confused with a later "cleansing" of a similar nature (Mt. 21:12–13). He charged: "Make not my Father's house a house of merchandise" (v. 16). John stated that when the disciples heard this, it reminded them that: "it was written" that "Zeal for your house shall eat me up" (Psa. 69:9). Incidentally, notice the distant expression, "your house," as the Lord prepared to deliver the Olivet discourse revealing the not-distant destruction of the holy city and its temple (Mt. 23:38). Observe the following.

First, for Christ to refer to the temple as "my Father's house" is a clear affirmation of his unique relationship to the Father (see also Mt. 17:24–27). Bernard observes that the expression "my Father" is used sixteen times in Matthew, four times in Luke, and twenty-seven times in John (1928, I.91). The use of the singular pronoun, "my," is an unequivocal suggestion of his deity (cf. Jn. 5:17–18; 20:17b).

Second, of the quotation from Psalm 69, John uses the phrase, "it was written" (*gegrammenon estin*—a perfect, passive form), indicating the permanent impact of the thing written. It is the equivalent of the more common form, *gegraptai* (cf. 8:17; some eighty-two times in the New Testament), and always is employed to reflect the "authority and present validity of what is written" (Balz and Schneider 1990, 261). It is used exclusively of inspired scripture in the New Testament (cf. Danker et al. 2000, 206).

Third, Psalm 69 has a primary application to David (cf. Rom. 11:9), and the sufferings to which he was subjected on account of his zeal for Jehovah. But both John and Paul (Rom. 15:3) see an ultimate fulfillment in Christ's sufferings. In fact, Psalm 69 is cited six times in the NT with a messianic application (cf. Jn. 2:17; 15:25; 19:28; Acts 1:20; Rom. 11:9–10; 15:3).

The disciples appear to have viewed the language of Psalm 69 as messianic in its ultimate import with the obvious application to Jesus as they observed his actions on this occasion (cf. Mal. 3:1ff). Some Old Testament prophecies have an initial application to the original author, but then an ultimate fulfillment in Christ. This is classified as a typological prophecy.

Johnson observed that in both the Hebrew and LXX texts the verb takes a past tense form—"has eaten me up"—while John changes it to a future tense, the design of which is "to show that he regards the psalm as Messianic, and this verse as a prediction of the zeal of Christ for the house of God" (1896, 323, cf. 77–78).

JOHN 6:31—PSALM 78:24

Following the miracle of the feeding of the five thousand (6:1ff), Jesus perceived that certain of the Jews were going to attempt forcing kingship upon him, so he withdrew to a secluded place on a mountain where he could be alone. The following day a multitude located the Savior at Capernaum and pressed close upon him. The Lord rebuked them, perceiving their interest as more physical (a desire for food) than spiritual. Christ cautioned that their preoccupation with "food" must go far beyond the material; rather, they must constantly "work for" that which provides soul life! When they asked about what they were required to "do" to obtain this life, Jesus explained they must "work the works of God." The term works "refers to the works God requires of those who please him" (Tenney 1981, 75). The principal work was the persistent exercise of belief, from which all obedience flows. There is no "faith only" dogma here.

The Jews pressed Christ for a "sign" (obviously wanting another miracle similar to the feat of the former day; cf. v. 14);

they armed their request with an appeal to Psalm 78:24, which refers to God's gift of manna for the Hebrews in the wilderness of Sinai: "[A]s it is written, 'He gave them bread out of heaven to eat.'" Several points are worthy of deeper reflection.

First, the Jews, though resisting a full faith in Christ, nonetheless acknowledged Psalm 78 as sacred Scripture (cf. "it is written" above). Moreover, they conceded the "manna" episode in the Old Testament to be genuine history, not a parable of sorts, reflecting the "secretion" of a substance from the tamarisk bush, or else the "excretion" of certain wilderness insects—as modern critical scholars allege. It is even more significant that Christ did not charge them with misunderstanding the miraculous nature of the Old Testament narrative.

Second, the subsequent narrative (vv. 32ff) clearly reveals that Jesus saw the supernatural provision of the "bread out of heaven" as a symbol of himself. The manna came not from Moses, but from God. The former was bread that could minister only to a physical person; Christ was the "true" (the genuine; various forms of *aletheia* are found forty-five times in John's Gospel; cf. 14:6; 15:1), providing nourishment for the eternal human soul. Bread (*artos*) becomes a metaphor for the sum of life's basic needs (cf. Mt. 6:11). He was the bread the Father provides (perpetually available) to all who are willing to "come" to him, i.e. "believe" on him (v. 35; note that "comes" and "believes" are parallel). The Lord clearly capitalized upon the Jews' use of Psalm 78 by affirming that anti-typically, he fulfills the passage, having come out of heaven himself for the purpose of providing eternal life for those who embrace him in obedience.

Third, observe that Jesus stresses his heavenly abode prior to the incarnation ("out of/down from heaven"—five times in vv. 31–38); he was not mere man. Note the selfless disposition of verse thirty-eight. The emphatic affirmation, "I am," is reminiscent of similar texts in the Gospel (cf. 8:12; 10:7, 14; 11:25; 14:6; 15:1; cf. 8:58).

JOHN 6:45—ISAIAH 54:13

The Jews caught the drift regarding Jesus' claim of being the "bread" that "came down out of heaven," and it irritated them. They argued that such could not be the case because the Jesus was "the son of Joseph" and Mary—not one who came out of heaven. The Savior went to the heart of their problem—it was ignorance. They needed to be taught and learn, and then they could, and must, come to him. In making his argument, as authority for his case, the Teacher declared: "It is written in the prophets, 'And they shall all be taught of God.' Every one that has heard from the Father, and has learned, comes to me" (6:45).

Note the familiar "it is written in the prophets," acknowledging the Old Testament text as sacred Scripture. Though the plural form "prophets" is used, the expression can refer to a specific reference (cf. Acts 13:40; 15:15), and this type of literary expression was common in the ancient world (Johnson 1896, 110). The "prophets" stands for their writings (cf. Lk. 16:29). The quotation is a free rendition, apparently from Isaiah 54:13 primarily, that conforms precisely neither to the Hebrew nor the LXX. These points are important to remember.

First, Christ acknowledged the authority of the Old Testament as Holy Scripture, and we must recognize the divine origin of the biblical documents as well. To not do so is to distance oneself from the Son of God.

Second, the Savior indicated that the "drawing" power of God is exercised through the teaching of his word, not by means of some non-definable influence of the Holy Spirit. If "draw" connoted an "irresistible force," then all would be saved, for later in this Gospel narrative the Lord says: "And I, if I be lifted up from the earth, will draw all men unto myself" (12:32). The "drawing" is a beneficent pull. The Lord said to ancient Israel: "I have loved you with an everlasting love: therefore with lovingkindness have I drawn you" (Jer. 31:3; cf. Sg. of Sol. 1:4).

Third, Jesus did not subscribe to the false notion that the "elect" had been chosen before the foundation of the world, hence salvation is entirely independent of human response. He affirmed that one must receive teaching, understand what is taught, and thereby "come" to him. The verb, "come," is a middle voice, present tense form, which indicates a sustained activity resulting from a personal action. The contention of Morris (1995, 328) and others, that the initiative is strictly by divine grace and cannot be resisted successfully by man, is entirely foreign to the truth (see Acts 7:51). Were that the case, all would be saved (Jn. 12:32). Robertson notes that it "is not enough to hear God's voice," one must learn it and obey it. "This is a voluntary response" (1930–33, V.109).

Simple logic provides a clear picture of the process. God draws; people come. Those who come, however, are those who have been taught, who have heard, and learned. Hence it is perfectly transparent that God draws sincere people by means of gospel instruction by which people are taught, hear, and learn. Professor Merrill Tenney wrote: "Verse 45 indicates that God would do his drawing through the Scriptures and that those who were obedient to God's will as revealed in the Scriptures would come to Jesus (1981, 76)."

Bernard also observed that the drawing was by "being taught" (1928, I.205). The term "heard" carries the idea of hearing with a view to being obedient (cf. Mt. 17:5; Acts 3:22).

We might add that the sequence of the conditions, i.e., learning before obeying, eliminates the digressive dogma of infant baptism.

JOHN 7:37–38—ISAIAH 58:11—PROVERBS 18:4

Now on the last day, the great day of the feast, Jesus stood and cried, saying, "If any man thirst, let him come unto me and drink. He who believes on me, as the scripture has said, from within him shall flow rivers of living water" (7:37–38).

The "feast" was that of Tabernacles (v. 2). This was a seven-day feast in the fall when the Hebrews lived in "booths" to commemorate their years of wandering in the wilderness of Sinai. During these days there were several processions involving water that doubtless served as the basis for the Lord's proclamation.

This is one of those passages that appear to cite Old Testament "substance" rather than "sentence." The method of citation may appear strange to the modern mind, but it was common in the ancient world (as Johnson demonstrated [1896, 103ff]), and the New Testament writers occasionally employed it as well (cf. Mt. 2:23; Eph. 5:14).

Of this text in John 7, Professor Johnson of the University of Chicago wrote:

> There is no passage in the Old Testament which contains just these words; but they express the meaning of all those passages which represent the salutary influence of a holy man under the image of flowing water, like Isa. 58:11: "Thou shalt be like a watered garden, and like a spring of water, whose waters fail not"; or Prov. 18:4: "The words of a man's mouth are as deep waters; The well-spring of wisdom is as a flowing brook." (1896, 113–114).

We are constrained to add that the Lord was not referring to a "baptism of the Holy Spirit," by which believers were made a part of the one body, the church, as some have alleged (Kaiser 1985, 96).

JOHN 10:34—PSALM 82:6

Jesus was in Jerusalem at the time of the feast of the Dedication (celebrating the cleansing of the Temple in 164 B.C., after the assaults of Antiochus Epiphanes). This was an eight-day celebration beginning on December 25th. The Jews pressed round about him (hemming him in, so to speak), demanding that he state explicitly whether or not he claimed to be "the Christ," i.e., the Messiah (10:24). The Lord did not answer precisely, but rather told them they already had ample evidence of his identity (cf. 5:33, 36, 37, 39, 46), yet they refused to believe.

Jesus then emphatically stated: "I and the Father are one" (10:30). The term "one" in the original is a neuter form; hence was an affirmation that he and the Father are one in essence or nature (Robertson 1930–33, V.186). The Jews perfectly understood his claim, and picked up stones for the purpose of killing him for this "blasphemy."

Courageously, Christ continued the discussion. He employed both the *ad hominem* and the *a fortiori* forms of argument. The former appeals to the Jews' own recognition of what the "law" said (cf. Mt. 12:11); the second reasons from a proposition with a greater objection, to one of a lesser objection (cf. Mt. 6:26, 30). If something is true in case A-plus, then surely it must be in case A-minus.

The Lord cited Psalm 82:6. "Is it not written in your law, 'I said, you are gods'?" (v. 34). Note the emphasis: "your law." In effect: "Will you repudiate your own law?" The term "gods" (Hebrew, *elohim*) occasionally was used accommodatingly for those who served by divine authority, even though they were flawed people (see Ex. 21:6; 22:8ff). As Morgan noted, certain Old Testament judges "were dignified with the very name of God, because they were the instruments through whom the Word of God came" (n.d., 184–185).

Since the Jews had no problem with this symbolic language used in their law with reference to frail men, why should they object to Christ's claim: "I am the Son of God," since he had been sent into the world by the Father, and set apart for a special redemptive mission? Westcott contended that in this use of Psalms 82, Jesus shows "that even in the Old Testament there was a preparation for that union of God and man which He came to complete" (1981, 160). Consider these points.

First, Christ clearly declared he possesses the very nature of God. When the Jehovah's Witnesses distort this text, alleging that Jesus claimed no more than being a "perfect man," they miss the point of the Lord's logical argument. This context, rather than nullifying the Savior's deity, powerfully demonstrates it.

Second, when Christ said: "I and the father are [*esmen*, plural] one," he clearly distinguished himself from the Father as a person. Thus, the Father and Son are not merely different "manifestations" of the "One-Person" God, as alleged by the "Jesus Only" sect.

Third, the Lord's use of "law" to embrace the entire Old Testament included the book of Psalms (cf. also 66:13). The "law" was abolished at the cross (Eph. 2:15), thus the Psalms may not be employed as a legal authority for worship under the New Testament regime. This recognition would exclude such things as the offering of animal sacrifices, the burning of incense, the holy dance, jubilant clapping in a worship context, and the use of mechanical instruments of music as implements of worship.

Fourth, in this connection, the Lord stated that "the scripture cannot be broken" (v. 35). Men may "break themselves," trying to overthrow Scripture, but Scripture itself remains steadfast.

JOHN 12:13—PSALM 118:25–26

On Sunday before he was crucified on Friday, Jesus made his way toward Jerusalem. A great multitude came forth to meet him. Extracting and mingling words from Psalm 118:25–26, the people cried out: "Hosanna [save now]: Blessed is he who comes in the name of the Lord" (cf. Mt. 21:9; Mk. 11:10; Lk. 19:38). A consideration of John's account of this event, combined with the synoptic records, reveals a remarkable collection of truths.

First, the original context in Psalm 118 is an address to Jehovah. The use of such on this occasion with reference to Jesus is telling indeed. This is "a supplication addressed to Jehovah by the worshipper, who is convinced that the proper time for full deliverance has now at last arrived" (Hendriksen 1953, II.188). In their minds the "deliverance" was to be accomplished by Christ. It was an acknowledgement of their conviction that he was coming in the Messianic role.

Second, the throng hailed him as "king" (Lk. 19:38) with a "kingdom" (Mk. 11:10), and also as the "Son of David" (Mt. 21:9; cf. 2 Sam. 7:12ff) who would "save" them. While their aspirations almost certainly were political (Jn. 6:15; Acts 1:6), the object of their worship is unmistakable! Though the joyous crowd did not appreciate the full significance of their chant, it seems clear that this "was something more than a mere blessing of welcome" (Bernard 1928, II.424); they were hailing him as the Messiah. The recent resurrection of Lazarus still was fresh in the minds of this multitude, and this impression likely fuelled this Messianic anthem of praise that suggested Jesus was entering the city "in the name of Jehovah" (Lenski 1943, 852).

Third, the expression "in the name of Jehovah," was a declaration that the Messianic mission of Jesus was by the authority of God, and it throws a floodlight on the rebellious attitude that would seize many of the Jews before this week expired.

It is clear that the apostle John, as he looked back upon these events later in his life when penning this account, viewed

Psalm 118:25–26 as previewing the triumphal entry. And it is not without significance that Jesus applied the text to himself in anticipation of his return to receive the faithful (Mt. 23:39). Note also John's use of the plural "these things," combining Psalm 118 and Zechariah 9 (see below), as addressing matters "written" about the Savior (Jn. 12:16).

JOHN 12:15—ZECHARIAH 9:9

As Jesus entered the holy city, he was riding upon the colt of a donkey. John declares that this was a fulfillment of what "is written" (v. 14b; cf. 16b). "Fear not, daughter of Zion: behold, your King comes, sitting on a donkey's colt." This is an abbreviated sentence from Zechariah 9:9. As one respected scholar observed:

> The freedom with which the inspired writers of the New Testament treat the text of the Old Testament sometimes quoting it with verbal accuracy, sometimes condensing two clauses into one, sometimes changing the tense of a verb to bring out more clearly its prophetic pertinence, and sometimes giving an implied thought for the one expressed—is by no means inconsistent with the highest reverence for the divine authority of that volume. This they uniformly show by the manner in which they refer to the ancient Scriptures. And so far as we can judge, they never attribute to an Old Testament writer any thought foreign to his language, or, indeed, any thought that is not fairly implied in his language (Hovey 1885, 250).

There are several thoughts to be gleaned from Zechariah's declaration—more than can be developed here from John's extraction from the ancient passage.

First, while Zechariah encourages the Hebrew people to "rejoice" in view of their coming king, John changes the wording to "fear not." Matthew simply says, "Tell the daughter of Zion" (21:9). One can only surmise why the language was altered. Perhaps the more jubilant "rejoice" gives way to the encouraging words, "fear not," in view of the cross that looms just ahead from the apostle's perspective. The fears of the faithful would be turned into rejoicing by virtue of the Lord's resurrection.

Second, the prophet urges, "Look, your King is coming." Jesus was a prospective king from the time of his birth (Mt. 2:2), but he was enthroned as king following his resurrection and ascension (Acts 2:30–31; Eph. 1:20–23; Heb. 1:3; 1 Pet. 3:21b-22). The "millennial" notion, that the reign of Christ has been postponed until the time of his second coming, has no basis in fact. When the Lord returns, his reign of mediation will be surrendered back to the Father in order that he may "be all in all" (1 Cor. 15:25–28).

Third, under the Old Testament regime, Jehovah had forbidden Israel to "multiply" horses, i.e., trust in these powerful animals as defense mechanisms instead of him (Dt. 17:16; cf. Josh. 11:6, 9), but David used horses for his chariots (2 Sam. 8:4). Additionally, Solomon marshaled a considerable depository of horses (1 Kgs. 4:26—though forty thousand appears to be a transcription error for four thousand; cf. 2 Chron. 9:25). Some of these were stabled at places like Megiddo. During the University of Chicago excavations at Megiddo (1925–39), Stratum IV was identified as Solomonic; and accommodations for four hundred fifty horses were discovered. While these stables currently are identified with the era of Ahab, it is likely they were first constructed in Solomon's day, and rebuilt during Ahab's administration (Vos 2003, 166).

How seemingly strange, therefore, that the greatest ruler who ever claimed the hearts of men, the King of kings, should make his final entry into Jerusalem on the back of a donkey—especially one that never had been ridden. In the midst of an excited crowd, "an unbroken animal remains calm under the hand of the Messiah who controls nature (8:23–27; 14:22–32)" (Carson 1984, 438). The deliberately planned entrance into the city was intended to be symbolic. It depicted the wonderful humility and meekness of our Savior. What a contrast to the bloody carnage of Mohammed whose philosophy was "convert" or "destroy."

JOHN 12:38—ISAIAH 53:1

As noted earlier (cf. Jn. 12:12ff), it was the final week before the Savior's death. The Pharisees were in a panic mode because of Jesus' mounting influence among the people (v. 19). With increasing hostility, the Lord's teaching (e.g., his claim of being the "Son of man"—a phrase with messianic overtones; cf. Dan. 7:13) was igniting heightened interest (v. 34). As the "Calvary clock" ticked toward the fateful hour, the Lord somehow was "hidden" so that his "hour" might be fulfilled precisely on time (v. 36b).

It is at this point that John provides his own inspired commentary on the spiritual state of many of the Jews of that era in Palestine. Of special interest for this study is the segment from verses thirty-seven through forty-three. Let us reflect upon the following matters.

First, the apostle declares that Christ had performed numerous miracles before the people. Later, by way of the figure known as hyperbole, John writes that the things Jesus did, if written, could not be contained in the books throughout the world (21:25). Thus, there was ample evidence of the true nature of the Lord. Excuses were not acceptable.

Second, in spite of the profuse and compelling evidence of Christ's claim of being the Son of God (20:31), his Hebrew kinsmen "believed not on him" (12:37). The imperfect tense verb suggests that "they continued not believing on him." They were "dug in" in disbelief.

Third, this rebellion was no surprise to God (as occasionally claimed by some dispensational millennialists); rather, it fulfilled the word of the prophet Isaiah, some seven centuries earlier. In that marvelous fifty-third chapter, which was a galaxy of messianic stars, the prophet asked: "Lord, who has believed our report? And to whom has the arm of the Lord been revealed?" (53:1). The question is plaintive, with a note of shock and sadness. It is rhetorical in that it suggests that few would believe, in contrast to the many that would not. Though the "arm of the Lord" (i.e., his mighty power as reflected in the works of his Son) provided ample evidence of Jesus' divine nature, he was being rejected.

Fourth, John proceeds to explain this steadfast state of disbelief by so many of the Jews. By this time, "they could not believe" (v. 39). The verb is a present tense form, suggesting they "could not sustain" belief. They were on-and-off; they waxed and waned—settling in with the latter. As Alfred Plummer once expressed it, "I will not" leads to "I cannot" (quoted by Morris 1995, 536). Lenski's note that it was "God's intention that the Jews should not believe in Jesus" (1943, 887) is utterly absurd. Repeated rejection hardens the heart (cf. Rom. 11:25; Eph. 4:19; 2 Tim. 4:2).

Fifth, John references a second quotation from Isaiah; this time the citation is from chapter six. Significantly, however, he begins with this phrase: "for that Isaiah said again." It is important to note that John, an inspired apostle, endorsed the fact that both chapters, six and fifty-three, were from Isaiah—not different writers as argued by modern liberal critics (see Willis 1980, 20ff). The reference in chapter six speaks to the fact that God had "blinded" the eyes of the Jews, and "hardened" their hearts. This phraseology employs a common biblical idiom whereby God is portrayed as actively doing what he merely permits. See such passages as: Jeremiah 4:10; Ezekiel 20:25; Matthew 6:13; 2 Thessalonians 2:11 (MacKnight 1954, 29).

Sixth, John states that Isaiah's words issued from the fact that he "saw his [Christ's] glory; and he spoke of him" (v. 41). A consideration of Isaiah 6:1–5 reveals the fact that the prophet had seen a personage who is called "Jehovah of hosts" (cf. 44:6). Thus, Jesus is worthy of the name "Jehovah" just as the Father is, for the Lord is likewise the self-existent, eternal God (cf. Ex. 3:14; cf. Jn. 8:58).

Seventh, though some of the Jews "believed on" Christ (v. 42), they refused to confess him because they feared the Pharisees. The statement is devastating to those who subscribe to the notion that "belief" (i.e., a mental disposition) is the sum of that required for salvation.

JOHN 13:18—PSALM 41:9

When Jesus was at the last supper with the disciples, he took advantage of the circumstances to teach his men an object lesson in humility. He washed their feet (normally a servant's task—1 Sam. 25:41) in order to impress upon them the reality that they should seek to serve others, rather than striving for positions of prominence (cf. Lk. 22:24ff). In this connection, the Savior repeated the obscure allusion hinted in verse ten—"not all" of the disciples were of the same quality (v. 18a). Clearly he is referring to Judas (vv. 21ff). He knew intimately the character of those he had chosen to be his apostles.

John then states that in order "that the scripture may be fulfilled," Jesus said: "He who eats my bread lifted up his heel against me" (v. 18b). The quotation is from Psalm 41:9. Hostile critics allege that in this setting, the phrase has been wrested from its original context; supposedly either Jesus misused the passage, or John misrepresented the circumstance. Consider the following points.

First, there is a common form of prophecy in the Old Testament known as a "type." A type can be a person, institution, office, action, or event "by means of which some truth of the Gospel was **divinely** foreshadowed under the Old Testament dispensations" (Terry 1890, 246; emphasis added). A number of the psalms contain typical representations that suggested Christ ultimately would "fulfill" the "manifold experiences" of humanity in both sufferings and victories (cf. Psalms 22, 35, 40, 69, 109, 118). These "typical word pictures" purposefully foreshadowed certain truths regarding Jesus in the Old Testament (Kirkpatrick 1906, lxxix; Kidner 1973, 22). The phrase, "that the scriptures may be fulfilled," negates the idea that there is a mere "accidental" similarity between the Old Testament phraseology and the New Testament occurrences; rather it connotes an "agreement" in the divine orchestration of the Scriptures (cf. Bengal 1877, 114). Christ did not make a bogus argument!

Second, originally Psalm 41 likely had to do with the treachery of Ahithophel, one of David's counselors, who betrayed the king and, in disgrace, subsequently hanged himself (2 Sam. 15–17). Such an incident becomes a prophetic type of the similar conduct of Judas towards the Lord. The psalmist's declaration thus reads: "Yes, my own familiar friend, in whom I trusted, who did eat of my bread, has lifted his heel against me" (v. 9). It is important to observe that when the Lord cited this passage, he omitted "my own familiar friend whom I trusted" (13:18), the reason being, he "knew from the beginning who they were that believed not, and who it was that should betray him" (Jn. 6:64). The Lord never trusted Judas. The prophecy, therefore, has an initial (personal) application with David, but an ultimate fulfillment in Christ. (Note: to speak of a prophecy having a "double fulfillment," as some writers do, is to use imprecise terminology. If an ancient context "fulfilled" [i.e., filled full] the meaning of a text, it hardly is appropriate to speak of a subsequent "filling" centuries later.)

JOHN 15:25—PSALM 69:4

Christ and his disciples (minus Judas) left the upper room where the Passover had been observed, and made their way eastward toward Gethsemane (Jn. 14:31). Along the way the Savior sought to prepare them for the difficulties that would lie in their paths, not the least of which was the "hate" to which they would be subjected (vv. 18ff). But they were not alone; their Master was hated, as well as the Father. And this animosity would vent itself in the death of the Son of God. It was in this context that Jesus, quoting Psalm 69, said: "But this is coming to pass, that the word may be fulfilled that is written in their law, 'They hated me without a cause'" (Jn. 15:25). (Note: the phrase is also found in Psalm 35:19, but 69:4 is most likely the context from which John quoted [Beasley-Murray 1999, 276].)

The superscription assigns the composition to David, and this likewise is the confirmation of Paul (Rom. 11:9–10). Quite obviously it was written in a time of distress when the author was being unjustly persecuted—perhaps during the time of Absalom's rebellion (2 Sam. 13–19). The psalmist desperately needed, hence solicited, the aid of his God. David is first speaking of himself, but also "under the guidance of the Holy Spirit" he speaks of things that are applicable to his own self in a limited sense, but which are "fulfilled perfectly in Christ" (Johnson 1896, 245). The following items are of interest.

First, again there is a reference to the fact that the citation is from the "law," i.e., the greater body of Old Testament literature (see the above discussion of Jn. 10:34). Too, there is that insinuating "their law" (cf. "your law"—8:17; 10:34), which seems to imply that Jesus was distancing himself from their interpretation of the law—which, by the way, excluded the Savior from their perception of the Messiah. See the similar language format in Isaiah 1:13–14, where the prophet steps away from the perverse practices of his people.

Second, within this same context Christ had declared that the world "hated" him (v. 18). This certainly was demonstrated by the repeated attempts to murder him during his personal ministry (Lk. 4:29; Jn. 5:16, 18; 8:59; 10:39, etc.). The perfect tense form suggests an abiding hate. "The world's hatred of Christ was no passing phenomenon" (Morris 1995, 602).

Third, the hatred of Jesus Christ, both then and now, is utterly "without cause." The Greek expression is *dorean*, which carries the idea of an antagonistic situation to which one has not contributed, hence is without "fault." The hatred was totally undeserved (Danker et al. 2000, 266). No wonder the Lord could challenge his adversaries, "Which of you can convict me of sin?" (Jn. 8:46).

Fourth, the "without cause" declaration also undergirds Christ's role as the "lamb without blemish and without spot" (1 Pet. 1:19), indeed who "did no sin"—the aorist form of the verb suggesting "not even once" (1 Pet. 2:22; cf. Heb. 4:15, etc.). Spiritual perfection was absolutely essential in Jesus' redemptive sacrifice—the totally innocent for the completely guilty (2 Cor. 5:21).

JOHN 19:24—PSALM 22:18

After Christ had been nailed to the cross, the four Roman soldiers, like vultures picking over remains, gathered up the Lord's clothes and began to divide them among themselves (Jn. 19:23)—most likely in violation of Roman jurisprudence. Soldiers could not arbitrarily confiscate the deceased's possessions, unless granted the privilege by the authority of the "governors" (Kostenberger 2002, 177). After the distribution of four garments, however, one piece remained—a seamless tunic, for which they cast lots rather than tear it apart.

John cites Psalm 22:18: "They parted my garments among them, and upon my vesture did they cast lots." The apostle is emphatic that this incident occurred "that the scripture might be fulfilled." Psalm 22 is a marvelous portrayal of the sufferings in connection with Jesus' crucifixion, together with the victory resulting from the ordeal. While some see the original narrative as "typical" of Christ, it may be more reasonably concluded that it is strictly predictive—having application to no one but the Lord Jesus. Kidner states that the "language of the psalm defies any naturalistic explanation" (1973, 105).

The psalm divides itself rather naturally into the following segments: (a) Christ is "forsaken" by the Father—in the sense that God did not intervene and rescue him from the cross (vv. 1–5); (b) the Savior's reproach by men (vv. 6–13); (c) the ordeal of the Savior's psychological and physical suffering (vv. 14–18); (d) a fervent prayer to God for deliverance (vv. 19–21); and (e) thanksgiving to the Father for the victory ultimately achieved (vv. 22–31). Here are some pertinent facts for reflection.

First, the writer of the book of Hebrews quotes verse twenty-two and explicitly gives it a messianic interpretation (2:12).

Second, ancient records indicate that the crucifixion victim was stripped of his clothes before being nailed to the cross (Kostenberger 2002, 177). The psalmist thus hints of this removal of garments a thousand years before the event, and centuries before crucifixion became a mode of capital punishment. The manner of death also is confirmed by this sentence: "They pierced my hands and my feet" (22:16b).

Third, there is the prophetic hint that there was some distinction between the garments—some were divided, another assigned by "lot." This was fulfilled by the four separate pieces versus the seamless "vesture" that could not be divided without destroying the fabric. Robertson suggested that the four items consisted of headgear, sandals, an outer garment (tallith with fringes), and a girdle—a sash or fabric belt (1930–33, V.302). Josephus mentions that the high priest wore a "seamless" garment (*Antiquities of the Jews* 3.6.4).

Perhaps this point is merely incidental, but it is interesting that Christ was in the process of being offered as a "sacrifice," and was on the threshold of entering his role as High Priest (Heb. 8:1; 9:11, 24; 10:19ff).

Fourth, the prophecy indicates that the distribution of Jesus' apparel was determined by the "casting of lots." Some have suggested that the Greek word really does not mean "to cast lots," but the evidence supporting the traditional rendition is ample (Danker et al. 2000, 581).

JOHN 19:36—EXODUS 12:46—NUMBERS 9:12

As the three crucified victims (Christ and the two thieves) hung upon their crosses, the Jews made request of Pilate that their legs might be broken to hasten their deaths, for the Sabbath, which in this instance was a "high day," i.e., a Sabbath associated with a festival, was near. How religiously sensitive were these Jews! They had just committed the vilest deed in the history of lawlessness, yet they were concerned about contaminating a "high Sabbath"! This is off-the-scale hypocrisy. The governor apparently conceded, for soldiers were dispatched to break the legs (incapacitating the victims' ability to breathe).

When the soldiers approached Jesus they discovered that he "was dead already," hence they did not break his legs (v. 33). John comments that "these things came to pass, that the scripture might be fulfilled, 'A bone of him shall not be broken'" (v. 36). What is the significance of this?

First, clearly this narrative is indirect testimony to the fact that the Passover lamb of the Mosaic Law was a type of Christ, who was "the lamb of God" (Jn. 1:29). Paul depicts Jesus as "our Passover" (1 Cor. 5:7). The death of the Passover victim, together with the application of its blood, saved the firstborn from death (Ex. 12:13). By the shedding of the blood of Christ, Christians are spared spiritual death (Rom. 6:11, 23), and are recognized as "firstborn" (Heb. 12:23).

Second, divine instruction specified that no bone of the sacrifice should be broken (Ex. 12:46; cf. Num. 9:12). Though various speculations have been offered as to why the bones were to remain inviolate, the Old Testament provides no explanation. One thing is clear, such was designed to foreshadow the prophetic reality that none of Christ's bones would be broken; and in the providence of the Almighty they were not! Alfred Edersheim, who was raised a Jew, remarked that had Christ's bones been broken, then Scripture also would have been "broken" (1947, 614), and that was not to be! (cf. Jn. 10:35).

Third, the fact that the soldiers did not break the Lord's bones is clear testimony to the fact that he really was dead, hence, not in a mere "swoon," from which he would be resuscitated by his disciples later, to announce his so-called "resurrection." The swoon theory is one of utter desperation that trashes all the facts of the case.

Fourth, the accuracy of the biblical record is supported by archaeological discovery. The remains of a man (approximate age of 24–28 years), who had been crucified during the time of Christ, were discovered in 1968 in the northern region of Jerusalem. The bones of one leg were fractured; the other was broken in pieces (Kostenberger 2002, 176, 180).

JOHN 19:37—ZECHARIAH 12:10

In connection with the foregoing, John continued: "Another scripture says, 'They shall look on him whom they pierced'" (Jn. 19:37). The language embraces two circumstances: (a) the piercing of his flesh by the nails (cf. Psa. 22:16b; Jn. 20:25b); and, (b) the puncturing of his side with the spear (Jn. 19:34). Some have alleged that Psalm 22:16 has been incorrectly translated in most versions, and that the original text actually says, "like a lion," instead of, "they pierced my hands and my feet." We have addressed this assertion elsewhere, to which we would refer the reader (Jackson 2001). But note the following.

First, writing in the early sixth century B.C., Zechariah produced an oracle that speaks of the "day" when Jehovah would "pour out" the "spirit of grace upon the house of David." Honest souls would "mourn" over the one whom they had killed. The murder was to be implemented by the victim being "pierced" (12:10). Happily, however, by that piercing, a "fountain" was opened for "sin and uncleanness" (13:1). John declared this was a prophecy of the death of Christ.

Second, it is intriguing that this piercing of Christ is, in fact, a wound rendered also to "Jehovah." Note the "thus says Jehovah" (v. 1), connected to "they shall look unto me whom they have pierced" (v. 10). A similar thought is expressed in Zechariah 11:12–13, where the insulting price of thirty pieces of silver was described as the sum paid for "Jehovah," as if he were the one being betrayed. He was—indirectly. Attacks against Christ are equally against his heavenly Father (cf. Lk. 10:16).

Third, again we must remind ourselves that a piercing, i.e., the shedding of blood, was a vital component in Heaven's plan of salvation. By sin man has forfeited his right to live (Rom. 6:23). If there was to be atonement for the lost, there must be the shedding of blood (Heb. 9:22), because blood is the depository of life (Lev. 17:11). Moreover, the atoning sacrifice must be without spiritual-moral blemish (Ex. 12:5). Christ, of course, fits all of the requirements perfectly (cf. 1 Pet. 1:19), and this allows the holy God to be both just and the justifier of those who, by means of the faith system, seek pardon through obedience to Christ (Rom. 3:21–30; cf. 1 Pet. 4:17–18).

As noted at the commencement of this study, the theme of John's Gospel is establishing the historical facts—that Jesus is the Christ, the Son of God (20:30–31). The inspired apostle achieves this goal in a number of remarkable ways—not the least of which is the employment of Old Testament inspired Scripture. What a wonderful component this fascinating document is in the overall scheme of revelation and redemption.

Chapter 19

The Sacred Canon of the Scriptures

"Written in the East, these characters live forever in the West; written in one province, they pervade the world; penned in rude times, they are prized more and more as civilization advances; product of antiquity, they come home to the bosoms of men, women, and children in modern times. Then is it any exaggeration to say that the 'characters of the Scriptures are a marvel of the mind'?"
— Robert Louis Stevenson (1850–1894)

Bible scholars refer to the "canon" of the Scriptures. What is meant by that expression? The term "canon" is an anglicized form of the Greek *kanon*. Originally, the word had to do with a straight rod or rule, to which a builder would compare his work for trueness.

Gradually, the term came to be employed figuratively of a "norm or standard." In ancient Greece, Polycletus, a spearman, "was regarded as the canon or perfect form of the human frame" (Kittel 1965, 597). In his letter to the Galatians, Paul referred to the "rule" (*kanon*) by which Christians are expected to live (6:16). Eventually, the expression came to signify that which has "passed the test."

When, therefore, the word is applied to the books of the Bible, it denotes those documents that, over a period of time, have passed the test of critical examination, hence, warrant the designation "sacred Scripture." In his *Commentary on Matthew*, Origen (ca. A.D. 185–254), one of the Greek "church fathers," alluded to the "canonized Scriptures" (section 28; Thiessen 1955, 4). Today, the "Canon" refers to those sixty-six books which constitute the common Bible.

But this introduces several questions. Who determined which books were to go into the Bible? Exactly when did that occur? And what are the Apocryphal books?

THE STANDARD OF DETERMINATION

The issue of which books belong in the Bible was determined gradually and on the basis of evidence. By "gradually" we mean that there was not a definite historical date when a synod or council made a determination—"These are the true biblical books!" Rather, over a period of years, by the application of reasonable tests, the documents truly inspired were separated from those works that are spurious. The evidence leading to this decision is classified as external and internal.

External evidence has to do with the testimony of those who had access to the documents originally. How did they view them, and why? Internal evidence relates to the nature of the material itself. Does it claim to be from God? Is it internally consistent? Does it harmonize with other documents that are perceived to be inspired? Is it characterized by a lofty tone, i.e., that essence which one would expect in a narrative that claims inspiration? Does it bear the marks of factual accuracy? These sorts of things, as applied by reasonable minds, ultimately separated the genuinely sacred books from those unworthy of that recognition.

OLD TESTAMENT BOOKS

Jewish tradition traces the collection of the Old Testament books to the time of Ezra (mid-fifth century B.C.). It may have been a while later before the entire canon was actually recognized. By the time Christ was born, there were two versions of the Old Testament.

The Hebrew canon consisted of the thirty-nine books that currently make up our Old Testament—though in the Palestinean version they numbered only twenty-four (due to a different arrangement—some books being combined).

The Septuagint version (a Greek translation from the third or second centuries B.C.) contained various other documents that were "bound up" with the regular thirty-nine books of the Hebrew Bible (the number of these extra books varying in different editions). While these additional books, called the Apocrypha, reflected some historical matters, they were not perceived as inspired by God, and, significantly, were never sanctioned by Christ nor any New Testament writer. Some of them, though, are incorporated into Roman Catholic editions of the Bible (see the chapter, "The Apocrypha").

Liberal critics claim that originally all the biblical docu ments were simply pieces of ordinary literature. They were eventually perceived as sacred, not because they merited the descriptive, but because inspiration was thrust upon them. One critic stated: "Every sentence in the OT was profane literature before it became canonical sacred scripture" (Pfeiffer 1962, 499). But this is not the way in which the writers of the Old Testament viewed their productions. For example, in the book of Leviticus the phrase, "the Lord called unto Moses," or a similar expression, is found about thirty-six in the twenty-seven chapters of the document. Moses was mentioned fifty-five times in the book.

One of the most significant evidences for the sacred nature of the Old Testament books is the manner in which they are quoted, or alluded to, in the New Testament, having the sanction of Christ and his sacred penmen. According to one computation (Horn 1960, 173), the New Testament contains 433 direct quotations from the Old Testament. No less than thirty of the thirty-nine books are definitely quoted, with numerous additional allusions. For a more detailed look at this matter, see the chapter elsewhere in this book, "How New Testament Writers Used the Old Testament in Their Teaching."

Moreover, it is not just the fact that the Old Testament is quoted; it is the way in which it is quoted that is significant. The technical phrase, "it is written" (used of an inspired work—cf. Thayer 1958, 121) is employed in seventy-three New Testament passages. In some twenty-one New Testament passages, the Old Testament documents are referred to as "scripture."

Quotations from at least eleven of the Old Testament books are attributed to God or the Holy Spirit. For example, Peter, quoting from Psalm 69, says that "it was needful that the scripture should be fulfilled, which the Holy Spirit spoke before by the mouth of David" (Acts 1:16ff). In some forty-six New Testament passages, the names of ten Old Testament books (or authors) are mentioned.

Again, let us emphasize that no Apocryphal book from the LXX is given endorsement, even though the New Testament writers were familiar with these books.

NEW TESTAMENT BOOKS

The New Testament authors considered their writings to be as authoritative as those of the Old Testament Scriptures. For example, Paul quotes from the book of Deuteronomy (25:4) and the Gospel of Luke (10:7) and classifies both of these as "scripture" (1 Tim. 5:18).

Peter places "all" of Paul's "epistles" in the same category as "the other scriptures" (2 Pet. 3:16). The word "other" translates the Greek *loipos*, which denotes "the rest of any number or class under consideration" (Thayer 1958, 382). Too, note how Peter puts the "apostles" in the same category as the "holy prophets" of Old Testament fame (2 Pet. 3:2).

The ancient church was unanimous in its acceptance of most of the New Testament books; for a while there was some dispute over James, 2 John, 3 John, 2 Peter, Jude, Hebrews and Revelation. Too, during this time period (second to third centuries), other books, which had generated some interest (e.g., the Epistle of Barnabas, the Shepherd of Hermas) were being eliminated. By the fourth century, it was a settled issue that the currently accepted twenty-seven books of our New Testament, and only these, are canonical.

It was not a matter of any official council deciding which books would be acknowledged as inspired; it was a matter of critically examining, sorting, sifting, and identifying what had become perfectly obvious. "The canon itself was produced, not by one act of men, so to speak, but gradually by God, who controls minds and seasons" (Loescher, as quoted by Green 1898, 111).

The writings of the New Testament were so profusely quoted by the ante-Nicene "fathers" (A.D. 325 and back), that it is said that if the whole New Testament were destroyed, it could be reproduced entirely from their citations—with the exception of about a dozen verses (Hastings 1980, 12).

We may have every confidence, therefore, that the sixty-six books which compose our present Bible are the true embodiment of the Word of God.

Chapter 20

The Apocrypha

"Education is useless without the Bible."
— Noah Webster (1758–1843)

In the ever urgent work of winning souls for Christ, the Christian occasionally will encounter members of the Roman Catholic Church who note, with perhaps some degree of pride, that their version of the Bible contains more books than standard translations used by non-Catholics. More often than not, the average Christian is at a loss to explain why there are forty-six books in the Old Testament of the Catholic Bible, yet only thirty-nine books in the Old Testament of the common versions. The qualified teacher needs to be able to give a reasonable explanation to his Catholic friends for the absence of those seven books in the versions we use.

THE DISPUTED BOOKS

The Apocrypha is a collection of documents, generally produced between the second century B.C. and the first century A.D., which were not a part of the original Old Testament canon. The names of these books are: I Esdras, II Esdras, The Rest of Esther, Song of the Three Holy Children, History of Susanna, Bel and the Dragon, Prayer of Manasses, Tobit, Judith,

Wisdom of Solomon, Ecclesiasticus, Baruch, I Maccabees, and II Maccabees. The last seven of these are incorporated into Roman Catholic editions of the Bible. The Catholic Council of Trent (1546) affirmed the canonicity of these books, as found in the Latin Vulgate, and condemned those who reject them.

The title, "Apocrypha," is a transliterated form of the term *apokruphos*, meaning "hidden." A plural form of the word is used in Colossians 2:3, where Paul declares that all the treasures of wisdom and knowledge are "hidden" in Christ. The adjective "apocryphal" has come to be applied to those books that do not bear the marks of divine inspiration. There are several reasons why the Apocrypha is to be rejected as part of the Bible.

GENERAL PRINCIPLES

There is abundant evidence that none of these books was ever received into the canon (that which conforms to "rule") of the Hebrew Old Testament. Though they appear in the Septuagint, that is not necessarily a reliable criterion. Professor G. T. Manley notes:

> [These books] do not appear to have been included at first in the LXX [third to second centuries B.C.], but they found their way gradually into later copies, being inserted in places that seemed appropriate" (1962, 39).

The apocryphal books are not in those most ancient works that allude to the Old Testament Scriptures. For example:

(1) Philo, the Jewish philosopher of Alexandria (20 B.C.–A.D. 50), wrote prolifically and frequently quoted the Old Testament; yet he never cited the Apocrypha, nor did he even mention these documents.

(2) Josephus (A.D. 37–95) rejected them. He wrote:

> We have not an innumerable multitude of books among us, disagreeing from and contradicting one another, but only twenty-two books, which contain the records of all the past times; which are justly believed to be divine" (*Against Apion* 1.8).

By combining several Old Testament narratives into a "book," the thirty-nine of our current editions become the twenty-two alluded to by Josephus.

(3) The most ancient list of Old Testament books is that which was made by Melito of Sardis (ca. A.D. 170); none of the apocryphal books is included (cf. Eusebius, *Ecclesiastical History* 4.26.14).

(4) In the early third century A.D., neither Origin nor his contemporary, Tertullian, recognized the books of the Apocrypha as being canonical.

(5) Though some of the apocryphal books were being used in the church services by the fifth century A.D., they were read only by those who held inferior offices in the church (Horne 1841, 1.436).

(6) The apocryphal books were produced in an era when no inspired documents were being given by God. Malachi concludes his narrative in the Old Testament by urging Israel: "Remember ye the law of Moses my servant, which I commanded unto him in Horeb for all Israel, even statutes and ordinances." He then projects four centuries into the future and prophesied: "Behold, I will send you Elijah the prophet before the great and terrible day of Jehovah come" (Mal. 4:4–5). This text pictured the coming of John the Baptist (cf. Mt. 11:14; Lk. 1:17). The implication of Malachi's prophecy is that no prophet would arise from God until the coming of John. This excludes the apocryphal writings.

Josephus confirms this when he declares:

> It is true, our history has been written since
> Artaxerxes very particularly, but has not been
> esteemed of the like authority with the former by
> our forefathers, because there has not been an exact
> succession of prophets since that time.

He further says that no one "has been so bold as either
to add any thing to them, to take any thing from them, or to
make any change in them" (*Against Apion* 1.8).

F. F. Bruce contended that there "is no evidence that these
books were ever regarded as canonical by any Jews, whether
inside or outside Palestine, whether they read the Bible in
Hebrew or in Greek" (1950, 157).

(7) Jesus Christ and his inspired New Testament penmen
quoted from, or alluded to, the writings and events of
the Old Testament profusely. In fact, some one thousand
quotations or allusions from thirty-five of the thirty-nine
Old Testament books are found in the New Testament
record. And yet, significantly, not once are any of these
apocryphal books quoted or even explicitly referred to
by the Lord or any New Testament writer. Noted scholar
Emile Schurer argued that this is really remarkable since
most of the New Testament habitually quoted from the
LXX (1849, 99).

> Despite the fact that New Testament writers quote
> largely from the Septuagint rather than from the
> Hebrew Old Testament, there is not a single clear-
> cut case of a citation from any of the fourteen apoc-
> ryphal books . . . . The most that can be said is that
> the New Testament writers show acquaintance with

these fourteen books and perhaps allude to them indirectly, but in no case do they quote them as inspired Scripture or cite them as authority (Unger 1951, 101).

(8) Finally, it must be observed that the apocryphal books, unlike the canonical books of the Old Testament, make no direct claims of being inspired of God. Not once is there a, "thus says the Lord," or language like, "the word of the Lord came unto me, saying." In fact, some of the documents actually confess non-inspiration! In the prologue of Ecclesiasticus, the writer states:

> Ye are entreated therefore to read with favour and attention, and to pardon us, if in any parts of what we have laboured to interpret, we may seem to fail in some of the phrases.

(9) Too, there is the matter of literary style. Dr. Raymond Surburg has written:

> When a comparison is instituted of the style of the Apocrypha with the style of the Biblical Hebrew Old Testament writings, there is a considerable inferiority, shown by the stiffness, lack of originality and artificiality of expression characterizing the apocryphal books (1980, 7).

EVIDENCE NEGATING INSPIRATION

The Apocrypha contains a great variety of historical, geographical, chronological, and moral errors. Professor William Green of Princeton wrote: "The books of Tobit and Judith abound in geographical, chronological, and historical mistakes" (1898, 195). A critical study of the Apocrypha's contents clearly reveals that it could not be the product of the Spirit of God. The following examples are ample evidence of this.

First, rather than the creation being spoken into existence from nothing by the word of Almighty God, as affirmed in the Scriptures (Gen. 1:1; Psa. 33:6–9; Heb. 11:3), the Apocrypha has God creating the world out of "formless matter" (Wisdom of Solomon 11:17).

Second, according to the prophet Jeremiah, Nebuchadnezzar burned Jerusalem on the tenth day, fifth month, of the nineteenth year of his reign (Jer. 52:12–13). Subsequent to this, both the prophet and his scribe, Baruch, were taken into Egypt (Jer. 43:6–7). According to the Apocrypha, however, at this very time Baruch was in Babylon (Baruch 1:1–2).

Third, there are two contradictory accounts of the death of Antiochus Epiphanes, that dreaded enemy of the Jews. One narrative records that Antiochus and his company were "cut to pieces in the temple of Nanaea by the treachery of Nanaea's priests" (2 Maccabees 1:13–16), while another version in the same book states that Antiochus was "taken with a noisome sickness" and so "ended his life among the mountains by a most piteous fate in a strange land" (2 Maccabees 9:19–29).

Fourth, Tobit is said to have lived 158 years (14:11), yet, supposedly, he was alive back when Jeroboam revolted against Jerusalem (931 B.C.), and then still around when the Assyrians invaded Israel (722/21 B.C.)—a span of some 210 years! (Tobit 1:3–5).

Fifth, the Apocrypha teaches the erroneous doctrine of the pre-existence of the soul, suggesting that the kind of body one now has is determined by the character of his soul in a previous life. "Now I was a goodly child, and a good soul fell to my lot; Nay rather, being good, I came into a body undefiled" (Wisdom of Solomon 8:19–20). The foregoing was a common belief among heathen peoples, but certainly it is contrary to the biblical view that the soul of man is formed with him at conception (Psa. 139:13–16; Zech. 12:1).

Sixth, the Apocrypha teaches that prayer may be made for the dead: "Wherefore he made the propitiation for them that had died, that they might be released from their sins" (2 Maccabees 12:45). Roman Catholics cite this passage to find support for their dogma of praying for the dead to be released from purgatory (obviously there is no New Testament passage to buttress the notion), but the effort is vain.

Seventh, the Apocrypha suggests that one may atone for his sins by the giving of alms. "It is better to give alms than to lay up gold: alms doth deliver from death, and it shall purge away all sin" (Tobit 12:9).

MORAL TONE

The moral tone of the Apocrypha is far below that of the Bible. Note some examples:

- It applauds suicide as a noble and manful act. Second Maccabees tells of one Razis who, being surrounded by the enemy, fell upon his sword, choosing "rather to die nobly" than to fall into the hands of his enemy. He was not mortally wounded, however, and so threw himself down from a wall and "manfully" died among the crowds (14:41–43).

- It describes magical potions which are alleged to drive demons away (Tobit 6:1–17).

- The murder of the men of Shechem (Gen. 34), an act of violence which is condemned in the Scriptures (cf. Gen. 49:6–7), is commended and is described as an act of God (Judith 9:2–9).

These, along with various other considerations, lead only to the conclusion that the Apocrypha cannot be included in the volume of sacred Scripture.

Chapter 21

Why is That in the Bible?

*"Every morning read seriously and reverently a portion
of the Holy Scriptures, and acquaint yourself with the
history and doctrine thereof; it is a book full of light and
wisdom, and will make you wise unto eternal life."*
— Sir Matthew Hale (1609–1676), Lord Chief Justice of England

There are hundreds of things in the Scriptures that obviously are crucial and clearly relevant to God's wonderful plan for human salvation. The devout student easily can discern such matters. On the other hand, there are other items in the sacred book the purposes of which are less discernable. Regarding such things the skeptic rails with obvious delight, alleging that these texts are absurd and meaningless—highly unworthy of a book that claims to be inspired of God. Even the reverent student occasionally may furrow his brow and ask: "Why is that in the Bible?"

In this chapter we will not profess to address all such instances in the sacred narrative. We will select a few examples that should be sufficient to illustrate the reality that things sometimes considered irrelevant, upon closer inspection, actually are quite meaningful.

GENEALOGIES

A genealogy is a record of a family lineage. It is a preserved documentation of a family's background that serves as a valuable historical and legal instrument. The general interest in genealogies in our modern world should signal the usefulness of such records and the value that people have attached to family lineages, including those of Scripture.

Some general facts regarding the biblical genealogies are: (a) Genealogies for the most part trace family histories through males. (b) The relationships frequently are father-son connections, though this is not always the case. (c) The genealogies of Scripture had both material and spiritual values. Let us briefly amplify these points.

First, while most of the genealogical lists deal with males, due to the patriarchal nature of the family as designed by God, occasionally women are mentioned. For example Matthew's record includes the names of Tamar, Rahab, and Ruth, and alludes also to Bathsheba (1:3, 5, 6). These women were a mixture of Gentile heritage and sin-stained lives. These inclusions likely suggest God's interest in nations beyond the Hebrew family and also his concern for the sinful. The sinless Son of God derived his physical existence from a sinful ancestry mingled with Gentile genetics. Christ thus became a light to the Gentiles and a Savior for sinful humanity.

Second, there obviously are some gaps in some of the genealogical records. A comparison of Ezra 7:3–4 with 1 Chronicles 6:6–10 reveals that six names are missing from Ezra's list. In Matthew's genealogy of Jesus—designed to demonstrate that the Lord was descended from Abraham and David (1:1)—four names are omitted between Joram and Uzziah (1:8). These deletions are known, of course, due to the fact that they are supplied in parallel lists. Minor deletions, however, do not nullify the primary objectives of genealogical proximity. Since there is a substantial genealogical record from Christ back to Adam (Lk. 3:23–38), when this reality is combined with our knowledge of post-Christian history, there is no reasonable way to dismiss the chronological data of Scripture in deference to the evolutionary theory that humankind has been on earth for several million years. As Professor John Klotz observed: "God apparently did want to show us that the earth is not billions of years old" (1970, 91; see Jackson 2003).

Third, the genealogies in the Genesis record that catalogue the great ages of the patriarchs demonstrate how the early earth could have been populated so rapidly (possibly seven billion souls by the time of the Flood; Morris 1976, 144). Additionally, the declining longevity of humanity highlights the gradual debilitating effects of sin upon mankind. Compare the ages of the pre-Flood patriarchs with those who followed (Gen. 5:1ff; 25:7–8; Psa. 90:10).

Fourth, the genealogies were important in maintaining the theocratic regime of the nation of Israel (through which Christ would descend), the substantial integrity of the Hebrew priesthood, and the preservation of tribal property rights under the Mosaic economy.

Fifth, some of the genealogies pertain principally to the nation of Israel and the development of the Messianic line. Certain Old Testament prophecies specifically had to do with the heritage of Jesus. Those lineage records establish the historical fact that Christ was of the Abrahamic and Davidic stream (cf. Gen. 49:10; Num. 24:17; Isa. 11:1). And here is another crucial point:

> Since . . . the period of their destruction as a nation by the Romans, all [Hebrew] tables of descent seem to be lost, and now [the Jews] are utterly unable to trace the pedigree of any one Israelite who might lay claim

> to be their promised and still expected Messiah.
> Hence Christians assert, with a force that no reason-
> able and candid Jew can resist, that Shiloh [Genesis
> 49:10] must have come (McClintock 1969, 771).

There are, therefore, important reasons for the several genealogical catalogs within the library of sacred literature. Let no one, therefore, criticize what he does not understand.

STRANGE LAWS

There are various laws in the early literature of the Bible that at first glance appear to be trivial in some cases, and almost bizarre in other situations. But before snap judgments are made and Scripture is thrust into a negative light, several principles need to be recognized.

First, the specific purposes of many of those regulations are shrouded in the obscurity of antiquity. It may not be possible to explain emphatically why certain ordinances were imposed. However all who have sufficiently studied the evidence so as to be convinced of the Bible's divine nature entertain no doubt that the Hebrews understood the purpose of those "strange" requirements—and learned from them. Our complete appreciation of them from this remote vantage point is not of great concern.

Second, God chose the nation of Israel for a special role in redemptive history. And from the time of its inception as a special people, it was nurtured from a child-like state towards a greater level of maturity. As with any development, the people failed on numerous occasions. In the more elementary stages of instruction, less sophisticated aids of teaching were necessary. Just as a small child learns his letters by pictures ("A is for apple"), even so "pictures" incorporated into certain laws were to instill concepts that would be foundational to subsequent development. An awareness of this fundamental instructive methodology is imperative to gaining some insight into the seemingly irrelevant minutia that was a part of the Mosaic legal system.

Let us now consider (for illustrative purposes) some of the "strange" regulations of Mosaic law.

First, in anticipation of Israel's entrance into Canaan, Moses laid down requirements regarding the planting of fruit trees (Lev. 19:23–25). For the first three years, the fruit was not to be eaten. The fourth year the crop was dedicated to God. Finally, the produce could be consumed the fifth year. R. K. Harrison noted that "the legislation forbidding the fruit of new trees to be eaten is based on sound horticulture principles" that permit the trees to mature. Even among the ancient Babylonians, "trees bearing fruit were seldom utilized for food until after the fourth year" (1980, 200–201).

Second, if an Israelite discovered a bird's nest with a mother bird brooding eggs, they were permitted to take the eggs, or even the young birds, but the mother was not to be disturbed (Dt. 22:6–7). What was the purpose in this regulation? One may only speculate. The lesson may deal with practicality. If both young and old are consumed, the species might soon become endangered and the people suffer the consequences. Phocylides, a Greek poet of the sixth century B.C., wrote: "Nor from a nest take all the birds away; The mother spare, she'll breed a future day." Thompson wondered if perhaps "reverence for motherhood in general" was behind the law (1974, 234). Jesus sometimes used birds as illustrations of God's care for humans (Mt. 6:26).

Third, in biblical days houses had flat roofs and these accommodated various activities (Josh. 2:6; 2 Sam. 11:2; Acts 10:9). The Law of Moses prescribed, therefore, that when a man constructed his house, there must be a railing around the roof edge (Dt. 22:8). Obviously this was for the protection of the man's family, and also for the sake of legal liability. It was a common-sense law to protect a man from his own neglect. The Babylonian Code of Hammurabi likewise had laws of liability that protected those who were victims of careless workmanship respecting houses (Pritchard 1973, 163–164).

Fourth, there are several laws in Deuteronomy 22 that require distinctions between certain objects. There must be a recognizable distinction between the way men and women dress (v. 5). Two different seeds might not be sown in one's vineyard. An ox and donkey might not be plowed together. And a garment woven of both flax and wool was forbidden (vv. 9–11).

The distinction in dress might have been directed at pagan ritualism. Male and female exchanges of clothing were a part of heathen ritualism, thought to cure infertility (Hoffner 1969, 48–51). The unequal yoking of beasts of burden might have been a polemic against the abuse of one's animals—the donkey being unable to compete with the ox in strength. The Septuagint translation of Leviticus 19:19 uses the term *heterozeugos*, an "unequal yoke," and such may have been designed to be a visual object lesson against forming harmful relationships with unbelievers (cf. 2 Cor. 6:14). Harris argued that the common perception that the cross breeding of animals was being prohibited (as reflected in the KJV, NIV, ESV) does not reflect the best explanation (1990, 606–607). The mixing of seeds and of garment fabrics could well be a "picture" reminder that reinforced the principle of keeping the sacred and secular separated (Harrison 1980, 199)—or perhaps that of preserving the distinction between the created order of things (Kalland 1992, 136).

Fifth, many have wondered why the rite of circumcision was required of males in the Old Testament (Gen. 17:9ff; Lev. 12:3). It was a special covenant "sign" between God and his people; it implied commitment to the Lord (Dt. 10:16; Jer. 4:4). Also, it may have signified that sexual activity was to be a sacred act within marriage, in contrast to the vile sexual rituals of heathenism (Laney 1997, 24). Some have noted the hygienic advantages as well (Watts 1951, 354–355).

ALLEGED TRIVIALITIES

Louis Gaussen, a Swiss scholar who served as Professor of Systematic Theology in Geneva, produced a classic volume, *Theopneustia—The Plenary Inspiration of the Holy Scriptures* (1840). In this work he responded to several criticisms often made against the concept of the Bible's verbal inspiration. One of these is "the apparent insignificance of certain details," that allegedly tends to nullify the lofty purpose claimed for the Scriptures (306ff). He addressed certain examples in the writings of Paul. I will consider a text from the Old Testament, and then one from the New.

There is a passage having to do with an incident in the life of David that is most intriguing. The Old Testament student is informed that when King David came to Mahanaim, three men, Shobi (an Ammonite), Machir of Lodebar, and Barzillai of Gilead:

> Brought beds, and basins, and earthen vessels, and wheat, and barley, and meal, and parched grain, and beans, and lentils, and parched pulse, and honey, and butter, and sheep, and cheese of the herd, for David and for the people that were with him (2 Sam. 17:28–29).

The critic is prone to ask: "Do we really need an entire 'grocery list,' in this book that purports to be a spiritual document that guides one from earth to heaven?" But the possible background of the passage could shed a floodlight of meaning upon this seemingly trivial list.

David's beloved son, Absalom, was a rebel at heart. He was envious of his father's success and wanted acclaim for himself.

Hence he carefully plotted to wrest the allegiance of David's subjects from him, and transfer the same to himself—and he was significantly successful. He "stole the hearts of the men of Israel" (2 Sam. 15:6).

Eventually, a full-blown rebellion was ignited. David, with his remaining loyalists, fled Jerusalem. The king, with head covered, barefooted, and weeping, abandoned his palace for the sheltered seclusion of the forests east of Jordan (2 Sam. 15:30; 17:22ff). Absalom hotly pursued his father, doubtless with the intention of assassinating the king. Such wretchedness! David and his people were hungry, exhausted, and without adequate provisions. What were they to do? Was there no assistance? Where was God?

Rather than acting directly (as in the case of dropping food from heaven for the Israelites [Ex. 16:4]), the Lord providentially intervened (i.e., through indirect means that appeared altogether natural) and sustained this man "after [his] own heart" in his time of distress. Some scholars believe that Psalm 23 might well have been written to celebrate the answer to David's prayers during this time of intense danger—especially verses five and six (Johnson 1981, 225; Kirkpatrick 1906, 124): "You prepare a table before me in the presence of my enemies; You anoint my head with oil. My cup overflows."

If there is no specific historical connection between the song and this episode in David's life, the latter at least certainly illustrates the former. The sneered-at "grocery list" becomes a prime example of one's "cup running over"—even in the looming shadow of a deadly enemy!

Another example of "triviality" that stirs the ire of the destructive critic is Paul's request from a Roman prison cell to his friend Timothy, urging the young man to join him as quickly as possible, and requesting that he bring the "cloak that I left at Troas with Carpus" (2 Tim. 4:13). Is this request of no importance? Is it bereft of spiritual value? The truth is, the phrase is brimming with information for those not too dull to detect it. From my recent commentary on Paul's letters to Timothy and Titus, I borrow the following thoughts (Jackson 2007).

Several questions are intensely stimulating. Why did the apostle leave his coat in Troas? Was he forced to flee quickly, and thus had no time to obtain it? We know that his ministry was fraught with dangerous circumstances that made rapid flight imperative on many occasions (cf. Acts 9:23–25).

The request is but another commentary on the sacrificial poverty of him who was willing to spend and be spent for the cause of Christ (2 Cor. 12:15). Think of it—a chilling winter in a Roman dungeon is approaching, and yet the apostle's only coat is a thousand miles away! Winters in Rome average in the low-to-mid forties. Paul was no stranger to "cold and nakedness" (2 Cor. 11:27), or to poverty.

Where were the saints in Rome during this time of Paul's physical need? Was there no one who could provide the beloved apostle with a coat to warm his frail frame? Where were those enthusiastic Christians who had rushed out of the city years earlier to meet the tireless preacher as he approached the imperial city? (Acts 28:15). Had persecution scattered many of them? Had others, like Demas (v. 10), forsaken the apostle? (cf. Phil. 1:15–17). At Paul's "first defense" (perhaps a preliminary procedure in his present legal ordeal), no one took his part; all forsook him (v. 16).

The passage is revealing of the fortitude and independence of the magnificent Paul. Tough as a pine knot, no word of complaint or whimpering escapes his courageous lips. No browbeating of neglectful brethren, and no pitiful solicitation from others is here in evidence. What a man!

The incorporation of this request into the sacred narrative is a reminder that God is concerned with the most intimate details of our lives. If he is attentive when a single sparrow falls to the ground (Mt. 10:29), is he not mindful when one of his saints is without the bare necessities of life? God cares! (cf. 2 Kgs. 20:5). Believe it, and be comforted thereby—even when discomfort surrounds you.

The text also reminds us, however, that our Father does not exempt us from the common distresses of life—even when we are faithful. Not even the apostle expected the Lord to provide him with a supernatural heat source to protect him from the cold. Rather, Paul knew that he must exercise his own ingenuity in the matter (by making a request of a devoted brother), and let Providence orchestrate the rest. Faith, without appropriate action, produces nothing.

Pity, therefore, the near-sighted, spiritually blighted soul who sees nothing in this apostolic comment but a piece of cloth!

Long ago I learned, when encountering a problem passage in the Holy Book, not to exasperatingly ask, "Why is that in the Bible?" Rather, I have come to view such texts as a thrilling challenge, and I absolutely delight in exploring the hidden treasures awaiting me. Such explorations have thrilled my soul more times than I can compute.

Chapter 22

The Integrity of the Biblical Text

"Yes, it is a press, certainly, but a press from which shall flow in inexhaustible streams the most abundant and most marvelous liquor that has ever flowed to relieve the thirst of men. Through it, God will spread His word; a spring of pure truth shall flow from it; like a new star it shall scatter the darkness of ignorance, and cause a light hithertofore unknown to shine among men."
— Johannes Gutenberg (1400–1468)

Do we really know that the text of our English Bible is essentially that of the original Hebrew, Aramaic, and Greek manuscripts? Happily, the science of archaeology has generously contributed to our confidence in the integrity of the biblical text.

THE OLD TESTAMENT TEXT

In the preface to his great volume, *A Scientific Investigation of the Old Testament,* Dr. Robert Dick Wilson declared,

> [I]t is my endeavor to show from the evidence of manuscripts, versions, and the inscriptions, that we are scientifically certain that we have substantially the same text that was in the possession of Christ and the apostles and, so far as anybody knows, the

same as that written by the original composers of
the Old Testament documents (1929, 8).

The man who made this confident statement concerning
the reliability of the Old Testament text was not some incom-
petent, know-nothing clergyman. He was, in fact, one of the
most accomplished language and Bible scholars of the preceding generation, or, as a matter of fact, any generation!

Robert Dick Wilson (1856–1930) graduated from Princeton
University in 1876, at the age of twenty. He went on to obtain
the MA and PhD degrees and then went to Germany where he
did two more years of postgraduate work at the University of
Berlin. Dr. Wilson was a brilliant language student. When he
was still in seminary, he could already read the New Testament
in nine different languages.

When Wilson was twenty-five years of age, he determined
that he would spend the balance of his life qualifying himself
so that he might be able to speak with authority in matters
relating to the text of the Bible. He figured, based upon the longevity of his ancestors, that he might live to be approximately
seventy years of age. If such were the case, he would have some
forty-five years left in which to work. Accordingly, he planned
his projected life-span into three periods of fifteen years each.
During the first of these periods, he would study all of the
ancient languages that had a bearing upon the text of the Old
Testament. Amazingly, in that initial fifteen years, he mastered
forty-five languages! He not only was an expert in Hebrew, and
all the cognate languages, but he learned all of the languages
into which the Bible had been translated down to the year
600 A.D. He once declared that if there was any language bearing upon the text of the Bible that he did not know, if someone
would show it to him, he would learn it! He was determined to
become so thoroughly qualified that no one could introduce a
problem that he could not investigate firsthand.

In the second fifteen years of his studies, Professor Wilson made a study of every consonant in the Hebrew Old Testament. (There are no vowels in the Hebrew text of the Old Testament.) There are about a million and a quarter of these consonants. He said of this monumental task:

> I had to read the Old Testament through and look at every consonant in it; I had also to observe the variations of the text, as far as they were to be found in the manuscripts, or in the notes of the Massoretes [a body of Jewish scholars dedicated to the preservation of the Old Testament] or in the various versions, or in the parallel passages, or in the conjectural emendations of critics; and then I had to classify the results. I prize this form of textual research very highly; for my plan has been to reduce the Old Testament criticism to an absolutely objective science; something which is based on evidence, and not on opinion. I scarcely ever make a statement which rests merely on my own subjective belief.

> In order to be a textual expert of this kind, it is necessary to be a master of paleography [the science which deals with ancient writings] and of philology; to have an exact knowledge of a dozen languages at least, so that every word may be thoroughly sifted.

Professor Wilson's expertise enabled him to show, for example, the accuracy of the Old Testament text as compared with some of the classical documents of antiquity. He wrote:

> I can remember when it was thought very unprofitable to read the long genealogies found in the first chapters of First Chronicles—nine chapters of proper

names. But today, in the scientific criticism of the Old Testament, proper names are of the profoundest significance. The way in which they are written—indeed, all that is connected with them—has come to be one of the very foundations upon which scientific criticism of the Old Testament is built.

Take the following case. There are twenty-nine ancient kings whose names are mentioned not only in the Bible but also on monuments of their own time, many of them under their own supervision. There are one hundred and ninety-five consonants in these twenty-nine proper names. Yet we find that in the documents of the Hebrew Old Testament there are only two or three out of the entire hundred and ninety-five about which there can be any question of their being written in exactly the same way as they were inscribed on their own monuments. Some of these go back two thousand years, some for four thousand; and are so written that every letter is clear and correct. This is surely a wonder.

Compare this accuracy with that of other writings. I have been blamed for not referring to the classical writings more frequently in my book on Daniel. Here is the reason—take the list made by the greatest scholar of this age, the librarian at Alexandria in 200 B.C. He compiled a catalogue of the kings of Egypt, thirty-eight in all, of the entire number only three or four of them are recognizable. He also made a list of the kings of Assyria; in only one case can we tell who is meant; and that one is not spelt correctly. Or take Ptolemy, who drew up a register of eighteen of the kings of Babylon. Not one of them is properly spelt; you could not make them out at all if you did not know from other sources to what he is referring. If any one talks against the Bible, ask him about the kings mentioned in it. There are twenty-nine kings of Egypt, Israel, Moab, Damascus, Tyre, Babylon, Assyria, and Persia, referred to, and ten different countries among these twenty-nine; all of which are included in the Bible accounts and those of the monuments. Every one of these is given his right name in the Bible, his right country, and placed in the correct chronological order. Think of what this means!

Dr. Wilson spent the final period of his life writing down the results of his many years of painstaking labor. He thus was able to firmly state:

> For forty-five years continuously, since I left college, I have devoted myself to the one great study of the Old Testament, in all its languages, in all its archaeology, in all its translations, and as far as possible in everything bearing upon its text and history. I tell you this so that you may see why I can and do speak as an expert. I may add that the result of my forty-five years of study of the Bible has led me all the time to a firmer faith that in the Old Testament we have a true historical account of the history of the Israelite people; and I have a right to commend this to some of those bright men and women who think that they can laugh at the old-time Christian and believer in the Word of God (Coray 1971, 39–48).

The accuracy of the text of the Old Testament has been forcefully demonstrated by the discovery of the Dead Sea

Scrolls. Prior to 1947, the oldest Hebrew manuscripts of any length did not date earlier than toward the end of the ninth century A.D., and the oldest complete Hebrew Bible is from about a century later. With the discovery of the Dead Sea documents, however, our history of the Old Testament text has been pushed back approximately one thousand years! They date during the first two centuries B.C. and the first century A.D. These scrolls have provided monumental evidence of the precision and accuracy of the Old Testament text. Note, for example, Gleason Archer's comment about the accuracy of the Masoretic Text as compared with the Isaiah scrolls of the Dead Sea find:

> Even though the two copies of Isaiah discovered in Qumran Cave 1 near the Dead Sea in 1947 were a thousand years earlier than the oldest dated manuscript previously known (A.D. 980), they proved to be word for word identical with our standard Hebrew Bible in more than 95 per cent of the text. The 5 per cent of variation consisted chiefly of obvious slips of the pen and variations in spelling (1964, 19).

To give a specific example of the quality of accuracy about which we are speaking, let us compare Isaiah 53 in the Masoretic Text with that of the Dead Sea Scrolls—and remember, the two are separated by a thousand years of time.

Of the 166 words in Isaiah 53, there are only seventeen letters in question. Ten of these letters are simply a matter of spelling, which does not affect the sense. Four more letters are minor stylistic changes, such as conjunctions. The remaining three letters comprise the word "light," which is added in verse eleven, and does not affect the meaning greatly. Thus, in one chapter of 166 words, there is only one word (three letters) in question after a thousand years of transmission, and this word does not significantly change the meaning of the passage (Geisler and Nix 1986, 263).

Edwin Yamauchi has commented concerning this matter:

> We were not sure how accurate the work of the Masoretes and their predecessors was. Some scholars dated the origin of the MT [Masoretic Text] to the editorial activities of rabbis in the second century A.D. Thanks to Qumran [the place where the Dead Sea Scrolls were found] we know that the MT goes back to a Proto-Masoretic edition antedating the Christian era, and we are assured that this reclension was copied with remarkable accuracy. This means that the consonantal text of the Hebrew Bible must be treated with respect and not freely emended (1972, 130).

W. J. Martin and A. R. Millard, professors of Hebrew and ancient Semitic languages at the University of Liverpool, affirmed that "the great significance of these MSS [manuscripts] is that they constitute an independent witness to the reliability of the transmission of our accepted text" (1980, 1538). Thus it may confidently be said that no other work of antiquity has been so accurately transmitted as that of the biblical text.

THE NEW TESTAMENT TEXT

Many people are surprised when they first learn that we possess none of the original documents (called autographs) of the New Testament. The loss of these original manuscripts is undoubtedly by divine design, for, without question, had they been preserved, foolish men would have made idols of them rather than being directed to God, whose will they set forth. In spite of this absence of the originals, however, thanks to the work of archaeologists and textual critics, we can express a total confidence in the reliability of the New Testament text. The original text of the New Testament is determined from three general sources: (1) Greek manuscripts, (2) ancient versions, and (3) quotations from the New Testament in the writings of the post-apostolic age.

Forty years ago there were approximately five thousand Greek manuscripts (in whole or in part) of the New Testament in existence (Metzger 1968, 36). A more precise number is now at 5,748. Some of these are very significant. Possibly the oldest fragment of the New Testament is the John Rylands Fragment acquired by B. P. Grenfell in 1920. It belongs to the early second century A.D. The story behind this and other discoveries is truly exciting.

The original New Testament documents were likely all written on papyrus rolls (or in the case of the smaller epistles, on a single sheet). Papyrus was a "paper" manufactured from the papyrus plant that grew along the Nile in Egypt. (Note: the little "ark" in which baby Moses was placed was of papyrus [Ex. 2:3].) Strips of the pithy inner stem of this plant were glued together to form sheets of paper, which, in turn, were frequently attached end to end to make long rolls. The longest known papyrus is the great Papyrus Harris I (ca. 1160 B.C.) in the British Museum. It is some 130 feet long. Papyrus was used from the beginning of Egypt's history, and from the beginning of the second millennium B.C. it was being exported to Palestine, Syria, and beyond. The extremely arid conditions of that part of the world facilitated the preservation of documents of this nature.

Between 1875 and 1895 large quantities of papyri were found in the Fayum province of Egypt, dating to the Roman period. Again, from 1895 and the years following, Drs. A. S. Hunt, B. P. Grenfell, and D. G. Hogarth, excavating in Egypt, acquired great quantities of papyri. Many of these helped to shed light on numerous New Testament words.

Two of the important papyri collections are the Chester Beatty collection (acquired in 1930–31), in Dublin, and the Bodmer collection in Geneva, Switzerland. A sampling of some of these materials may be arranged as follows.

The Gospels

The Chester Beatty Papyrus of the Gospels (ca. 250 A.D.) contains large sections of Luke and Mark and somewhat less of Matthew and John. In the John Rylands Library in Manchester, England is the fragment referred to above. Known as P52, this fragment from the eighteenth chapter of John is dated by paleographers in the first half of the second century A.D. This discovery, of course, utterly destroys the claims of the liberal critics that the fourth Gospel was not written until about 160 A.D.; for by the early part of the second century it had already been in circulation long enough to reach the interior of Egypt! Accordingly, such modernistic scholars as John A. T. Robinson are having to concede that the books of the New Testament were in fact written in the first century (1977). Too, the Bodmer Papyrus II (ca. 200 A.D.) contains the Gospel of John with some missing sections in chapters fourteen through twenty-one. Bodmer Papyrus XIV-XV, second century, contains Luke 3–14 and John 1–15.

The Acts of the Apostles

The Chester Beatty Papyrus has parts of Acts 5:30–17:17; P48 (in Florence), third century, contains Acts 23:11–29; P38 (in Ann Arbor, Michigan), third or fourth century, embraces Acts 18:27–19:6 and 19:12–16.

The Epistles

The Chester Beatty Papyrus contains considerable parts of Romans, Hebrews, 1 Corinthians, 2 Corinthians, Galatians, Ephesians, Philippians, Colossians, and 1 Thessalonians. The

Bodmer Papyrus VII-VIII contains Jude, 1 Peter, and 2 Peter. (Note: the Chester Beatty Papyrus also contains Revelation 9:10–17:2.)

The importance of the discovery of these manuscripts is two-fold. First, it sheds an abundance of light on the meanings of words in the New Testament. It demonstrated that Koine (i.e., New Testament Greek) was the language of the common man on the street in the first century, and that the New Testament was not written in a language of the Holy Ghost as some had supposed. Second, as suggested earlier, these manuscripts demolish the critical claims of a late composition for the New Testament writings.

Though we are somewhat departing from the field of archaeology proper at this point, we do want to mention that there is an abundance of additional material from many centuries past which further establishes the reliability of the text of the New Testament. For example, there are some 250 uncial (a style of writing that approximates English capital letters) manuscripts on parchment. These date from the fourth to the tenth century A.D., and though they are later in composition than the papyri, they are much more extensive in their containment of Scripture. Also, there are numerous minuscule (a smaller, script-like writing) manuscripts (out-numbering the uncials about ten to one), but they are of a later period. The earliest is from 835 A.D. (It is the oldest New Testament manuscript containing a date.) Too, there are some fifty manuscripts known as palimpsests (from two Greek words meaning, "I scrape again"). These are documents originally containing one message which was later erased and a new inscription was recorded on the parchment.

In addition to the above, there are near ten thousand versions (translations) of the New Testament in ancient languages, and some of these reach back into the second and third centuries A.D. Moreover, another important source of information on the New Testament text is the quotations in the writings of the Greek and Latin "church fathers." Dr. J. H. Greenlee has stated: "These quotations are so extensive that the N.T. could virtually be reconstructed from this source alone" (1975, 707). In fact, the whole of the New Testament, with the exception of less than a dozen verses, can be found scattered throughout these writings.

A survey of this evidence reveals two very important facts. First, a vast amount of material to establish the text of the New Testament is now available. Second, these discoveries are of great antiquity. Perhaps this can best be appreciated by comparing the New Testament to some of the classics, the authenticity of which no scholar dreams of questioning. Some of the classics are dependent upon one old manuscript (or at the most a very few) for their existence; and usually these are several centuries removed from the original source. For instance, manuscripts for the works of Homer are from fifteen centuries this side of the blind poet. There is a gap of eighteen hundred years between the manuscripts of Herodotus' works and the era in which the ancient historian lived. Similar examples could be multiplied many times over. (I have detailed some of this material in my book, *Fortify Your Faith* [1974, 70–75].) John Warwick Montgomery points out that:

> to be skeptical of the resultant text of the New Testament books is to allow all of classical antiquity to slip into obscurity, for no documents of the ancient period are as well attested bibliographically as the New Testament (1971, 29).

We can only stand in awe of how the Lord God providentially preserved his holy Word as it has survived the dusty ages of the past, and how grateful we are to many tireless archaeologists who brought these thrilling discoveries to light.

Chapter 23

Does Modern Scientific Understanding Disprove the Bible?

"That grand old Book of God still stands; and this old earth,
the more its leaves are turned over and pondered, the
more it will sustain and illustrate the Sacred Word."
— James D. Dana (1813–1895), American geologist and Yale professor

Various views are entertained regarding the Bible. Some hold it to be a strictly human document—respectable with age, but certainly not an inspired revelation from God. It is considered to be but one of the unusual, enduring literary efforts of antiquity.

Others feel the Scriptures have a vague sense of the "divine," but they do not believe the Bible is a book from God. It may contain some sacred truth, they allege, but it also has a mixture of purely human ideology. They contend, therefore, that much of the biblical information is flawed—certainly it is "scientifically" obsolete. Neither of these views is consistent with the Bible's claim for itself. "All scripture is inspired of God" (2 Tim. 3:16); the "sum" of it is truth (Psa. 119:160 ASV). If God is the Author of nature, and if he is the ultimate Source of the Scriptures, the two will be in harmony, for he is not a Deity of confusion (1 Cor. 14:33). Our focus in this chapter is: has "modern science" disproved the Bible's claim of being the Word of God?

In 2003 Victor Stenger, an adjunct professor of philosophy at the University of Colorado, wrote a book titled, *Has Science Found God?* Therein he argued that evidence for the existence of God is "inadequate." Recently the professor issued his latest book, *God: The Failed Hypothesis—How Science Shows That God Does Not Exist.* In this volume he contends that the battle is over. "Science has advanced sufficiently to be able to make a definitive statement" (2007, 11)—the God of the Bible has been vanquished. Science demonstrates the Book itself is a fraud. What amazing discoveries! As Shakespeare's Cassius inquired: "Upon what meat doth this our Caesar feed, That he is grown so great?" And we must add: in just four years! To get some idea of the professor's logical acumen, note his claim of a few years back:

> [T]he universe is probably the result of a random quantum fluctuation in a spaceless, timeless void. . . . [T]he earth and humanity are not conscious creations but an accident. . . . [I]t is not sufficient merely to say, "you can't get something from nothing." While everyday experience and common sense seem to support this principle, if there is anything that we have learned from twentieth-century physics, it is this: Common sense is often wrong, and our normal experiences are but a tiny fraction of reality (1987, 26–27).

Common sense and atheism are not amicable companions! (Psa. 14:1). Even the Scottish skeptic David Hume was reserved enough to declare: "I have never asserted so absurd a proposition as that anything might arise without a cause" (1932, 187).

In his newly-published book, *The Dawkins Delusion*, Oxford scholar and former atheist, Alister McGrath (PhD in molecular biology) has an entire chapter titled "Has Science Disproved God?" He vigorously denies that "science" is even capable of such (2007, 33–51). And Professor McGrath is not a "fundamentalist."

Then there is the testimony of the late Sir Peter B. Medawar, a Nobel Prize winner and self-acknowledged rationalist. In his book, *The Limits of Science*, published not long before his death, he confessed that there are questions that "science" simply cannot answer, including: "How did everything begin?" "What are we here for?" and "What is the point of living?" (1985, 66).

The truth is, the scientific "hall of fame" is studded with the names of some of the world's most brilliant minds—Kepler, Pascal, Newton, Boyle, Faraday, Pasteur, etc.—who believed in God, and revered the Bible as Holy Scripture (though with varying degrees of understanding). For example, Sir Isaac Newton wrote regarding the Bible:

> [T]he labors of the centuries have established
> its Divine origin, and developed in all its order
> and beauty the great plan of human restoration
> (Northrop n.d., 338; see also Graves 1996).

THE BIBLE: NOT A BOOK OF SCIENCE

It occasionally is said that the Bible is not a book of science. There is, of course, truth in that. The Scriptures were not designed to set forth the law of gravity, or to explain that water is composed of two gases, oxygen and hydrogen. It generally is the case, however, that such a statement is intended to convey the impression that the Bible is scientifically vulnerable; that it contains, in fact, outmoded "scientific" data. Such is not the case.

While the Scriptures do not constitute a science textbook, when they do incidentally touch on issues that relate to physical or material areas of knowledge, one has every right to expect the sacred documents to be unblemished by error. For example, the Bible is not a book of mathematics. It does not teach us how to add, subtract, or do fractions. Nevertheless, when it does introduce numerical relationships, we expect it to be mathematically accurate. In Daniel's prophecy of the eventual death of the Messiah, he predicted that certain events would be fulfilled in "seventy weeks"; the sum then was segmented into sixty-two, seven, and one (9:25–27). We do not expect a math mistake in such summations. This does not ignore the fact that the Bible sometimes rounds numbers, just as we commonly do.

THE BIBLE'S SCIENTIFIC PRECISION

It is an amazing fact that though it was completed some twenty centuries ago, the biblical record is always consistent with the ongoing discoveries of science. This certainly cannot be said for any modern textbook dealing with scientific issues. Science books become obsolete rather quickly.

When the renowned physicist George Gamow published the second edition of his book, *Biography of the Earth*, he had to write a special preface correcting errors in the first edition, because as he noted, "many changes have taken place [during the past seven years] in our ideas concerning the origin of the planetary system" (1959). (He still had a galaxy of errors in the revised work.) Thus consider the following.

First, many have argued (and a rare few still do) that the universe is eternal; supposedly, there never was a time when it did not exist. But Moses wrote: "In the beginning God created the heavens and the earth" (Gen. 1:1). Dr. Robert Jastrow, an agnostic, confesses: "Modern science denies an eternal existence to the Universe" (1980, 15). This is one of the implications of the Second Law of Thermodynamics. Everything is "running down." Thus the universe must have been "wound up" at some point in the past; it had a commencement.

Second, Genesis states that Jehovah's creation activity concluded with the sixth day of the initial week (2:1–2). Accordingly, there is no creation of matter being implemented today. This is consistent with the First Law of Thermodynamics, which indicates matter is not being created now. This further suggests matter cannot create itself. It may be altered in form (e.g., from a solid to a liquid or a gas), but it neither is being created nor destroyed. Contrast these facts with the contention of atheist Bertrand Russell—just fifty years ago:

> There is no reason why the world could not have come into being without a cause; nor, on the other hand, is there any reason why it should not have always existed (1957, 7).

These statements are manifestly absurd. The Bible is wonderfully current.

Third, consider Paul's statement in his address to the philosophers of Athens. "[H]e [God] made of one every nation of men to dwell on all the face of the earth" (Acts 17:26 ASV). The expression "of one" translates the Greek phrase *ek henos*, literally "out of one male." The word "blood" (KJV) does not appear in the older Greek texts. The inspired apostle affirmed that the entire human family descended from one man—Adam. This asserted the unity of humanity, which was contrary to ancient Greek ideology that boasted the Athenians were an indigenous people—a special creation—and all others were considered barbarian (cf. Rom. 1:14).

This idea has had a modern counterpart. Charles Darwin, who popularized evolutionary theory, argued that "Caucasian races" are superior. From this concept Adolf Hitler developed his notion of the "master race." As late as World War II, the U.S. Red Cross segregated blood (for transfusion purposes) according to race types. It now is known that there is a basic unity shared by all ethnic families of the earth. Anthropologist Dr. Ashley Montague declared that "all the ethnic groups of man must have originated from a single ancestral stock." He says: "The more we study the different groups of man the more alike they turn out to be" (1950, 184).

ALLEGED INACCURACIES

Unbelievers charge that there are scientific blunders in the Scriptures, which ought not to be if the narrative derived from God. Here are a few instances commonly cited.

First, in Genesis 1:6 Moses wrote: "And God said, Let there be a firmament in the midst of the waters" (KJV). It is charged that this passage suggests the notion of a "solid, inverted dome which holds back the waters above it" (Willis 1979, 84). There is a mistaken notion all right, but it can be traced back to the Septuagint (the Greek Old Testament of the third century B.C.). Those translators were influenced by the erroneous ideas of their day in their rendition of the original term. However, the Hebrew word *raqiya* simply means an "expanse" (cf. NASB); it does not imply a "solid" sky (Harrison 1982, 306–307).

Second, it is contended that the Bible contains references to the unicorn, a mythical, one-horned creature (cf. Num. 23:22 KJV). Again the problem is one of inaccurate translation. It is now known that the Hebrew word *re'em* in this context refers to a species of extinct wild ox. The biblical animal actually had "horns" (Dt. 33:17), but was pictured in Babylonian and Egyptian relief carvings in profile. Hence the Septuagint translators mistakenly rendered *re'em* by the Greek *monokeros* (one horn; see Klotz 2003, 83). No mistake in the original text.

Third, some allege that Scripture contains a scientific blunder when it refers to the "four corners of the earth" (cf. Rev. 7:1). Supposedly, this is a mistake from those days when unenlightened man believed the earth was flat. But the biblical phrase is simply a figurative expression for the extremities of the planet. Some time back the U.S. Marine Corps published a brochure affirming that this branch of the military has men "serving the flag at the four corners of the earth." Does our government not know the shape of the earth? Isaiah spoke of God as sitting above the "circle of the earth" (40:22). Though many scholars deny the specificity of this descriptive with reference to the shape of our globe, others have pointed out that the Hebrew word for "circle" (*chuwg*) "is compatible with the notion of the earth as a sphere" (Archer 1962, 637).

FALSE SCIENCE NOT IN THE BIBLE

Invariably, strictly human writings reflect the "science" of their day. Even today, science books have to be revised every few years. It would be unthinkable to use a science text published just ten years ago. Yesterday's science is often tomorrow's superstition. Amazingly the Bible does not incorporate into its records the pseudo-science of the antique world. This is evidence of its divine character. But note the following.

First, Aristotle said the brain is a "compound of earth and water." He further taught that the human brain "is larger in men than in women." He suggested that the "region of the heart in man is hotter" than in animals (*On Man and the Universe*, chapter 7). The truth is, most birds and many mammals have warmer internal heat than humans. The philosopher's "science" was less than precise.

Second, as noted in a previous chapter, in the famous *Papyrus Ebers*, an Egyptian medical text (sixteenth century B.C.), there is a prescription to prevent losing one's hair:

> When it falls out, one remedy is to apply a mixture
> of six fats, namely those of the horse, hippopota-
> mus, the crocodile, the cat, the snake, and the ibex.
> To strengthen it, anoint with the tooth of a donkey
> crushed in honey (McMillen 1963, 11).

Though Moses was raised in Egypt, and was "instructed in all the wisdom of the Egyptians" (Acts 7:22), when he penned the Pentateuch he incorporated no superstition into his narrative. In fact, the Old Testament record is astoundingly ahead of its time. The sanitation regulations incorporated into certain portions of the Law (which presuppose a knowledge of the existence of germs), cannot be explained except by the fact that God was behind the message (cf. Lev. 13).

When one argues that the Bible is scientifically flawed he speaks beyond the capacity of his knowledge. As world-renowned archaeologist W. F. Albright once noted: "[I]t may be seriously doubted whether science has yet caught up with the Biblical story" (1948, 135).

Is the Bible Obsolete?

"In this age of space flight, when we use the modern tools of science to advance into new regions of human activity, the Bible—this grandiose, stirring history of the gradual revelation and unfolding of the moral law—remains in every way an up-to-date book."
— Wernher Magnus Maximillan von Braun (1912–1977),
father of the American space program

"**H**ow can the Bible be accepted as universal when certain aspects of it are obsolete by reason of the ancient cultures out of which it arose? In view of its historical setting, how can it be practical today? How can it function as a guide for contemporary humanity?"

These are questions that trouble many. In considering these issues there are several factors that must be taken into consideration.

First, if the one posing this objection were concerned about arguing a consistent position, he would be forced to contend that God could never give a written revelation to mankind, because history does not stand still. There always has been, and ever shall be, changes in cultural conditions. Thus, according to the logic advanced above, any written communication from Heaven would become obsolete in a relatively rapid time frame.

For that matter, if the premise were valid, all historical documents would be worthless because the modern student would be unable to understand them due to evolving circumstances. The initial questions, therefore, have a built-in presumption that reflects upon the very nature of God, namely that the Creator was unable to anticipate historical changes in the preparation of a divine revelation. The argument is fundamentally skeptical in nature.

Second, in order to correctly address the alleged problem of biblical obsolescence, one must recognize the following facts (which could be argued effectively independently, but for the convenience of this brief discussion, will be merely stated):

- God exists.

- He is the Creator of humankind.

- He had (and has) an ideal goal for Adam's offspring. But humanity, irresponsibly exercising its freedom of choice, rejected that ideal and plunged itself into a state of sin and suffering.

- Out of divine love, a plan for man's redemption was initiated.

- That plan was revealed progressively across the ages of history.

- From the nature of the case, the record of that purpose has been embedded in developing history.

- By his infinite power, the Lord was able to adapt the facts and conditions of his purpose to a universal mode of communication that was/is capable of being understood in any era, in spite of the fluctuations of historical circumstances.

Let us consider the following factors.

First, much of the Bible has its roots in the land of Canaan, that special parcel of real estate that God gave to Abraham and his offspring in preparation for the coming Messiah. One of the remarkable characteristics of this small territory (smaller than the state of Massachusetts) is its versatility. Palestine has a broad variety of geographical features—from high mountains, e.g., snowcapped Hermon (almost ten thousand feet high), to the sweltering region of the Dead Sea area (thirteen hundred feet below sea level).

The land has hosted a vast conglomerate of forests, plants, and animals (both wild and domestic). This unusual diversity, together with the fact that much of the imagery by which biblical ideas are conveyed is drawn from the conditions of the region, has provided an ideal means of accommodating a wide range of cultures (both ancient and modern). It is hardly a coincidence that Jehovah chose this region as a preparatory arena for the unfolding of his revelation by means of the Holy Scriptures.

Second, Jesus expected the people of his generation to understand the requirements of Moses' law, even though that religious system had been initiated fifteen hundred years earlier. For instance, Christ rebuked the Sadducees, charging that they were ignorant of the Scriptures. Then, in establishing the case for the resurrection of the dead, he anchored his argument from a text in the book of Exodus (see Mt. 22:29–30). It is obvious that the Lord did not endorse the notion that the clarity of the Old Testament documents had been shrouded in obscurity by virtue of the passing of some fifteen centuries.

Similarly, Paul declared that "whatsoever things were written aforetime were written for our learning, that through patience and through the comfort of the scriptures we might have hope" (Rom. 15:4). He too was oblivious to the modern notion that divine revelation is made obsolete by the passing of time.

Third, many truths are timelessly transparent, in spite of the culturally grounded language in which they are clustered. When the Pharisees and scribes saw Jesus extending friendship to sinners and tax collectors, they harshly criticized him (Lk. 15:1–2). And so, in one of his parables the Savior told of a man who had a hundred sheep, one of which wandered into the wilderness and became lost. With loving concern, the shepherd went after the imperiled creature and tenderly brought it home. Though most of us are not in the sheep business today, it does not require an advanced degree in animal science to understand the lesson being conveyed.

Who can miss the spiritual point in the parable of the Good Samaritan (Lk. 10:25ff), in spite of the fact that the imagery in which the lesson is nestled arises from an environment of twenty centuries ago?

Are the common truths enshrined in Aesop's fables without value today, merely because (presumably) a Greek slave who lived more than twenty-five hundred years ago wrote the composition? Who has attempted to argue such a flawed proposition?

The charge that the Bible cannot be understood, and therefore is irrelevant today, is without merit. This is but another of those shallow rationalizations that take their rise from the twisted logic of those who seek to avoid responsibility to their Creator. Such is but a thinly veiled attempt to fashion a religious system of human flexibility that permits a man to "direct his own steps" (Jer. 10:23).

Bibliography

Aland, Kurt, et al. 1983. *The Greek New Testament*. Third edition. London, England: United Bible Society.

Albright, W. F. 1948. The Old Testament and Archaeology. *Old Testament Commentary*. Herbert Alleman and Elmer Flack, eds. Philadelphia, PA: Muhlenberg Press.

Alexander, J. A. 1953. *A Commentary on the Prophecies of Isaiah*. Grand Rapids, MI: Zondervan.

Allis, Oswald T. 1950. *The Unity of Isaiah—A Study in Prophecy*. Philadelphia, PA: Presbyterian & Reformed.

Archer, G. L. 1962. Isaiah. *The Wycliffe Bible Commentary*. Charles Pfeiffer, Everett Harrison, eds. Chicago, IL: Moody.

Archer, G. L. 1964. *A Survey of Old Testament Introduction*. Chicago, IL: Moody.

Archer, G. L. 1975. Biblical Criticism. *The Zondervan Pictorial Encyclopedia of the Bible*. Grand Rapids, MI: Zondervan.

Balz, Horst and Gerhard Schneider. 1990. *Exegetical Dictionary of the New Testament*. Vol. 1. Grand Rapids, MI: Eerdmans.

Barbieri, Louis A. 1983. *The Bible Knowledge Commentary— New Testament*. John Walvoord and Roy Zuck, eds. Wheaton, IL: Victor Books.

Barclay, William. 1956a. *The Gospel of John*. Philadelphia, PA: Westminster.

Barclay, William. 1956b. *The Gospel of Luke*. Philadelphia, PA: Westminster.

Barclay, William. 1957. *The Gospel of Matthew*. Vol. 2. Philadelphia, PA: Westminster.

Barclay, William. 1959. *The Master's Men*. Nashville, TN: Abingdon.

Barclay, William. 1976. *And He Had Compassion*. Valley Forge, PA: Judson Press.

Batey, Richard. 1969. *Letter of Paul to the Romans*. Austin, TX: Sweet Publishing.

Bauckham, Richard. 1983. *Jude, 2 Peter*. Waco, TX: Word.

Beale, G. K. and D. A. Carson, eds. 2007. *Commentary on the New Testament Use of the Old Testament*. Grand Rapids, MI: Baker.

Beasley-Murray, G. R. 1999. *John—Word Bible Commentary*. Second edition. Waco, TX: Word.

Blaiklock, E. M. 1966. *St. Luke*. Grand Rapids, MI: Eerdmans.

Blaiklock, E. M. 1972. *The Pastoral Epistles*. Grand Rapids, MI: Zondervan.

Bengal, John A. 1877 *Gnomon of the New Testament*. Vol. 1. Edinburgh, Scotland: T. & T. Clark.

Bernard, J. H. 1928. *The Gospel According to John—The International Critical Commentary*. Edinburgh, Scotland: T. & T. Clark.

Blunt, J. J. 1884. *Undesigned Coincidences in the Writings Both of The Old Testament and New Testament*. London, England: John Murray.

Boyd, Robert T. 1969. *A Pictorial Guide to Biblical Archaeology*. Grand Rapids, MI: Baker.

Bromiley, G. W. 1986. *The International Standard Bible Encyclopedia—Revised*. Vol. 3. Grand Rapids, MI: Zondervan.

Bruce, A. B. 1956. *The Expositor's Greek New Testament.* Grand Rapids, MI: Eerdmans.

Bruce, F. F. 1950. *The Books and the Parchments.* London, England: Pickering & Inglis.

Bruce, F. F. 1977. *Paul: Apostle of the Heart Set Free.* Grand Rapids, MI: Eerdmans.

*Bulletin of the American School of Oriental Research.*1953, Vol. 129.

Bullinger, E. W. 1968. *Figures of Speech in the Bible.* Grand Rapids, MI: Baker.

Buttrick, George. 1952. *The Interpreter's Bible Commentary.* Vol. 1. New York, NY: Abingdon.

Cadbury, Henry J. 1955. *The Book of Acts in History.* New York, NY: Harper & Bros.

Callaway, Joseph. 1973. *The Broadman Bible Commentary.* Nashville, TN: Broadman.

Carson, D. A. 1984. *Matthew—The Expositor's Bible Commentary.* Vol. 8. Frank Gabelein, ed. Grand Rapids, MI: Zondervan.

Carson, D. A., Douglas Moo, and Leon Morris. 1992. *An Introduction to the New Testament.* Grand Rapids, MI: Zondervan.

Cassuto, Umberto. 1961. *The Documentary Hypothesis.* Jerusalem, Israel: Magnes Press.

Cheyne, T. K. 1899. *Encyclopedia Biblica.* London, England: A. & C. Black.

Clark, G. H. 1975. Miracles. *The Zondervan Pictorial Encyclopedia of the Bible.* Vol. 4. Merrill C. Tenney, ed. Grand Rapids, MI: Zondervan.

Collett, Sidney. n.d. *All About the Bible.* London, England: Revell.

Coray, Henry W. 1971. The Incomparable Wilson—The Man Who Mastered Forty-five Languages. *Which Bible?*

David Otis Fuller, ed. Grand Rapids, MI: Grand Rapids International Publications.

Cruden, Alexander. 1840. *Cruden's Explanations of Scripture Terms.* London, England: Religious Tract Society.

Danker, F. W., et al. 2000. *A Greek-English Lexicon of the New Testament.* Chicago, IL: University of Chicago.

Davidson, A. B. 1902. *A Dictionary of the Bible.* Vol. 4. James Hastings, ed. Edinburgh, Scotland: T. & T. Clark.

Davies, G. Henton, et al. 1955. *The Twentieth Century Bible Commentary—Revised.* New York, NY: Harper & Bros.

Douglas, J. D., ed. 1974. *The New Bible Dictionary.* Grand Rapids, MI: Eerdmans.

Eddy, Mary Baker. 1934. *Science and Health with Key to the Scriptures.* Boston, MA: The First Church of Christ, Scientist.

Edersheim, Alfred. 1947. *The Life and Times of Jesus the Messiah.* Vol. 2. Grand Rapids, MI: Eerdmans.

Encyclopedia Britannica. 1958. Tacitus. Vol. 6. London, England: Encyclopedia Britannica, Inc.

Evans, Craig A. 1980. *Luke—New International Biblical Commentary.* Vol. 3. Peabody, MA: Hendrickson.

Fairbairn, Patrick. 1859. *Hermeneutical Manual— Introduction to the Exegetical Study of the Scriptures of the New Testament.* Philadelphia, PA: Smith, English & Co.

Fee, Gordon. 1988. *New International Biblical Commentary—1, 2 Timothy, Titus.* Peabody, MA: Hendrickson.

Ferm, Vergulius. 1945. *An Encyclopedia of Religion.* New York, NY: The Philosophical Library.

Findlay, A. F. 1906. Gospels (Apocryphal). *A Dictionary of Christ and the Gospels.* Vol. 1. Edinburgh, Scotland: T. & T. Clark.

Fosdick, Harry Emerson. 1924. *The Modern Use of the Bible.* New York, NY: Macmillan.

Foster, R. C. 1971. *Studies in the Life of Christ.* Grand Rapids, MI: Baker.

Frank, H. T. 1964. *An Archaeological Companion to the Bible.* London, England: SCM Press.

Freeman, Hobart. 1968. *An Introduction to the Old Testament Prophets.* Chicago, IL: Moody.

Friedman, Richard E. 1997. *Who Wrote the Bible?* San Francisco, CA: Harper.

Gaebelein, Frank. 1950. *The Meaning of Inspiration.* Chicago, IL: InterVarsity.

Gamow, George. 1959. *Biography of the Earth.* New York, NY: Mentor.

Gaussen, Louis. 1840. *Theopneustia—The Plenary Inspiration of the Holy Scriptures.* Chicago, IL: Moody.

Gealy, Fred D. 1955. 1, 2 Timothy, & Titus. *The Interpreter's Bible.* G. A. Buttrick, ed. New York, NY: Abingdon.

Geike, Cunningham. n.d. *Hours With the Bible.* Vol.1. New York, NY: Hurst.

Geisler, Norman and William Nix. 1986. *A General Introduction to the Bible.* Chicago, IL: Moody.

Geisler, Norman. 1999. *Baker Encyclopedia of Christian Apologetics.* Grand Rapids, MI: Baker Books.

Girdlestone, Robert. n.d. *Synonyms of the Old Testament.* Grand Rapids, MI: Eerdmans.

Glaussen, L. n.d. *Theopneustia—The Plenary Inspiration of the Holy Scriptures.* Chicago, IL: Moody.

Goodpasture, B. C. 1970. Homer Sometimes Nods. *The Gospel Advocate.*

Goodspeed, Edgar J. 1946. *How To Read the Bible.* Philadelphia, PA: John C. Winston.

Graves, Dan. 1996. *Scientists of Faith*. Grand Rapids, MI: Zondervan.

Green, Michael, ed. 1977. *The Truth of God Incarnate.* Grand Rapids, MI: Eerdmans.

Green, Michael. 1980. *The Second Epistle of Peter and the Epistle of Jude.* Grand Rapids, MI: Eerdmans.

Green, William H. 1898. *General Introduction to the Old Testament: The Canon.* New York, NY: Scribner.

Greenleaf, Simon. 1899. *A Treatise on the Law of Evidence.* 16th edition. Vol. 1. Boston, MA: Little, Brown, & Co.

Greenleaf, Simon. 1903. *The Testimony of the Evangelists Examined by the Rules of Evidence Administered in Courts of Justice.* Newark, NJ: Soney & Sage.

Greenlee, J. H. 1975. *The Zondervan Pictorial Encyclopedia of the Bible.* Vol. 5. Merrill Tenney, ed. Grand Rapids, MI: Zondervan.

Gregory, C. R. 1907. *Canon and Text of the New Testament.* New York, NY: Scribners.

Gundry, Robert H. 1981. *A Survey of the New Testament— Revised.* Grand Rapids, MI: Zondervan.

Guthrie, Donald. 1975. Biblical Criticism. *The Zondervan Pictorial Encyclopedia of the Bible.* Merrill Tenney, ed. Grand Rapids, MI: Zondervan. Five Volumes.

Hamilton, Mark. 2006. Transition and Continuity: Biblical Scholarship in Today's Churches of Christ. *Stone-Campbell Journal,* Fall.

Harrelson, Walter. 1964. *Interpreting the Old Testament.* New York, NY: Holt, Rinehart, and Winston.

Harris, R. Laird. 1990. Leviticus. *The Expositor's Bible Commentary.* Vol. 2. Frank Gaebelein, ed. Grand Rapids, MI: Zondervan.

Harris, T. George. 1989. Mysticism Goes Mainstream. *Psychology Today.*

Harrison, R. K. 1963. *The Archaeology of the Old Testament.* New York, NY: Harper & Row.

Harrison, R. K. 1980. *Leviticus—Tyndale Old Testament Commentaries.* Vol. 3. Downers Grove, IL: InterVarsity Press.

Harrison, R. K. 1982. *The International Standard Bible Encyclopedia—Revised.* Vol. 2. G. W. Bromiley, ed. Grand Rapids, MI: Eerdmans.

Harrison, R. K. 1983. *The New International Dictionary of Biblical Archaeology.* E. M. Blaiklock and R. K. Harrison, eds. Grand Rapids, MI: Zondervan.

Harvey, Van A. 1964. *A Handbook of Theological Terms.* New York, NY: Macmillan Co.

Hastings, H. L. 1890. *The Inspiration of the Bible.* Elgin, IL: Brethren Publishing House.

Hendriksen, William. 1953. *Commentary on the Gospel According to John.* Grand Rapids, MI: Eerdmans.

Hiebert, D. Edmond. 1984. *First Peter—An Expositional Commentary.* Chicago, IL: Moody.

Hillycr, Norman. 1992. *New International Biblical Commentary—1, 2 Peter, Jude.* Peabody, MA: Hendrickson.

Hoffner, H. 1969. *Tyndale Bulletin,* 20.

Holladay, Carl. 2005. *A Critical Introduction to the New Testament.* Nashville, TN: Abingdon.

Horn, S. H. 1960. *SDA Bible Dictionary.* Washington, DC: Review & Herald.

Horne, Thomas H. 1841. *An Introduction to the Critical Study and Knowledge of the Holy Scriptures.* Philadelphia, PA: Whethan & Son.

Hovey, Alvah. 1885. *Commentary on the Gospel of John.* Philadelphia, PA: American Baptist Publication Society.

Hume, David. 1932. *Letters.* Vol. 1. J. Y. T. Greig, ed. Oxford, England: Clarendon.

Hunington, Oliver R. 1892. Inhabitants of the Moon. *Young Woman's Journal.*

Jackson, Wayne. 1974. *Fortify Your Faith.* Stockton, CA: Christian Courier Publications.

Jackson, Wayne. 1988. *Biblical Studies in the Light of Archaeology.* Stockton, CA: Courier Publications.

Jackson, Wayne. 1997. *Jeremiah & Lamentations.* Stockton, CA: Courier Publications.

Jackson, Wayne. 1999. The Code of Hammurabi. *Christian Courier,* March.

Jackson, Wayne. 2001. *Does Psalm 22 Prophecy the Crucifixion of Christ?* Stockton, CA: Christian Courier Publications. http://www.christiancourier. com/articles/read/does_psalm_22_prophesy_the_ crucifixion_of_christ.

Jackson, Wayne. 2002. *Was Matthew Mistaken in the "Nazarene" Prophecy?* Stockton, CA: Christian Courier Publications. http://www.christiancourier. com/articles/read/was_matthew_mistaken_in_the_ nazarene_prophecy.

Jackson, Wayne. 2003. *Creation, Evolution, and the Age of the Earth.* Stockton, CA: Courier Publications.

Jackson, Wayne. 2007. *Before I Die—Paul's Letter to Timothy & Titus.* Stockton, CA: Christian Publications.

Jackson, Wayne. n.d. *Daniel's Seventy Weeks.* Montgomery, AL: Apologetics Press.

Jastrow, Robert. 1980. *Until The Sun Dies.* New York, NY: Warner.

Jevons, W. Stanley. 1928. *Elementary Lessons in Logic.* London, England: Macmillan.

Johnson, Franklin. 1896. *The Quotations of the New Testament From the Old*. Philadelphia, PA: American Baptist Publication Society.

Johnson, G. H. S. 1981. Psalms (23). *The Bible Commentary*. Vol. 4. F. C. Cook, ed. Grand Rapids, MI: Baker.

Kaiser, Walter C., Jr. 1985. *The Uses of the Old Testament in the New*. Chicago, IL: Moody.

Kalland, Earl S. 1992. Deuteronomy. *The Expositor's Bible Commentary*. Vol. 3. Frank Gaebelein, ed. Grand Rapids, MI: Zondervan.

Kennedy, D. James. 1980. *Why I Believe*. Waco, TX: Word Books.

Kidner, Derek. 1973. Psalms 1–72. *Tyndale Old Testament Commentaries*. Vol. 14a. Downers Grove, IL: InterVarsity Press.

Kirkpatrick, A. F. 1906. *The Book of Psalms*. Cambridge, England: University Press.

Kitchen, Kenneth. 1966. *Ancient Orient and the Old Testament*. London, England: Tyndale.

Kitchen, Kenneth. 1980. *The Illustrated Bible Dictionary*. Vol. 1. J. D. Douglas, ed. Wheaton, IL: Tyndale House.

Kittel, Gerhard. 1965. *Theological Dictionary of the New Testament*. Vol. 3. Grand Rapids, MI: Eerdmans.

Klotz, John. 1970. *Genes, Genesis, and Evolution*. St. Louis, MO: Concordia.

Klotz, John. 2003. *Wycliffe Bible Dictionary*. Charles Pfeiffer, Howard Vos, John Rea, eds. Peabody, MA: Hendrickson.

Kostenberger, Andreas J. 2002. John. *Zondervan Illustrated Bible Backgrounds Commentary*. Vol. 2. Clinton Arnold, ed. Grand Rapids, MI: Zondervan.

Kramer, Samuel Noah. 1959. *History Begins At Sumer*. Garden City, NY: Doubleday.

Laney, Carl. 1997. *Answers to Tough Questions.* Grand Rapids, MI: Kregel.

Lenski, R. C. H. 1943. *The Interpretation of St. John's Gospel.* Minneapolis, MN: Augsburg.

Lewis, C. S. 1947. *Miracles.* New York, NY: Macmillan.

Lightfoot, J. B. 1889. *Essays of the Work Entitled Supernatural Religion.* London, England: Macmillan.

Machen, J. Gresham. 1923. *Christianity and Liberalism.* Philadelphia, PA: The Sunday School Times Co.

MacKnight, James. 1954. *Apostolical Epistles.* Nashville, TN: Gospel Advocate.

Manchester, William. 1978. *American Caesar—Douglas McArthur, 1880–1964.* Boston, MA: Little, Brown.

Manley, G.T. 1962. *The New Bible Handbook.* Chicago, IL: Inter-Varsity.

Marsak, Leonard M. 1961. *French Philosophers from Descartes to Sartre.* Cleveland, OH: World Publishing Company.

Martin, John A. 1985. *The Bible Knowledge Commentary— Old Testament.* John Walvoord and Roy Zuck, eds. Wheaton, IL: Victor Books.

Martin, W. J. and A. R. Miller. 1980. *The Illustrated Bible Dictionary.* Vol. 3. J. D. Douglas, ed. Wheaton, IL: Tyndale.

Mayor, Joseph B. 1979. *The Epistles of Jude and II Peter.* Grand Rapids, MI: Baker.

Mays, James, et al. 1988. *Harper's Bible Commentary.* New York, NY: Harper Collins

McBirnie, William S. 1973. *The Search for the Twelve Apostles.* Wheaton, IL: Tyndale House.

McClintock, John and James Strong. 1969. *Cyclopedia of Biblical, Theological, Ecclesiastical Literature.* Vol. 3. Grand Rapids, MI: Baker.

M'Clymont, J. A. 1893. *The New Testament and Its Writers.* London, England: Adam & Charles Black.

McGarvey, J. W. n.d. *Sermons.* Cincinnati, OH: Standard.

McGarvey, J. W. 1875. *Commentary on Matthew and Mark.* Delight, AR: Gospel Light.

McGarvey, J. W. 1881. *Lands of the Bible.* Philadelphia, PA: J. B. Lippincott & Co.

McGarvey, J. W. 1910. *Biblical Criticism.* Cincinnati, OH: Standard.

McGarvey, J. W. 1956. *Evidences of Christianity.* Nashville, TN: Gospel Advocate.

McGrath, Alister and Joanna C. 2007. *The Dawkins Delusion.* Downers Grove, IL: InterVarsity Press.

McLay, Timothy R. 2003. *The Use of the Septuagint in New Testament Research.* Grand Rapids, MI: Eerdmans.

McMillen, S. I. 1963. *None of These Diseases.* Westwood, NJ: Fleming Revell Co.

McNab, Andrew. 1954. *II Peter- The New Bible Commentary.* F. Davidson, ed. Grand Rapids, MI: Eerdman.

Medawar, Peter B. 1985. *The Limits of Science.* Oxford, England: Oxford University Press.

Metzger, Bruce. 1965. *The New Testament—Its Background, Growth, and Content.* Nashville, TN: Abingdon.

Metzger, Bruce. 1968. *The Text of the New Testament.* New York, NY: Oxford University Press.

Mitchell, T. C. 1988. *The Bible in the British Museum.* London, England: British Museum.

Montague, Ashley. 1950. *Human Heredity.* New York, NY: Mentor Books.

Montgomery, John Warwick. 1971. *History and Christianity.* Downers Grove, IL: InterVarsity Press.

Morgan, G. Campbell. n.d. *The Gospel According to John.* Westwood, NJ: Fleming Revell.

Morris, Henry. 1976. *The Genesis Record.* Grand Rapids, MI: Baker.

Morris, Leon. 1995. *The Gospel According to John—Revised—The New International Commentary on the New Testament.* Grand Rapids, MI: Eerdmans.

Morton, J. S. 1978. *Science in the Bible.* Chicago, IL: Moody.

Mounce, William D. 2000. *Pastoral Epistles—Word Biblical Commentary.* Nashville, TN: Nelson.

Myers, Allen C. 1987. *The Eerdmans Bible Dictionary.* Grand Rapids, MI: Eerdmans.

Newton, Thomas. 1831. *Dissertations on the Prophecies.* London, England: Blake, Bell-Yard, Temple Bar.

Nicole, Roger. 1958. New Testament Use of the Old Testament. *Revelation and the Bible.* Carl F. H. Henry, ed. Grand Rapids, MI: Baker.

Northrop, Stephen Abbott. n.d. *A Cloud of Witnesses—The Greatest Men in the World for Christ and the Book.* Cincinnati, OH: John F. McCurdy.

Otten, Herman. 1965. *Baal or God?* New Haven, MO: Leader Publishing.

Pache, Rene. 1969. *The Inspiration and Authority of the Scriptures.* Chicago, IL: Moody.

Paley, William. 1839. *The Works of William Paley.* Edinburgh, Scotland: Thomas Nelson.

Payne, J. Barton. 1973. *The Encyclopedia of Biblical Prophecy.* New York, NY: Harper & Row.

Pfeiffer, Charles. 1966. *The Biblical World.* Grand Rapids, MI: Baker.

Pfeiffer, R. H. 1962. *The Interpreter's Dictionary of the Bible.* Vol. 1. Nashville, TN: Abingdon.

Plummer, Alfred. 1896. *The Gospel According to Luke.* Edinburgh, Scotland: T. & T. Clark.

Price, George M. 1934. *Modern Discoveries Which Help Us To Believe.* New York, NY: Fleming H. Revell.

Price, Ira. M. 1920. *The Monuments and the Old Testament.* Philadelphia: American Baptist Publication Society.

Pritchard, J. B. 1955. *Ancient Near Eastern Texts.* Princeton, NJ: Princeton University Press.

Pritchard, J. B. 1973. The Code of Hammurabi. *The Ancient Near East—An Anthology of Text and Pictures.* Vol. 1. Princeton, NJ: Princeton University.

Ramsay, William. 1979. *The Bearing of Recent Discovery on the Trustworthiness of the New Testament.* Grand Rapids, MI: Baker.

Randi, James. 1987. *The Faith Healers.* Buffalo, NY: Prometheus.

Rawlinson, George. 1877. *The Historical Evidences of the Truth of the Scripture Records.* New York, NY: Sheldon & Co.

Rienecker, Fritz. 1980. *A Linguistic Key to the Greek New Testament.* Vol. 2. Grand Rapids, MI: Zondervan.

Robertson, A. T. 1930–33. *Word Pictures in the New Testament.* Nashville, TN: Broadman.

Robinson, Edward. 1855. *Greek-English Lexicon of the New Testament.* New York, NY: Harper Bros.

Robinson, George L. 1954. *The Book of Isaiah—Revised Edition.* Grand Rapids, MI: Baker.

Robinson, John A. T. 1977. *Redating the New Testament.* London, England: S. C. M. Press.

Russell, Bertrand. 1957. *Why I Am Not A Christian and Other Essays.* New York, NY: Simon & Schuster.

Sadler, William S. 1929. *The Truth About Mind Cure.* London, England: George Allen & Unwin.

Sarna, Nahum. 1960. *Understanding Genesis*. New York, NY: Schocken Books.

Sarton, George. 1959. *A History of Science*. Cambridge, MA: Harvard University.

Schurer, Emile. 1849. Apocrypha of the Old Testament. *Schaff-Herzog Encyclopedia of Religious Knowledge*. Vol. 1. Phillip Schaff, ed. New York, NY: Funk & Wagnalls.

Sidlow, Baxter. 1966. *Explore the Book*. Vol. 5. Grand Rapids, MI: Zondervan.

Simpson, Cuthbert and Walter Bowie. 1952. *The Interpreter's Bible*. Vol. 1. G. A. Buttrick, ed. Nashville, TN: Abingdon.

Smick, Elmer B. 1988. *Baker Encyclopedia of the Bible*. Grand Rapids, MI: Baker.

Smith, G. A. 1928. *The Book of the Prophets*. New York, NY: Harper.

Stenger, Victor. 1987. Was the Universe Created? *Free Inquiry*, Summer, vol. 7, no. 3.

Stenger, Victor. 2007. *God: The Failed Hypothesis: How Science Shows That God Does Not Exist*. Amherst, NY: Prometheus Press.

Stoner, Peter W. 1963. *Science Speaks*. Chicago, IL: Moody.

Surburg, Raymond. 1980. The Untenability of Ecumenism's Attempt To promote the Apocrypha as Word of God. *The Christian News*, November 24.

Swete, H. B. 1914. *Introduction to the Old Testament Greek*. Cambridge, England: Cambridge University Press.

Tenney, Merrill. 1981. *The Gospel According to John—The Expositor's Bible Commentary*. Frank Gaebelein, ed. Vol. 9. Grand Rapids, MI: Zondervan.

Terry, Milton. 1890. *Biblical Hermeneutics*. New York, NY: Eaton & Mains.

Thayer, J. H. 1958. *A Greek-English Lexicon of the New Testament*. Edinburgh, Scotland: T. & T. Clark.

Thiessen, Henry C. 1955. *Introduction to the New Testament*. Grand Rapids, MI: Eerdmans.

Thomas, W. H. Griffith. 1939. The Resurrection of Jesus Christ. *International Standard Bible Encyclopedia*. Vol. 4. James Orr, ed. Grand Rapids, MI: Eerdmans.

Thompson, J. A. 1974. Deuteronomy. *Tyndale Old Testament Commentaries*. Vol. 5. Downers Grove, IL: InterVarsity Press.

Unger, Merrill. 1951. *Introductory Guide to the Old Testament*. Grand Rapids, MI: Zondervan.

Unger, Merrill. 1954. *Archaeology and the Old Testament*. Grand Rapids, MI: Zondervan.

Unger, Merrill and William White. 1980. *Expository Dictionary of the Old Testament*. Nashville, TN: Thomas Nelson.

Vis, William R. 1950. Medical Science in the Bible. *Modern Science and the Christian Faith*. Wheaton, IL: Van Kampen Press.

Vos, Howard. 2003. *Wycliffe Geography of Bible Lands*. Peabody, MA: Hendrickson.

Ward, Ronald. 1978. *Survey of the New Testament*. Waco, TX: Word Books.

Watts, J. W. 1951. *A Survey of Syntax in the Old Testament*. Nashville, TN: Broadman.

Watts, John. 2003. Circumcision. *Wycliffe Bible Dictionary*. Charles Pfeiffer, Howard Vos, John Rea, eds. Peabody, MA: Hendrickson.

Westcott, B. F. 1981. *The Gospel of John. The Bible Commentary*. Vol. 8. F. C. Cook, ed. Grand Rapids, MI: Baker.

Wheaton, David H. 1970. *2 Peter—The New Bible Commentary—Third Edition*. D. Guthrie and J. A. Motyer, eds. Grand Rapids, MI: Eerdmans.

White, N. J. D. 1956. *The Expositor's Greek Testament*. W. Robertson Nicholl, ed. Grand Rapids, MI: Eerdmans.

Willis, John T. 1979. *Genesis*. Abilene, TX: ACU Press.

Willis, John T. 1980. *Isaiah. The Living Word Commentary*. Abilene, TX: ACU Press.

Wilson, Robert Dick. 1929. *A Scientific Investigation of the Old Testament*. New York, NY: Harper & Brothers.

Wiseman, D. J. 1980. Belshazzar. *The Illustrated Bible Dictionary*. Vol. 1. Wheaton, IL: Tyndall House.

Wuest, Kenneth. 1946. *The Practical Use of the Greek New Testament*. Chicago, IL: Moody Press.

Yamauchi, Edwin. 1972. *The Stones and the Scriptures*. Philadelphia, PA: Holman.

Young, Brigham. 1854–75. *Journal of Discourses*. Vol. 13. Liverpool, England: F. D. Richards.

Young, Edward J. 1958. The Canon of the Old Testament. *Revelation and the Bible*. Carl F. H. Henry, ed. Grand Rapids, MI: Baker.